WAL
10|20

# HOW TO TEACH CLASSICS
## TO YOUR DOG

# HOW TO TEACH
# CLASSICS
# TO YOUR DOG

A Quirky Introduction to
the Ancient Greeks and
Romans

PHILIP WOMACK

ONEWORLD

**A Oneworld Book**

First published in Great Britain and North America by Oneworld Publications, 2020

ISBN 978-1-78607-814-8
eISBN 978-1-78607-815-5

Typeset by Fakenham Prepress Solutions, Fakenham, Norfolk, NR21 8NL
Printed and bound in Great Britain by Clays Ltd, Elcograf S.p.A.

Oneworld Publications
10 Bloomsbury Street
London, WC1B 3SR
England

Stay up to date with the latest books,
special offers, and exclusive content from
Oneworld with our newsletter

Sign up on our website
oneworld-publications.com

# Contents

# Contents

*This book is dedicated to Nicola Shulman:* docta puella amicaque discipulaque, *with whom so many of these conversations began.*

*And also, to Una,* optima canis.

# Introduction

In the summer of 2011, Google, the search engine colossus, launched a social network, Google+, which threatened to rival Facebook.

Mark Zuckerberg, Facebook's CEO, took an aggressive position. This was a hostile incursion into his rightful territory. Facebook would have to resist. He flooded the campus of the company he'd founded with inspirational posters.

Did they show memes from popular TV shows? Or grinning emojis? Did they display the famous Facebook thumb, pointing upwards?

Did they hell.

In displaying his imperial ambition, Marcus Zuckerbergus Libervultus* selected a phrase that issued from the mouth of a Roman senator over 2,000 years ago: 'Carthago delenda est', topped by the sinister silhouette of a helmeted Roman soldier.

Carthage must be destroyed. This city was the great and ancient enemy of Rome. The statesman Cato thought it had grown too rich; it was menacing Rome from right across the Mediterranean Sea.

---

* Latin for 'Book of Face'.

1

Cato ended every speech he made in the Senate with these words, whether they were relevant or not. Relentless, bold, militaristic: the tag perfectly captures Zuckerberg's overweening desire to crush all his competitors.

The Roman Empire may no longer exist, but excessive ambition always will. Empires come and go in different forms. Google+ vanished, crushed under the might of the Zuck and his myriad legions. *Google delenda est*!

Being a classicist can be a precarious business. Sometimes I feel like a soldier in the city of Troy, just after they'd hoisted in the wooden horse, feasted, fallen into a drunken stupor, and been roused by the clang of enemy metal. 'But they *said* it was a present!' went the cry round the streets of Troy, as their palaces and houses burned around them.

Large, brutal forces are ranged against the classicist, which seem all-powerful. Our enemy believes in 'irrelevance'.

How, they wonder, is it possible to understand what happened so long ago? What is even the point of trying to learn and understand languages that have been six feet under for centuries?

People often regard Classics with slight amusement, as they do your eccentric great-aunt Millicent, who still reads paper newspapers, writes with an ink fountain pen and worries about missing the post. They always ask me: but why be a classicist?

'Latin is a dead language, as dead as dead can be: it killed off all the Romans, and now it's killing me!' As for Ancient Greek – well, it doesn't even use the same alphabet, so what's the point of that? It's so obscure, nobody's even bothered to make up a disparaging jingle.

Latin and Greek are, of course, *not* dead. They have been bursting with life throughout the centuries. Imagine a river, with more than one mouth, and several tributaries, all flowing into the great sea of literature and culture. The texts and mythologies that form the study of Classics are as relevant now as they ever were.

As I prepare this book for publication, the comedians Steve Coogan and Rob Brydon are recreating the journey of Odysseus, for a TV show about male identity and friendship. The writer and hip-hop artist Akala recently investigated the same poem, travelling around the Mediterranean in search of its origins. He concluded that Homer's oral culture wasn't far off today's rap battles. The Duke and Duchess of Sussex have named their charitable foundation Archewell, after the Greek word '*arche*'. They claim it means 'source of action'; it does, but it means 'rule', too, hence the word 'monarchy' and so on. It's a shame, then, that they didn't have a classicist on their staff, who could have told them that 'arche' has a hard 'ch', and is pronounced 'ark-eh'.

Prince Harry wasn't paying attention in his Greek classes. But the subject flourishes. In private and grammar schools, it has been a traditional plank of the system for generations, though sometimes the teaching hasn't changed in the last fifty years (I do not joke). Increasingly, the state sector is getting involved. Visit the website of Classics for All, a charity that provides funding for the teaching of Classics, and you'll find videos of children across the country getting excited by conjugating verbs. 'Latin is the language of the future,' as one of the teachers, from Blackpool, says. And she means it.

This *libellus*, or 'little book', will provide all you need for a general understanding of the subject. If you want to be able to tell your Odysseus from your Oedipus, then this book is for you. If you did a bit of Latin at school, then this book is for you.

If you did Classics at university, and have forgotten everything you learned, then this book is for you. If you have an interest in literature, poetry, history, mythology or philosophy, then … this book is for you.

If you're a sceptic who puts Latin on a par with wearing ruffs, singing madrigals and learning the lute, then give us a chance. After all, if the Emperor of the Internet divined something useful in this apparently dusty old subject, then you might as well.

The following chapters cover the essentials in the study of Classics. There's an excellent Latin phrase to describe the topics: *sine qua non*. You wouldn't study it at all without touching on these points. The discussions take the form of conversations with my dog, Una, over the course of a few months, from the middle of August to the beginning of January.

We discuss the big as well as the small. We'll see how mythology underpins literature and philosophy; we'll look at how the great epic poems that stand at the very beginning of civilisation developed, and what they mean. We'll enquire into the workings of history; and we'll talk about love poems and tragedies.

On the human scale, you'll find devoted inscriptions to pet dogs; you'll encounter people whose job it is to fatten peacocks; you'll meet crazed (or not) emperors; you'll see transformations into dogs and wolves; and you'll taste the vastness and complexity of the ancient world.

You can find terrifying battles, passionate loves and awe-inspiring turns of fortune, just as much as you can enjoy a joke about someone not pronouncing their 'H's, or a pompous ex-slave who uses silver bottles to pee in.

No other subject offers such breadth; no other subject has been engaged with so deeply by so many people across so many different societies and countries over the centuries.

# Introduction

A Roman lady in the early Empire would be able to have a meaningful discussion with a modern teenager about the letters of Cicero or the poems of Sappho. It's the closest thing we have to time travel. To ignore Classics, to suppress its study, would be like amputating a limb from the intellectual, imaginative and spiritual body of the world.

Sometimes antiquity seems so tantalisingly close that you could step out of the front door and into the forum at Rome, the swish of togas and the shouts of orators almost audible; sometimes it appears impossibly distant.

There is always a continuum: we are living in a classical world, and I am a C-la-ssical girl, as Madonna might have sung; her own name, of course, being a contraction of the Latin *Mea Domina*: My Lady.

Classics has been my companion for nearly all my working life. I began as a private tutor in London in 2003, almost as soon as I had left Oxford University, where I read Classics and English at Oriel College, and now my pupils are scattered all over the globe.

As well as the usual face-to-face encounters, the advance of technology means I can now appear as a disembodied presence, much like some minor god might manifest, only instead of magical swords or hats that make you invisible, I dispense irregular verbs.

A pupil might be in Hong Kong or Singapore or America, whilst I utter the words of the ancients from my study in London. Nouns, verbs and grammatical constructions flit and hum and crackle along the electronic wires, swift as thought, in a manner that would probably not have been so astonishing to the ancients. They had their goddess, Fama (Rumour), who spread her chatter all over the planet from her house on top of a mountain.

Latin is spreading: *in totum orbem*, or into the whole world.

When I teach, my pupils and I speak aloud the same words that emerged from the minds of the orator Cicero, the poets Virgil and Homer, the philosopher Plato, and countless others.

That, to me, is astonishing. A language is only truly dead when it is no longer on lips, in minds, in hearts.

Una, my dog, raised an eyebrow. Dogs are past masters at raising their eyebrows.

*So when you say 'sede' to me in your lessons, and I sit, like a* bona canis, *or good dog, I'm actually demonstrating that Latin is very much alive, and if not kicking, then at least putting up a good show?*

Yes indeed, I answered. *Bona canis.*

I gave her a pat.

Una is not above self-congratulation. Her feathery tail waggled from side to side.

In the following pages, Una and I meander through the dirty, busy streets of north London, and over the semi-rural hills of Hampstead Heath, but in our minds we are walking past the Parthenon in Athens, painted in all its glory, or peering in at some senators in the Senate House at Rome, when Cicero condemns the villain Catiline, or just lazing in a courtyard playing dice. To join us, you won't even need your walking boots.

Now, there's only one thing for it. *Carpe diem.*

*Carpe what?* said Una.

Ah… well, it doesn't mean quite so much seize the day, as *harvest* it.

You can read this book in whatever way you want: dipping into chapters that catch your fancy, or all the way through. Academics, classicists and ancient historians spend their whole lives immersed in all the aspects of the subject that I discuss here, and every section will lead you, I hope, to explore those avenues in more detail. Secondary sources are footnoted or in the bibliography, and you can follow up any of the research or theories that way. All mistakes are my own.

Now, get ready, and harvest this book.

*Carpe librum.*

## Chapter I

# THESE ARE THE DOG DAYS
## An Introdogtion

It was the dog days of early August, and it should, by rights, have been blazingly hot.

There was one slight problem, however. I was not luxuriating on a Greek island, sunning myself by the wine-dark sea, or inhaling cocktails in the purview of a Roman ruin.

The only thing that bore even the slightest resemblance to wine-dark was the raincloud looming above me. I was, of course, in England.

A rainstorm had been in unrepentant swing for quite some time, as Una and I huddled miserably under a tree near the bottom of Parliament Hill, on Hampstead Heath, which is the closest thing to the countryside you'll find in London.

Some dogs were grappling with each other a few feet away: a ball of fur and heads, they resembled Cerberus, the three-headed hound of Hades, and were certainly making enough noise to trouble the dead. I said as much to Una.

She regarded me with a very particular expression that she brings out maybe three or four times a day. It registers mild disdain.

*Cerberus?* she said.

Earlier that morning, Una had shoved me out of the house, all but exploding with energy. Now, she couldn't see why a tiny spot of rain should stop us.

If one got wet, it was possible to dry oneself by shaking one's entire body from nose to tail, and, failing that, to use the base of the sofa at home. Why couldn't we carry on?

Una, I should mention, is an elegant black-and-white lurcher.

She huffed. A glimpse of a squirrel was making her twitch.

'Cerberus,' I said to Una. 'You know, the monstrous guard dog of Hades? Heracles had to drag him up from the Underworld?' My thin shirt was already soaked through.

Una sighed.

I was wondering how much longer we might have to wait, and was even thinking about braving the rest of it, when, at last, the torrent gave way to a fine mizzle, and the black rainclouds rolled apart.

A ray of sunshine pierced, spear-like, through the sky, and then the gorgeous bow of Iris, one of the messengers of the gods, appeared.

Una blinked at me, her long, fine lashes quivering in a way that means only one thing.

That I've made yet another classical reference.

Around us, the Heath relaxed. The joggers, plugged into their little musical pods, continued on their rounds. The schoolchildren in fluorescent tabards, hunting for tiny, brightly coloured flags. Teenagers doing tricks on bicycles.

And everyone else staring down at their phones, waiting for their next message to appear.

I turned to Una.

*Iris?* she suggested, with a flick of her tail, which waves, flag-like, when she is interested in something, although that is usually a decomposing vole.

'Iris, the rainbow, was a messenger god, along with Hermes. The ancient world, much like ours, was powered by messages. People prayed to the gods, and sent curses. Heralds and embassies brought offers of peace or threats of war. In Athenian drama, the speech given by a messenger is one of the dramatic cruxes of the play.'

The sun was now fully out, the rainbow fading, the dark clouds pushing off to water the more distant suburbs. Iris, having done her duty, was heading back to Mount Olympus for a well-earned rest, a cup of ambrosia and a gossip with her fellow immortals.

'Our idea of the rainbow as the kitsch preserve of fluffy unicorns is not at all the same as the ancients'. For Homer, Iris is "storm-footed"; she's also the sister of the Harpies, vicious half-birds half-women.'

We pottered up Parliament Hill, beginning to dry off a little. Una took the opportunity to rub herself on a bit of grass; she only succeeded in making herself look more bedraggled.

'It's all about messengers,' I continued. 'The rainbow is a celestial phenomenon, marvelled at by generations. We've been trained to think of it as light refracted into seven distinct colours. But look at how Virgil describes Iris, in his epic poem the *Aeneid*.' I pulled the quote up on the SPQR app.

> *Ergo Iris croceis per caelum roscida pennis*
> *mille trahens varios adverso sole colores*
> *And dewy Iris, on rosy wings, through the sky*
> *Came pulling a thousand colours…*

At this point the goddess is zooming to Earth, on a heavenly mission. She is described as '*roscida*' – dewy; on '*croceis pennis*' – rosy wings; and she drags with her '*mille colores*' – a thousand colours.

*A thousand?*

Una can't really see colours, but she was still a bit confused.

In Homer's *Iliad*, Iris is '*porphureen*'.

*Does that mean 'purple'?*

It does, Una. But that's not what Homer was thinking of.

Let's look up the word in Liddell and Scott. This is an Ancient Greek dictionary, first published as recently as 1889, and still essentially in the same form. Things used by classicists are none of your shoddy flat-pack stuff: they are built to last, which is more than can be said for dishwashers.

This Liddell, incidentally, was the father of the Alice Liddell who inspired Lewis Carroll's *Alice in Wonderland* (which has been translated into Latin as *Alicia in Terra Mirabilis*). I have had my Liddell for over twenty years. There even used to be jokes in it.

*Really? In a dictionary?*

Yes. If you looked up *sykophantes* in the first edition, you'd find the meaning 'false accuser'; then that it referred to people who accused others of stealing their figs. 'This,' says Liddell, 'is probably a figment.'

*Tumbleweed*, said Una.

Ahem. They removed it from subsequent editions. Rather than lugging about a heavy volume, I have it all on my phone.

I looked up '*porphureos*', and read it out for Una:

---

\*    Charles Lutwidge Dodgson Latinised his first two names into Carolus Lewis, and then switched them round as if seeing them in a mirror. See, Latin gets everywhere.

'of the swoln [sic]…'

*Sick?*

No, sic. It means 'thus'. It's Latin. It's when something looks odd, or is a mistake, and you put it there to show that it's what was actually written down.

I continued with the definition: 'swoln sea, *dark-gleaming, dark*; of blood; of death in battle; of stuff, cloths, etc., *dark, russet*; of the rainbow, prob. *bright, lustrous*; and of serpents *glittering*. Homer seems not to have known the *porphura*, so that the word does not imply any definite colour.'

The '*porphura*' is the murex, a shellfish that, when crushed, produced purple dye – an expensive process, which is why it was the colour associated with wealth and emperors.

Note, though, that 'the word does not imply any definite colour'. The rainbow is not purple; Iris is certainly not entirely purple.

Iris shows us quite how different the ancients were. To us, a rainbow is a process of physics. To them, it had a sense of movement, and of brightness, that 'rainbow' does not even begin to convey.

Look at the rainbow and you might see just seven colours, because you've been trained to do so. Perhaps now you'll see a thousand.

Una was tugging at her lead. A squirrel, grown bold, had appeared a mere few feet away. It paused, bright-eyed, and glanced at us.

*You*, it seemed to be saying to Una, *can't catch me.* Then, just in case, it scampered up a tree trunk to safety.

Deflated, Una turned to me. *You're always banging on about Classics. So what is it? And why is it called Classics? Is it like my favourite books?*

What are your favourite books? I asked.

Una considered. She was about, I could tell, to say *Dog Quixote*. But then she thought better of it.

The Latin word '*classis*' meant, amongst other things, a group of Romans who had reached a particular level of wealth – in other words, a class. It then spawned the adjective '*classicus*'.

*What does that mean?*

Excellent. A1. Top-hole. The bee's knees.

*The dog's pyjamas?*

Exactly. Classics is the study of what, over time, readers, writers and critics came to know as the Top Drawer of Literature from the Greco-Roman era. Specifically, the many surviving texts from fifth-century-BC Athens, and the first centuries BC and AD in Rome.

We have enough poetry, prose, plays, philosophical treatises, histories and other texts to fill the Colosseum many times over. One day you could be reading a light-hearted poem about a battle between frogs and mice; the next, a disquisition on ethics; the day after, an early effort at science fiction in which someone visits the moon. Most students will begin with the literature, with a dash of philosophy thrown in to add some spice.

There is also a joke book, the *Philogelos*.

*Tell me a joke from it?*

'A pupil asks an incompetent teacher the name of Priam's mother. At a loss, he answers, "Well, out of politeness we call her Ma'am."'

*I can see that one going down well.*

You couldn't hope to read every single text in one lifetime. You'd have to be immortal. And only jellyfish are immortal, and they can't read. As far as I know.

Yet even so, the survival of a text is a precarious business.

For centuries, the Greek lyric poet Sappho was on our radar, but we had none of her poems.

Only in the nineteenth century did fragments of Sappho appear in, of all places, a rubbish dump in Egypt. This is no reflection on what people thought of her: merely that the papyrus was used and reused, scribbled on and over until it was discarded.

A scene in Ronald Firbank's twentieth-century novel *Vainglory* demonstrates the frustration of deciphering scraps of a manuscript.

Here is a professor, announcing to a roomful of eager guests the latest discovery, apparently from Sappho. They are all expecting something sublime.

What they hear is rather different:

'…the Professor declaimed impressively the imperishable line.

"Oh, delicious!" Lady Listless exclaimed, looking quite perplexed. "Very charming indeed!"

"Will anyone tell me what it means," Mrs Thumbler queried, "in plain English! Unfortunately, my Greek—"

"In plain English," the Professor said, with some reluctance, "it means: 'Could not' [he wagged a finger] 'Could not, for the fury of her feet!'"'

Torn from its context, this sentence might as well have beamed down from outer space.

These days, we've pieced the fragments together, and Sappho's verse delights millions of readers. A Sappho bot on Twitter zaps out her (translated) verse, bringing a touch of the ancient world smack bang into the modern.

*So if you want to learn Classics, where do you start?*

Language. The first stop, the *fons et origo*—

*The what?*

Sorry – the fount and source for this mammoth subject is the languages in which these texts were composed.

*Can't you read them in translation?*

You can. I'm often asked what's 'the best' translation of the *Iliad,* which is like having to choose which Mozart symphony you prefer. Here's Alexander Pope's verse *Iliad*:

'Achilles' wrath, to Greece the direful spring

Of woes unnumber'd, heavenly goddess, sing!' says Pope.

But listen to E.V. Rieu's prose version:

'The Wrath of Achilles is my theme, that fatal wrath which, in fulfilment of the will of Zeus, brought the Achaeans so much suffering…'

Rieu[†] doesn't even mention the goddess until a few lines later. Comparing translations is a way into tasting the flavour of the texts, but to enjoy the full banquet, it's worth tackling the languages themselves.

The classicist studies Classical Latin and Ancient Greek, their grammar, syntax and vocabulary. You can also delve into what Latin looked like before it became Latin (answer: really strange), and search deeply into the roots of words, finding parallels between Latin and Greek, stretching back to their theoretical sources.

And whilst you're learning the language, you'll also be sampling the texts. With texts, like two sides of the same *sestertius,* come contexts.

---

†    E.V. Rieu also wrote light verse for children. Sample:
    'Said the Shark to the Flying Fish over the phone:
    "Will you join me tonight? I am dining alone.
    Let me order a nice little dinner for two.
    And come as you are, in your shimmering blue."'
    He is not much remembered for this.

The discipline requires a good dash of ancient history. If literature is the steak, then background is the Béarnaise sauce. Studying the Roman poet Virgil gains toothsome spice when you know that he composed the *Aeneid* with the Emperor Augustus looming over him.

*So what's the period you cover?*

You can begin with pre-Greek societies in around 2700 BC, and gallop all the way through the Athenian Empire, the Roman Empire, and come hurtling into the end of the Byzantine Empire (which was an extension of the Roman) in AD 1453.

Una thinks in dog years, which are rather shorter than human years, so for her that was almost unimaginable.

*Crumbs*, she said, her nose quivering.

You may well invoke those morsels of disbelief. During this immense stretch of time, both Greek and Latin were hale and hearty, throughout Europe and even the rest of the world. There exists a titanic corpus. Latin was an international mode of communication, even in the most surprising places. A sixteenth-century Aztec, for example, sent a letter to the King of Spain written in Latin.

The story of Stephen Parmenius illustrates this dimension. He was born in Hungary in the sixteenth century, and visited most of the universities in Europe, before rocking up in Christ Church, Oxford. He joined the explorer Sir Humphrey Gilbert on a trip to North America, and wrote an embarkation poem in Latin hexameters. Unfortunately he was drowned. But who knows – had he survived, we might have an epic poem based in what would become the USA.

Even today, the Pope has a dictionary in which modern phenomena are given Latin names.

*He never,* said Una.

He certainly does. There's a word for train and everything.

*What is it?*

'*Hamaxostichus.*' Countless books are translated into Latin and Ancient Greek, my favourite being *Winnie Ille Pu.*

And you know, Una, if somebody is sitting in a room trying to construe 'Harry took his wand out' into Latin, then I think we can agree that it's not a dead language, or even a zombified one.

*People still use it?* asked Una. She looked a tad surprised.

They do. That's not even thinking about the countless Latin tags and mottos that abound. A thriving subculture exists on YouTube, with Latin songs, lessons and parodies. Look up 'Agamemnon' by Rathergood, which pairs the mighty leader of the Greek armies with a leg of lamb called Legolambnon. 'I sailed to Troy with the navy,' sings the king. 'I taste good with spuds and gravy,' answers the roast joint. Radio Bremen regularly broadcasts bulletins in Latin, known as *Nuntii Latini* (Latin News).[‡]

There is a version of Wikipedia in Latin, *Vicipaedia,* with updated Latin news. On Saturday mornings, you'll usually find me scratching my head over the Latin crossword in *The Times* – it's called *O Tempora!* (O the Times!). I'm also a member of a Classics reading club, Pindr, which meets fortnightly: we've been reading Plutarch's *Life of Mark Antony,* in Greek, as well as some poems by Horace.

*Why is it called Pindr?*

---

[‡] The headline at the time of going to press: *Negotia de Europaeis auxiliis contra coronavirus composita* – (lit.) The negotiation concerning European allies, against coronavirus, has taken place.

After the poet Pindar. We regularly communicate in Latin. A sample exchange:

'*Si ancillam filio invenire potero, veniam!*'

Or in English: 'If I can find a babysitter for my son, I'm coming.'

*Lollius Maximus*, said Una.

Giovanna Chirri, an Italian news reporter, wangled a scoop because she was the only person who understood the Pope when he announced in Latin that he had just resigned.

*Sterling stuff*, said Una. *And really, terribly useful.*

I gave her my best stern look.

The languages are important. But there's another aspect, too, which is equally valid. Many people, as I did, come to Classics by way of enchantment.

There was an Usborne book, called *Animal Stories*. My mother had bought it for me. It retold Aesop's fables, and other tales of origin, but I yearned for the section on magical animals.

Here I met (and pitied) the kraken, a sea monster who drags unwary sailors to their deaths; here, the unicorn, enticed from hiding by a Tibetan girl; here, the monstrous, ox-eating griffin. I was particularly affected by the cockatrice, the deadly serpent born from a cockerel's egg, which devastated living things with its breath. For many years afterwards I was nervous around henhouses.

But these were all by the by, *amuse-bouches* for the main event.

I was feeling a little dewy-eyed, overcome with the memory of being five years old, wrapped up in a blanket, immersed in a fantastical world.

*Which was? The main event, you say?* Una butted my calf.

Sorry, Una. She brought me back to the present with her usual elegance. Which was the story from Greek myth, of the hero Bellerophon and the winged horse Pegasus.

Even at that young age, I sensed something deeper and more resonant than the other stories. It said something urgent and important about the world.

I still have the book, now much battered. The illustrations seem comically crude. Everybody wears laurel wreaths and togas, which the ancient Greeks certainly didn't do, and the story is much compressed, for the ears of the child audience.

In the Usborne version, Bellerophon is sent away by a king who hates him, for reasons undisclosed, to kill a monster called the chimera. He is helped by the goddess Athena (who appears as a woman with film-star looks). She provides him with a magical bridle, and orders him to tame Pegasus.

Pegasus really caught my imagination, his broad feathery wings so incongruous and yet so fitting. He is so potent a symbol, and I did not know then that he had sprung from the blood of the slain gorgon's head.

*Really?*

Yes! That's why you sometimes see Perseus, who slew the gorgon, riding the horse. The two heroes are confused. Pegasus had a brother, you know, called Chrysaor – he was born from the gorgon's head at the same time as Pegasus. Not a horse. No wings. Just a man. But he did become the father of a three-headed giant, so, you know. Swings and roundabouts.

Pegasus has a long afterlife – you can see him, guarding the gates of the Inner Temple in London, cast in bronze, hooves upreared to the skies. That combination of the beauty of the horse and the elegance of the wings is unparalleled in Greek myth.

What was disquieting – and thus interesting – was that Bellerophon, after he'd killed the chimera by filling its throat with boiling lead, grew too big for his buskins.

Returning home, one imagines, with the body of the chimera lashed to the winged horse's back, he quaffed ale, ate plenty of roast oxen, roister-doistered and told anyone who'd listen that he was a famous hero, whilst belching and smelling slightly of body odour. His muscles, once taut, would begin to turn into wobbly fat.

*A bit like yours*, said Una.

Now now. He would become rather a bore, propping up the bar in his local taverna. His friends would find that they had other appointments.

'Did I tell you,' he would slur, over his third bowl of wine, 'that the chimera had three heads?' He had probably made a rug out of it, or at least nailed the heads above his dining room table.

'Excuse me, I've got to see a man about a dog…'

'Go on then,' one of the remaining listeners might have said. 'If you're so special, why don't you go and tell Zeus all about it.'

His pride would have been wounded. These silly fools did not know what he, Bellerophon, had gone through. He'd killed a monster! The nearest any of them had come to that was herding a distressed goat. Perhaps he was of divine birth. Perhaps he ought to go up to the skies and claim his birthright.

So the hero did. He put down his flagon of beer, sploshing foam onto the table, wiped his mouth with the back of his hand (as boozy heroes always do), mounted Pegasus and soared up to the skies, towards Mount Olympus, the home of the gods.

But Zeus spotted him from a distance. There's no keeping anything from Zeus.

He had heard of this fellow Bellerophon, and had half an eye on him. This was really too much. A mere mortal, trying to breach the heavenly heights?

He ordered a bee to go and torment his ride.

Pegasus, maddened, hurled Bellerophon from his back, and the boasting hero plummeted down to his death.

So much for Bellerophon.

Zeus, meanwhile, decided he rather liked the look of Pegasus, and retained him to pull his chariot. (Quite why the gods needed chariots when they could materialise at will has always bothered me, but I suspect it's to do with showing off. Like those oligarchs who have seventy sports cars and a mega-basement just to put them in.)

Bellerophon's death was an early intimation that the world of the ancients was not so simple. It wasn't just about bumping off a monster, marrying a maiden and ruling a kingdom. I could marvel at Bellerophon's prowess, but at the same time this was complicated by his stupidity.

I didn't know it then, but I had been introduced to one of the classical world's major concepts: hubris.

This term is widely considered to mean prideful behaviour leading to a fall. The ancient understanding of hubris was more complex, meaning an act done to shame somebody. Bellerophon's flight to Olympus would bring shame on the gods, and so he had to go.

There are many other facets to this story. One of the more profound is the way in which the philosopher Plato transmuted it. Plato's version sees a charioteer, symbolising the soul, driving two winged horses up to heaven. One of the horses is wild, and threatens to pull the driver back towards the Earth below; the other is good, and heaves him up to the heavens. Reining horses becomes a common metaphor for reining in the self: we also see it in a tragedy by Euripides, where Hippolytus loses control of his chariot and is killed.

This is the struggle of man, illuminated by myth and metamorphosed into philosophy. Anybody can find relevance in that image.

We shall meet Bellerophon again, when we talk about Homer, and when we talk about tragedy.

But for the moment, we are back to Iris and the messengers. The tale of Bellerophon, even in its bowdlerised and truncated form, still conveyed something resonant.

Myths are about transmission, marking moments when the nature of the world shifts, and yet providing universal truths about human experience.

In reading the ancient texts, in trying to absorb what has gone before and how it relates to where we are today, we are engaged on a quest for the essence of reality, to understand who we are, why we are, and what made us.

I paused. We began to make our way up the hill.

Una, however, did not hurtle away into the distance, as is her wont. Instead, she padded along by my side, nose twitching.

*That all sounds great and everything. But are there any more dogs in all this?* she asked.

Dogs? Oh yes, I replied. Plenty.

*Well go on then.*

Let's see. How about the gender-bending tale of Procris and her magical dog?

*That,* said Una, *sounds like a great place to start.*

## Chapter 2

# CAVE CANEM
## Dogs in Classical Life
## and Literature

Earlier, before the rain had caught us, as Una and I were saunter-ing up to the Heath, with a song in our hearts and a braid in our hair—

*A braid in our hair?*

You know what I mean. It's an expression, isn't it? It means 'joyfully', doesn't it?

*I suppose so.*

We'd passed many houses with '*Cave Canem*' on their gate-posts, usually accompanied by a picture of a snarling beast that looked as if it would give you what for, should you come within reach of its jaws.

Actually open the gate, however, and you'd probably find a wimpy cockapoo inside with no more biting power than a damp blanket.

*Some of my best friends are cockapoos.*

That may be so. But nevertheless. There is a pleasing brevity to the phrase *Cave Canem*, much lacking in our more plodding 'Beware of the Dog.' In fact, it is a perfect illustration of the ele-gance and concision of Latin.

R.J. Yeatman,[*] one of the authors of *1066 and All That*, a spoof history textbook, painted 'CAVE CANEM' on his gate. He neglected, however, to provide a picture of a dog.

Somebody pointed out to him that burglars might not be as well versed in Latin as he was.

'Well', he replied, 'then they are not the sort of burglars we want.'[†]

Dogs have always been used as guardians – whether for show, as most of the dogs in London are, or for extra muscle. There is a picture at the House of the Tragic Poet in the ruins of Pompeii of a dog so fierce that he appears to scratch furrows into the ground, desperate to tear out your throat. He's black, with white patches, a bit like Una. Also at Pompeii, excavators found the remains of a guard dog, still with its collar on. The poor thing had perished, tied up, during the eruption of Vesuvius in AD 79.

The Roman writer Columella advises that the first thing a farmer should do when setting up is to buy a dog, and it should be white so that you don't mistake it for a wolf at night. You should also give your sheepdog a short name, two syllables being best. These are Columella's more sensible ideas: you'll also find him telling you to get rid of caterpillars by sending a menstruating girl to walk barefoot round your garden. But dogs, he says, will be your prime guardians, and I think we can trust him on that.

---

[*] Who was an Oriel man, and therefore a Good Thing.
[†] Letters to *The Times*, 27 November 2017.

Una is excellent at sniffing out postmen, and can sense them a mile off. She growled, as if to show that she too, if called upon, could tear out an intruder's throat.

If you stand by the entrance to the Heath at any time of day, you'll see a parade of dogs, from prinking poodles to lolloping Labradors.

Una, being a lurcher and therefore half-aristocrat, half-gypsy, is descended from the ancient sighthound known as the *vertragus*. The swift Laconian (or Spartan), on the other hand, hunted by scent.

Una's sense of smell is notoriously bad. Whole cavalcades of squirrels can pass by behind her, and she won't notice when she's turned round. Yet if something flashes by in the distance, she'll be after it like a javelin hurled from the hand of a rampaging Goth.

Arrian, the biographer of Alexander the Great, owned a *vertragus*, whom he called 'most swift and wise and divine'. Her name was Horme, which means 'A violent movement onwards, an assault, attack, onset'.

*Quite right too*, said Una, who certainly is swift and wise and divine, though I would never let her know that, as it might go to her head. But I hesitate to imagine what residents of the Heath would think if I had named Una 'Attack!'

'Silver! Silver!' A woman hurried by, alternately looking down at her iPhone in that manic way that people have, as if there's a chain attached to the screen, and up to scan the park. I turned, to see where her dog was.

A little girl came scrambling towards her. Silver was her daughter. This is Hampstead, after all.

Alexander the Great himself named a city after his dog, Peritas, so he must have been devoted to him. Peritas was meant to have saved Alexander from death, and died in his master's lap.

Una was very put out. *Why don't you ever name cities after me?*

Er, well... anyway. Moving on. The writer and soldier Xenophon composed a treatise on hunting with dogs, the *Cynegeticus*, in which he discusses different breeds of hunting dogs, the Castorian and the Vulpine, the latter of which was apparently a cross with a fox.

Una made a slightly appalled flick of her tail.

Well, I did say apparently. He mentions it was the twin gods Apollo and Artemis who gave the gift of hunting to Chiron the centaur.

*Who was he?*

An ancient schoolmaster who taught many heroes, including the warrior Achilles and Cephalus, whom we're about to meet. Xenophon provides plenty of detail on the best way to hunt hares.

*I could tell you that,* sniffed Una.

Aristotle mentions the enormous Molossian mastiff, heavier than the hunting dogs, from Molossus on the Greek mainland (whose first king was said to be a descendant of Achilles), and praises them for bravery. Virgil too says that you need never fear wolves or brigands with a Molossian hound at your back. The Roman Emperor Marcus Aurelius (he of the slightly twee *Meditations*) fitted them out with collars and spikes and trained them to attack in formation, so that they really were dogs of war.

Dogs were often burned with the dead body of their owner, so that they could accompany them into the afterlife. It was common across both Latin and Greek cultures to bury dogs with honours: Theophrastus' fourth-century-BC text *Characters* talks of a man of petty ambition, who dedicates an epitaph to his little Maltese dog, called Barker – only there it's a little bit of a snide dig at his pretensions.

A marble epitaph to a dog called Margarita Pearl is a poem as if written by the dog herself, detailing her biography.

Here, the love for the hound is deep and sincere: she has never been chained up, and her snow-white body has never endured a beating; she used to lie on her master's and mistress's soft laps.

The close connection between dog and human, it seems, is a constant. Another charming example is the tombstone put up for the dog Helena, who lived sometime in the second century AD. The inscription refers to the hound as a 'foster daughter'.[‡]

One of the loveliest things to have appeared from antiquity so far is a mosaic, from Alexandria in the second century BC. It shows a dog, white with black spots and a red collar, sitting by a jar that's been knocked over, we assume, recently. The expression on the hound's face shows exactly the kind of mixture of love, surprise and remorse we recognise in our doggy friends when they've done something they know they shouldn't have.

The Romans bred dogs and introduced new varieties: it's estimated there were about ten thousand pet dogs roaming the streets of, er, Rome.

*Ahem*, said Una.

We can imagine the streets heaving with them: the historian Suetonius talks of a stray that brought an actual human hand into the dining room of the Roman Emperor Vespasian. Which I imagine put him off his roast dormouse.

*Yuck. Though dormouse sounds nice.*

---

‡   Michael MacKinnon, 'Pack animals, pets, pests, and other non-human beings', in *The Cambridge Companion to Ancient Rome*.

Indeed. They fattened them up in special jars. And we can well imagine a Roman lady with her little Maltese toy dog, much as you might see a fashionista with a little dog poking out of her handbag today.

*Well*, said Una. *You know what I think about those sorts of dogs.*

I was perspiring a smidgeon at this stage. It was still hot, and the Heath teemed with Londoners. Una's tongue was out, and she licked my hand warmly, which meant something along the lines of, *I hope you give me a monument when I'm gone.*

Dog saliva was considered to have healing properties, and many dog statues have been found at religious sites, perhaps because of their therapeutic role. Anyone who's ever been licked by a dog will recognise the rightness of this.

Canine loyalty is evident throughout history. The historian Plutarch tells of the evacuation of Athens when the Persians were about to invade. The departing Athenians looked back on shore and saw their dogs, all running to the sea, howling. One, belonging to Pericles' father, dashed into the waves and swam by the ship's side until it reached Salamis.

*That's nice*, said Una.

Well, not really. The old fellow died as soon as they landed.

We retreated to a quiet, shady place, sat down on a bench (or at least, I did) and watched the parade of hounds: bounding Alsatians whose knowledge of Latin left a lot to be desired, and a bichon frise that might have been the toy of an empress.

A while ago I mentioned how far from sizzling we were, though it was the dog days of August. W.H. Auden's poem 'Under Sirius' describes a vivid picture of a listless summer. A legion's spears grow rusty, the scholar's brain is empty, and even the prophetess, the sibyl, can't perform her oracles properly. I once recited this in a ruined Roman theatre at Leptis Magna in Libya, causing some consternation amongst the tourists, who were unsure whether this mad Englishman was part of a show or not.

Sirius is the dog star, the brightest star in the firmament, and its appearance in the sky during August whilst the sun is out is supposed to add a bit of extra oomph to the heat. Supposed to, I muttered, looking up.

Una knows Sirius very well, since in doglore he came down to Earth to ask all the dogs if they wanted to go and live with him on his star.[§] The dogs refused, of course, wishing to remain with their humans. There's another dog-legend that the star was forced to take dog form on Earth, punished for a crime that he didn't commit.[¶] The star is within the constellation of Canis Major, and there are many stories about how this particular doggy arrangement came to be, which I'll tell you in a minute. At one point in the *Aeneid*, a flame around the hero Aeneas is compared to the brightness of the dog star, showing his brilliance and semi-divinity; when Achilles in the *Iliad* is similarly described, it also has sinister associations.

Perhaps the most famous dog in classical, if not all, literature is Argus, the loyal hound who waits for his master Odysseus to return home and then, once he's recognised him (after a whole twenty years, let us not forget), quietly expires. We'll look at that scene later when we talk about the *Odyssey*. Argus, incidentally, may well have been a Laconian; whereas the dogs of the swineherd, Eumaeus, who rush towards Odysseus and almost tear him limb from limb, were probably Molossians.

---

§   Dodie Smith, *The Starlight Barking*.
¶   Diana Wynne Jones, *Dogsbody*.

Dogs rather ran in the family. One of Odysseus' ancestors was a man called Cephalus. The whole story is found in Ovid's Latin poem *Metamorphoses*, which we'll discuss in more detail later; there you'll find the characters' Latin names, such as Aurora for Eos; I'll use the Greek, because they came first.

The dawn goddess, Eos, took quite a shine to Cephalus.

*A shine? That's your worst joke ever.*

Well, she's the dawn, isn't she, and she's literally 'taking a shine' to him when she appears…

*I know how it works. I'm just saying…*

All right. Eos… took a fancy to him.

*Better.*

Mortals never seem to learn it's unwise to refuse a deity. The voice of love was calling Cephalus; but he was deaf to it, and was not as free with his favours as Eos might have wished.

The dawn goddess, in an almighty huff, informed him that his wife, Procris, was a whore and would sleep with anyone for gold.

'Ridiculous!' you can imagine Cephalus saying, but perhaps feeling a tiny bit nervous and wondering about all the times he'd been away or out late hunting with his mates. Eos promptly disguised him, and he managed to tempt Procris into bed with a golden crown.

Unfortunately, or fortunately, depending on how you look at it, this meant he lost his bet with Eos, and had to sleep with her.

Which was bad luck in the end for Cephalus, as Procris became insanely jealous and abandoned him, flouncing off to Crete.

Now I know you've been wondering where dogs come into this, and you'd be quite right to do so. King Minos of Crete was the proud possessor of a hound called Laelaps ('whirlwind'), which the goddess Artemis had bestowed on him. This is the King Minos you may have heard of, the constructor of the labyrinth, the enormous maze complex Daedalus designed in order to imprison the Minotaur, the half-man half-bull. But he doesn't come into this part of the story.

Laelaps was a remarkable creature, who, like Dudley Do-Right, never failed to catch his man. Minos, despite being married with children, was utterly charmed by Procris, and he decided he would give her Laelaps, along with a dart (or a javelin) that never missed its mark.

Procris was duly seduced. What says love more than a supernatural dog and a weapon that can't fail to kill?

*Diamonds don't cut it*, interjected Una.

Procris grew worried about her affair with Minos, and especially that his wife Pasiphaë (the mother of Ariadne and the Minotaur) might put a spell on her. So, pre-empting Shakespeare by several centuries, she returned to Athens dressed as a boy.

She became best friends with Cephalus, and joined him on a hunting expedition, which is one way, I suppose, to keep your husband in order. Cephalus must have been taken down a number of pegs. Every time his own dog bounded on ahead, snatching at its quarry with its jaws, along came Laelaps, leaping in front.

Naturally Cephalus coveted Laelaps and the dart, so he offered Procris a vast sum of money for the gifts.

But Procris (remember, disguised as a boy) wouldn't part with them – quite rightly – apart from for love.

And so Cephalus went to bed with him. Or rather, her.

After Cephalus discovered that Procris was actually Procris, the happy couple were reunited, because what says 'I love you' more than pretending to be a boy to get your husband into bed?

Cephalus got to keep Laelaps and the dart, too, and everything was tickety-boo. **

The only hiccup was that now Artemis, the originator of the gifts to Minos, became annoyed at her magical bounty being bandied about in such a base fashion. When Cephalus gallivanted off to go hunting after midnight, she put it into Procris' head that he was sneaking away to see that hussy Eos.

Procris followed him, and Laelaps, sensing her, growled and stiffened.

Cephalus, not knowing who it was, hurled the dart.

And of course, since it never missed its mark, there and then it killed Procris.

Una, crestfallen, lowered her tail. *So it's the dog's fault?*

I suppose so. Cephalus was banished for the murder, and departed, distraught, to Thebes, the city of Oedipus.

You would have thought that Cephalus had learned his lesson about lending stuff that belonged to the gods, but no. You might be tempted to say something about spots and leopards. As Thebes was being ravaged by a giant fox, in revenge for the death of the Sphinx, he lent Laelaps to Amphitryon (Heracles' mortal father).

Una stiffened. She knows what it's like to have her territory invaded by a vulpine interloper.

---

** Although it's not related directly to the myth, it's interesting to note that Spartan wives would dress as boys to sleep with their husbands. *Why?*

Well, up until then they had been in a male-only society, developing sexual relationships with older boys. So the wives shaved their heads and wore cloaks to make them feel at home.

This was a vixen. She was so bloodthirsty that a child was sacrificed every month to appease her, much good though it did. And what's more, her fate was never to be caught.

*But…* said Una, wrinkling her brow, as her brain cells cranked into gear.

You're there before me, I replied. Laelaps was fated to catch whatever he chased. Amphitryon set Laelaps loose, and the result was like one of those paradoxes that occasionally keeps the internet amused for five minutes before everyone goes on to screeching about something else.

*What happened?* asked Una.

The universe couldn't work it out. So a *deus ex machina* was required. A god from the machine. And it was the Big Kahuna himself.

Zeus was exasperated by the contradiction. He did the only possible thing, and turned Laelaps into stone, setting him amongst the stars as Canis Major. Where, in truth, he is always in eternal pursuit.

*And the fox? She's not still ravaging and demanding human sacrifice?*

I gave Una a reassuring pat. Oh don't worry, she's up there too. There is another story about Canis Major: that this constellation was the bronze dog, fashioned by Hephaestus, that guarded Zeus when he was a baby, and he was set into the stars as a reward.

*I like that one better,* said Una. *But what does it all mean?*

The Procris and Cephalus story is a minor myth, although you will find plenty of pictorial representations, including one by Gerard Hoet featuring a dog very like you, Una. Robert Graves, in his exhaustive compendium *The Greek Myths*, even asserts that it's passed more into folktale and anecdote than myth. His theory about myths was that they encoded memories of ancient rituals and raids. He thinks this particular one is a way of recording a ritual marriage between a Cretan king and an Athenian priestess, with Pasiphaë representing an angry moon goddess, whilst the fox records raids in search of child sacrifices.

But then Graves also believed Jesus Christ lived till the age of eighty and invented spaghetti.[††] Which is not, as far as I know, in the Bible. But Graves's broad thesis is a compelling one, and when you encounter myths, it is helpful to think of them as commemorating some shift in a culture, perhaps from one mode of worship to another, or even one form of government to another.

The story also includes an origin for Canis Major. Many myths do similar things: and especially if you look up into the night sky, you'll see them in the constellations. This kind of myth is known as an aetiology.

*Eetiology*? said Una, chops stumbling over the unfamiliar word.

Yes, that's how you pronounce it.

We passed the ladies' bathing ponds, full of determined figures, heads bobbing up and down as they persevered through the weedy waters. We cannot embark upon a discussion of dogs in the classical world, I continued, without mentioning Artemis (Diana to the Romans) and Actaeon. Artemis is the closest thing to a goddess of dogs.

*I know*, said Una. *I'm a dog.*

I'm sorry, I forgot that for a minute. You'll know then that she's the queen of the hunt, usually depicted with a pack of hounds at her heels; she was also a virgin goddess (her acolytes were virgins too, which becomes important in Euripides' *Hippolytus*, where the titular hero's fanatical devotion to her causes problems).

Hunting was always an aristocratic sport. Proving yourself in the field was a way of showing strength and valour. One of the great ancient myths (though it's not particularly noised about today) concerns the Calydonian Boar Hunt. A variety of heroes (including Jason, Theseus, the twins Castor and Polydeuces, Meleager and Atalanta) go chasing after a huge boar.

*Wait a minute – Castor and Polydeuces? I thought it was Castor and Pollux.*

That's right, Una – Polydeuces is the Greek name (from Sparta); it became, in Rome, Podlouques, and thus, by a process of telescoping, Pollux. Say them in turn, and you'll see how it happened.

The hunter Actaeon (grandson of Cadmus, and a member of the tragic royal house, which we will consider later) was hunting a deer in the woods with his hounds, the prime example of a gentlemanly youth.

Ovid provides a beautiful description of his dogs, translated by Arthur Golding in the sixteenth century. A few taps summoned it onto my phone, and I read it out to Una.

> His hounds espied him where he was. And Blackfoot first
>     of all
> And Stalker, special good of scent, began aloud to call.
> This latter was a hound of Crete, the other was of Spart.
> Then all the kennel fell in round, and every for his part
> Did follow freshly in the chase more swifter than the
>     wind:

Spy, Eatall, Scalecliff, three good hounds come all of
   Arcas' kind;

Strong Killbuck, currish Savage, Spring and Hunter fresh
   of smell,

And Lightfoot, who to lead a chase did bear away the bell;

Fierce Woodman, hurt not long ago in hunting of a boar,

And Shepherd, wont to follow sheep and neat to field
   afore,

And Laund, a fell and eager bitch that had a wolf to sire;

Another bratch called Greedygut with two her puppies by
   her,

And Ladon, gaunt as any grew'nd, a hound in Sycion
   bred;

Blab, Fleetwood, Patch, whose fleckèd skin with sundry
   spots was spread;

Wight, Bowman, Roister, Beauty, fair and white as winter's snow,

And Tawny, full of dusky hairs that over all did grow;

With lusty Ruffler, passing all the residue there in strength,

And Tempest, best of footmanship in holding out at
   length;

And Coal and Swift and little Wolf, as wight as any other,

Accompanied with a Cyprian hound that was his native
   brother;

And Snatch, amid whose forehead stood a star as white as
   snow,

The residue being all as black and sleek as any crow;

And shaggy Rug, with other twain that had a sire of Crete

And dam of Sparta – t'one of them called Jollyboy, a great

And large-flewed hound, the t'other Churl, who ever
   gnarring went;

And Ringwood with a shirl loud mouth, the which he
   freely spent;
With divers mo whose names to tell it were but loss of
   time.

*Neat.*

Yes, it is, rather, isn't it?

*No, I mean – Shepherd is wont to follow sheep and neat. What
does that mean?*

Oh – neat means 'cattle'. Even filtered through the lens of
Golding, we can see what's important in a dog to the Roman.
We would have had much to say to Ovid's Actaeon, Una.
Appearance, ability to scent, pedigrees; appetites. You can sense
the pride in their physical attributes, such as their teeth and
their coats and in their talents as hunters – Killbuck is who you
want on your side when you are dashing after deer.

His dogs come from Crete, Sparta, Arcadia, all across Greece.
Scalecliff is wonderful – I can imagine a particularly nimble,
fearless hound, able to pursue its quarry up any height. There's
a sheepdog in there, naturally, and the joy in Beauty still reso-
nates today. I've always especially enjoyed Roister, and 'little
Wolf, as wight as any other'.

*What does wight mean?*

Strong. Maybe Actaeon gave him this name because of his
wolf-like demeanour. It could even be ironic, because he is the
smallest. We see that in a real dog, Taurus, or 'bull', the name of
a small Maltese lapdog. There are some lovely dog names in
antiquity: Lampourgos, 'firetail', for a sheepdog. Columella suggests Ferox, Lupa, Cerva, Tigris – Fierce, She Wolf, Hind and
Tiger. But for every one of those kinds, there's also a Kalathine
– which means 'small enough to be carried in a handbag'. And I

would have liked to meet Melissa, Myia and Acris – Bee, Fly and Grasshopper.

This kind of love in the rearing of dogs is evident in the *Odyssey*. It's all the more poignant when you consider what actually happened to Actaeon. He named all his dogs, knew them intimately, probably fed them from his own table. And then...

## EPIC POEMS RANKED BY DOGGINESS

1. The *Odyssey* by Homer. The doggiest of epics. Sitting by the Aga, on a stinky blanket, with a belly full of beef. The chocolate Labrador of epic poetry.
2. The *Iliad* by Homer. Dogs slink around the camp; Achilles keeps pet dogs. (He must be a good guy.) Keen, mean, fast. The lurcher of epic.
3. *Metamorphoses* by Ovid. Plenty of hunting scenes and a delight in the power and swiftness of dogs. Though only one transformation into an actual dog.
4. The *Aeneid* by Virgil. Dogs are hardly in evidence. Almost a cat.

Actaeon stumbled upon the goddess Artemis as she was bathing. Her nymphs shrieked; she, horrified, transformed him into a stag. It's one of Ovid's more memorable descriptions.

As Actaeon changes, he tries to call out the names of his dogs. But his mouth, now with a thickened tongue, turning into a muzzle, can't form the sounds.

His own dogs don't recognise him: baying, they leap at him, and tear him apart.

Una's ears drooped.

So what does it mean? An excellent scholarly article describes how the story took on different layers over time.[‡‡]

In early tradition, Actaeon dies because either he tries to court Semele (mother of Dionysus), and Artemis executes Zeus' vengeance on him, or, in familiar style, he boasts: he's better at hunting than she is.[§§] Whichever way, his death is caused by hubris. In Euripides' play *Bacchae*, Actaeon is punished for bragging about his hunting ability. He was initially viewed as a tragic hero suffering the consequences of his excess.

The deadly bath scene was introduced by another poet. There were powerful taboos against men being present at the ritual bathing of the statue of a goddess. Here, Actaeon innocently violates the taboo in spying on the real goddess. There is no voyeuristic element to this. No Peeping Tom he.

Ovid runs with the baton, using the story as part of a cycle built around the House of Cadmus, in which the gods take disproportionate vengeances on mortals. A later epic poem introduced an erotic element: Actaeon becomes maddened with desire for Artemis. The version you see painted so evocatively by Titian, hanging in the National Gallery, is only one image from a much more fluid tradition.

---

[‡‡] Carl C. Schlam, 'Diana and Actaeon: Metamorphoses of a Myth'.

[§§] Boasting is a feature of myths: Arachne boasts that she's better at weaving than Athena, and gets turned into a spider; Niobe boasts her children are more beautiful than Apollo and Artemis, and so she gets turned into a rock, and so on.

The dogs are a constant. Creatures that Actaeon has trained, fed, hunted with, probably even slept beside, turning on him, unable to identify him. A terrible irony.

*That's a sad story*, Una said. *I would never do that to you.*

I know.

Una trotted up close to me and placed her head just next to my right thigh. I returned the gesture with a tickle behind the ear.

It was time to head home. We had a lot to get through on the morrow.

*More stories then?*

But before I replied, she'd already bounded away, disappearing amongst the trees, glorying in her swiftness. I rose, and followed on behind.

# Chapter 3

# A DOG~~GOD~~LY DIGEST
## Who's Who in Myth

It was a broadly sunny morning towards the end of August. I was in bed, half-dozing, whilst Una was poking her nose over the windowsill to look outside, which is what she does when she's telling me she wants a walk. Then she patters over to nudge me. Una would be really good in charge of the government's nudge unit.

Lie-ins on a Saturday are not an option when a lurcher's wet muzzle is coming into contact with your face at regular intervals. It was time to get up.

Once we were ready...

*Once you were ready.*

Yes, thank you, Una... we headed down towards Regent's Park, past a group of teenagers smoking on the corner of the street.

Benson and Hedges, I said.

*What?* said Una.

Torvill and Dean. Little and Large. Classics and mythology. You can't have one without the other. But they are not the same. The popular conception of Classics is that there exists a book, containing every myth, a kind of Bible, which is what you study.

There isn't such a thing, alas. Myth is a complex beast, pieced together from myriad sources in time and space, interpreted and reinterpreted over the years. The Romans were not so hot on their own myths (which they termed '*fabula*', from which we get the word 'fabulous' – note that it really means 'unbelievable'. Think on that next time you compliment someone's dress) and only had a few of their own, whilst assimilating those of the Greeks.

The word '*mythos*', in Ancient Greek, means 'word, speech or message' (remember Iris, and that shimmering transmission of thoughts and ideas). It later expanded to mean a story, and one that wasn't necessarily entirely reliable.

Myths were inescapable in the ancient world: shown on temples, altars, frescoes; they would have been told as women sat at their weaving, or during dinner parties, the year dotted by festivals to one god or goddess or another.

The Amyclae Throne in Sparta, which was probably constructed in the sixth century BC, is an example of the literal presence of myth. It was decorated with the whole shebang: to list them all would take the rest of the morning. Everyone's there, from the Graces, the seasons and the ancient monsters to the Olympians, the heroes Theseus, Perseus, Heracles, and all the way through to the Trojan War.[*]

Spartans saw this every day, and were reminded of their mythical heritage constantly. And crucially, they would have talked about these myths and celebrated them.

Across the sea in Italy, and later on in time, Romans played out mythical scenes in the Colosseum. This could be done in quite brutal fashion. The story of the Minotaur's conception is

---

[*]   See Appendix E for the full list.

gruesome enough in the imagination. It involves Pasiphaë, the wife of King Minos, concealing herself in a specially built wooden cow so that a bull could mate with her. (Poseidon made her lust for the bull for the usual divine reasons.)

I sometimes wonder how Pasiphaë went about asking Daedalus to construct this for her.

'Oh hey, Daedalus. You know I'm a queen and everything, and I have pretty much everything I want. But the one thing that I'm really lacking is a life-size cow made out of wood.'

Daedalus, presumably, just rolled his eyes and got on with it. The scene was often acted out, usually with the cow standing empty. The Emperor Nero, says Suetonius, put a woman in there.

*Awful!* said Una.

Absolutely – if it's true. We only have Suetonius' word for it. This suggests that the general populace (known as the *plebes*) in Rome knew the stories well.

Petronius' later Latin novel, the *Satyricon*, shows it was as possible to be pretentious about myth in antiquity as it is now.

The freed slave Trimalchio is giving a feast, where excess is the norm. He wants to boast about his silver: he's got some three-gallon bumpers, which show Cassandra killing her sons, and the boys are lying there dead; very lifelike. He has a bowl, left to him by his patron, displaying Daedalus shutting Niobe into the Trojan Horse.

Except, of course, he's wrong on every point: it was Medea who killed her sons, not Cassandra, who was a prophetess fated to tell the truth and have nobody believe her; it was Daedalus who shut the Minotaur into the labyrinth; and Niobe wept when all her children were killed by Apollo and Artemis, and was turned into stone, and had never been anywhere near the Trojan Horse in her life, honest, guvnor.

Trimalchio's intention is to add grandeur, to show himself a member of the educated classes, but he fails. Trimalchio also shows his bad taste when he goes to the baths: he pees into a silver bottle. Not quite the done thing, you see.

Myths were an essential part of literature. Almost every Greek tragedy has a mythical basis. Poetry not only tells and retells the stories, but also illuminates daily life with mythical allusion. Legal speeches employ examples from myth to damn or praise their targets; philosophy, as we have seen, transforms it for its own purposes. To take just one example: Medea—

*How do you pronounce Medea?*

Medea, my deah, is how one Oxford don suggests it should be done.

Medea pops up in the myth of Jason and the Argonauts, then stars in her own tragedy, in which, after killing her children, she scarpers in a chariot drawn by dragons to Athens.

She appears too in Ovid's *Metamorphoses*, in agony over her love for Jason. Cicero uses Medea as an unflattering comparison for Clodia Metelli, a woman he's trying to smear as a murderer. If you followed all the allusions to Medea, you'd have a whole book.

The myths in popular culture have been standardised. Ancient myth was much more elastic. One man's Helen might be sitting quietly in Troy, pining for her husband Menelaus; another version sees her snatched away to Egypt, leaving a phantom behind, and hard cheese on everyone who thought they were fighting for her.

Many figures of myth have now metamorphosed into brand names and products, completely untethered from their original powers. The goddess Nike is a straightforward personification of victory, often shown with wings (and confused with Iris). But her name is now synonymous with a manufacturer of plimsoles. Hermes is a postal delivery company; and you can still buy posters from Athena online.

Because of the importance of myth to Classics, it's helpful to have an idea of who's who.

The characters resemble a series of aristocratic families engaged in permanent internecine strife. Only they're not just worried about inviting Great-Aunt Millicent to a wedding because she's been feuding with Cousin Theodore about a silver cow creamer that's gone missing in suspicious circumstances. They are feuding because one of them castrated his father and sprinkled the ocean with the resulting blood.

*Yipes.*

Many of Una's male friends have suffered the same thing. Though, it must be said, at the hands of the vet. She winced with sympathy, and her tail darted between her legs.

I'll stick to the most common names from the Athenian dialect, because frankly who's heard of Pohoidan?[†]

Most of the ones familiar to us from mythology have percolated down via the Latin tradition, which is why we, usually, say Hercules, instead of Herakles/Heracles, although I've chosen to stick to Heracles here. Even trying to transliterate Greek names from the Greek alphabet results in differences.

The Greek gods, like the invaders of Britain, arrived in waves. The first lot were massive primaeval personifications of things that we, even today, find difficult to envisage.

---

† A dialectal form of Poseidon, god of the sea.

A Doggodly Digest

Let's imagine a conversation between two travellers, each on a different journey, coming together in company in a tavern. We know there were wayside houses; such a situation is most probable. One is a heavy-set farmer, on his way back from selling off a few bullocks. The other is a tired scholar, returning to his family estate after some taxing business in Athens, looking forward to taking up his researches again.

They have polished off a bowl of wine, devoured some cheese and olives, and are gazing, dreamily, into the fire. A Molossian hound whimpers quietly, drooling a little. The farmer reaches forwards to pat its head.

The circularity of the drinking bowl reminds them of the world, and then of how it sprang into being.

'Chaos was the first thing, and Night was born from it,' says the farmer.

'Oh no, I'm fairly sure that Eurynome was the first?' The scholar is surprised; his investigations have shown him something different.

'Who's Eurynome when she's at home?' The Molossian lifts its head and wheezes; another traveller enters; the discussion turns to the price of corn.

Even the ancients could not agree. So let's stick with one story. The farmer's will do.

Chaos. At first there was Chaos – not the eternal state of my desk, but the original state, or rather non-state, of the universe, which gave form to Gaia.

The scientist James Lovelock's theory that the Earth is a conscious, self-regulating organism would have resonated. Gaia is fertile Planet Earth, and she promptly popped out a son, with whom she had (there not being anyone much else around) plenty of children.

The most important of these was the one who still makes schoolchildren snigger, and gives his name to a distant planet.

Uranus managed to reign supreme over the universe for about five minutes, before his eldest son, Cronus, lopped off his genitals with a sickle. Perhaps understandably, he retired, leaving the family business to his children, the Titans.

Cronus took charge.

For now. Tension between generations is a trademark of the ancient gods. Cronus married his sister Rhea and, very sensibly, for fear of being overthrown, gobbled up all his six children (three boys and three girls). History does not recall whether he used salt, or a handful of mint, or what he washed them down with, or, indeed, whether they agreed with him, but I imagine that he might have suffered a tiny bit of indigestion.

Rhea wasn't best pleased with this arrangement, and so she set about rescuing one of the children. She wrapped up a stone in some swaddling clothes, which lucky Cronus swallowed instead, and concealed the infant Zeus on an island, where he was brought up by a goat.

Later on, when Zeus was fully grown and ready to take on his father, Rhea administered an emetic to Cronus, and he vomited up all his children. They emerged not only whole but prepared to fight, and then proceeded, along with Zeus, brought back from exile, to topple him.

Down several steps on the divine ladder for Cronus; up to the very top for Zeus and his siblings.

We sometimes find Cronus, post-usurpation, presiding over a Golden Age; he is a model for the Roman god Saturnus, who was the civiliser of the Romans. There is a contradiction between these two stories (on the one hand: violent eater of children! on the other: benevolent bringer of laws!). This is probably because they came from different places, and ended up being conflated.

Either way, Cronus was pensioned off, whether to the Isles of the Blessed, or to Tartarus, an unfashionable place in the furthest depths of the Underworld. We can only hope, for Cronus' sake, that it was the former. People sometimes confuse him with 'Chronos'. The latter is a word simply meaning 'time', and not to be mixed up with the baby-swallowing Titan. Time swallows all; Cronus only swallowed his children.

One or two well-behaved Titans did continue to hang about after Zeus and his siblings seized the chariot-reins of power.

We strolled past a poster advertising a production of *A Midsummer Night's Dream*, to be performed in the open air. A lovely sight, I thought, at dusk, when things turn eerie and magical. The queen of the fairies, Titania, is named after the Titans. She's no butterfly-winged gauzy thing, but a powerful entity.

There's only one Titan you need to know about, and that is Prometheus. His name means 'forethought', and his fate, once he stole fire from heaven to give to mankind, for whom he felt rather sorry as we sat shivering and scoffing raw food, was to be chained up on a mountainside and have his regenerating liver pecked out, eternally, by an eagle.

*That doesn't seem very fair*, said Una.

It's not. This has been the subject of many plays, including Aeschylus' (dubiously attributed) *Prometheus Unbound*. He's understandably fascinating for writers and artists, a myth about the tension between creativity and power. We'll see this very same tension at play when we get to Virgil's *Aeneid*.

Prometheus' grandson, Hellen, was one of the founders of the Greek people – which is where the name Hellenes, still in use today, derives from. In Prometheus' story we encounter

Pandora's box, which the girl opened, allowing evils into the world (as well as, some add, hope). Classical pedants note: it probably wasn't a box, but a jar or a vase. Pandora's vase doesn't have quite the same ring to it.

Back to Zeus. Jupiter; his Roman name is, like 'Zeus', connected to the word for 'day' – or what you can see in the day, the 'Sky'. He is a supremely ancient god. The -piter suffix is related to 'pater', which means Zeus/Jupiter is the Skyfather.

In the *Iliad*, Homer frequently calls Zeus 'Son of Cronus' – a constant reminder of the horrors he committed to achieve power, and of the possibility of the same thing happening to him. Which he was not very keen on. Being a sole ruler, he is a harbinger of the monotheistic religions that came after him; but he's hardly an omnipotent god.

His sister Hera, or Juno to the Romans, was also his wife, which made her the most powerful goddess, with an ancient cult. Her province was marriage and women. Zeus had many other consorts, one of whom he turned into a fly and then swallowed; but Hera was his official spouse. That's why, in literature, she's usually portrayed as jealous and watchful. You can hardly blame her.

Far from being a lesser divinity than Zeus, she was royal, beautiful and sometimes even surpassed him. A statue in Olympia shows a regal Hera ensconced on a throne, her husband standing beside her.

According to Virgil, she couldn't stand the Trojans, understandably enough, because Zeus had abducted the handsome young Trojan prince Ganymede to be his cup-bearer.

'Are you sure there's nothing going on between you and Ganymede?' Hera might ask one morning in the Olympian bedchamber, glancing at her husband sideways. He'd come in late last night, as usual, smelling of wine and nectar.

'No, no… of course not…'

'Are you sure?'

'I like him for his conversation.'

She bore a real dislike for Heracles, one of the many illegitimate sons of Zeus. His name was in itself a goad to her pride, as it can be taken to mean 'Glory of Hera'.

As a Roman, Juno was in charge of the mint, which was not a breath sweetener, as one of my pupils believed for a surprisingly long time, but the place where they produced coins. Plus her chariot was drawn by peacocks, which is pretty mint if you ask me.

We have largely forgotten about Hestia, although her role as goddess of the hearth was vital for both the Greeks and the Romans, who called her Vesta. The hearth was absolutely central for any household (in Latin, the word for it is *focus*). Yet as she languished indoors all the time, she features in hardly any stories. She was said, though wrongly, to have given up her place on Olympus to a raffish interloper from the East, Dionysus (although he was no interloper). In later years, whenever someone lit a Swan Vesta match, it was a reminder of this once powerful goddess. A small act of worship every time someone had a fag.

In Rome a body of six aristocratic women, the Vestal Virgins, tended to her worship. They exerted considerable political power, though the less said about their status as virgins the better.

Demeter, the third sister, whose Roman name, Ceres, you invoke every morning when you take your cornflakes—

*I don't eat cornflakes*, said Una.

Her daughter Persephone was snatched into the Underworld by the god Hades. This grim tale is called the 'Rape of

Persephone', 'rape' here meaning 'abduction', from the Latin *rapio*, 'I seize'. Persephone ends up dividing her time: she spends six months amongst the ghosts, and six months up on Earth with her mother.

*Is that about the seasons?* asked Una.

It was really about the way that plants grow hidden underground for half the year, and then it became linked to the seasons. A fine example of a myth that seeks to explain natural phenomena.

Demeter and her daughter could move between the Underworld and this world. Those who penetrated that border were always of especial interest to the ancients: the promise of a glimpse behind the veil was as thrilling then as it is now.

This meant they were the subject of the sacred mysteries at Eleusis, lying a few miles from Athens, and every year people would descend from all over Greece to celebrate at the festival.

*What did they learn?*

If only we knew – initiates were all sworn to secrecy, on pain of death. We think that initiates were given a guide to negotiating the borders between life and death. The temple at Eleusis was enlarged by the Athenian Pericles; and Marcus Aurelius had it rebuilt many centuries later. But the fourth century AD Emperor Theodosius put an end to them: although some say that Greek peasants simply transferred the rites to St Demetrius of Thessaloníki.

Zeus' three sisters, therefore, were not to be trifled with. His male siblings had to be dealt with, too.

When Zeus performed his hostile takeover of the heavens, the rest of the world was parcelled out to his brothers in the universe's first power-sharing arrangement: Poseidon (Neptune) collared the sea. This elemental, watery divinity also caused earthquakes. As father of the Cyclops, he has a big role in the *Odyssey*, where he is one of the main causes of the hero's troubles. Poseidon's job description also included horses – either because he was the first god to tame them, or because he fathered the first one.

The third brother, Hades, who perhaps wasn't paying attention, or was of a naturally gloomy disposition, ended up as ruler of the Underworld. I always think of him as a bit like Hamlet, swathed in black and standing slightly off to the side, making sarcastic comments. Pluto, his Latin name, means 'wealth'.

*Gold?* asked Una. *All that gold in the mines?*

No, souls. Which is ironic, since it's not like they do anything under there. Hades doesn't bother Olympus much, and there aren't many images of him. He's not simply the god of the dead, but also the embodiment of death, and so a pretty terrifying chap. The gates to his kingdom, Una, are guarded by the three-headed dog Cerberus.

*Cerrrberrruss.* Una growled. *Why is he guarding the Underworld? Who would want to get in?*

There's a meme that did the rounds of the internet a few years ago, showing Cerberus as a puppy, guarding the gates to heck. Fully grown Cerberus is a little bit more frightening to those wanting to leave. Generally speaking, nobody wants to get in, apart from various heroes bent on asking favours from Hades. He must have got jolly irritated with all those people constantly bothering him for one thing or another. Never a moment's peace.

Some people believe that Cerberus' name means 'Spotty', but that is very unlikely. Although he did greet newly dead souls with a wag of his tail. Quite cheering, I should think, especially after that dreary boat ride with the ferryman Charon across the River Styx.

The conversation would not have been particularly stimulating, I imagine, although Charon of all people should have known the gossip. It's not a great job, going back and forth for ever. He Styx with it, though.

Una rolled her eyes.

Cerberus was there to stop people getting out. A more plausible explanation for his name is that it means 'Growler'.

Una nodded. That seemed more likely to her, too.

The Greek poet Hesiod calls Cerberus the 'bronze-voiced hound of Hades', and gives him fifty heads. But don't let that get in the way of your image of him. He had a brother, Orthrus, who only had two heads.

*What happened to him?*

He was slain by Heracles, collateral damage in one of his labours. Still, at least he had a snake's tail, which is more than can be said for Cerberus.

*Oh. But how did all the other gods come about?*

I settled down on a bench and took up a stick, much as Odysseus did when he wanted to impress Calypso and drew diagrams of his Trojan campaigns in the sand.

Here are the rest.

### SOME GODLY BIRTHS

Born from the foam made by the castrated penis of Uranus – **Aphrodite, goddess of love**

Born from the union of Zeus and Dione – **Aphrodite, also**

Twice born. Once, snatched from his dying mother's womb – **Dionysus, god of wine**

The second time, snatched from the thigh of Zeus – **Dionysus, god of wine**

Born from Zeus' splitting headache – **Athena, goddess of weaving and war**

Not born from Zeus' splitting headache – **Athena's twin brother, who remained inside Zeus' head**

Born from the actual marriage of Zeus and his sister/wife Hera – **Ares, god of war**

Born from Zeus and the nymph Maia – **Hermes, messenger god and trickster**

Born from Zeus and the nymph Leto – **Apollo and Artemis, twin gods of light, hunting and various other things**

Born by Hera's parthenogenesis (virgin birth) – **Hephaestus, the smith and fire god**

Zeus and Hera only produced one legitimate child: Ares, the war god. Sharks are capable of parthenogenesis – that is, of virgin birth, from the Greek words 'parthenos', meaning 'maiden', and 'genesis', meaning 'birth'. And so was Hera, who, terribly indignant when Athena leapt out from the head of her husband, managed to produce the lame god Hephaestus as an eternal rebuke.

There were two stories about Aphrodite's birth, which illustrates the plasticity of myth. The first was Uranian Aphrodite, in which she's a primaeval force of love. Because she rose from her father's genitals, this aspect of her was in charge of male–male love.[‡] You'll see this birth in Botticelli's painting of Venus, as she wafts onto shore, borne in a shell, though the severed pudenda of her father lie well out of sight.

Aphrodite was, in the second story, the daughter of Zeus and the goddess Dione. She is both Aphrodites at the same time, as well as being Venus for the Romans (exceptionally important as she was the mother of Aeneas, from whom they claimed descent). She's a powerful force: in Lucretius' philosophical poem *De Rerum Natura* she's invoked both as the mother of the Roman race and as the supreme generative force.

Gods and goddesses are fluid. They take on aspects from other gods, merging with them, perfectly capable of being more than one thing at any one time. It's one of the perks of being divine, you see.

*What are the other perks?*

Immortality, of course. Although this seems to be not as clear-cut as it might be. But you could have your pick of any mortal. And the ability to influence the affairs of men, whilst remaining untouched by any deep care or sorrow.

Now I know you're wondering, what about Cupid? The impish cherubic figure flutters in from Roman tradition. His power has almost completely vanished through cartoonification and commerce: the big-eyed, simpering baby who brings lovers together on Valentine's Day. He has been conflated with

---

‡   This is why nineteenth-century homosexuals called themselves Uranians.

the Greek Eros – quite literally, Love – who in Greek myth was a supremely important figure. He's either one of the more ancient gods or he is the son of Aphrodite. He pops up in many stories with his ability to cause gods and men to fall in love, often mischievously. There's also the delightful tale of Cupid and Psyche, in which he accidentally shoots himself.

*Eros. Isn't there a statue of him in Piccadilly Circus?* Una certainly knows its smells, and has even left some of her own at its base.

That's actually not Eros.

*It's not?*

No. It's Anteros, his brother, a different god, his twin, who represents mutual love. Though Anteros is usually shown with butterfly wings, and Eros with bird equivalents, the statue in Piccadilly does look very birdlike. Its sculptor was clear, though, that this was the more mature, reflective brother.

*Huh*, said Una. *Are there any others?*

Not that I know of. But there were many different forms of love, which the philosophers tried to categorise: Plato, for example, distinguished between two types of Eros: Vulgar and Divine. The first is the attraction of the body; the second is connected to the first, but transcends the material to move towards the appreciation of Beauty itself in ideal form. Eros here is a way of helping human nature to move towards the divine.

'Cupid and Bacchus, my saints are…' I mused. 'Let drink and love still reign…' It was the start of a poem by the Earl of Rochester, innocent-sounding enough; however, its ending was probably a little too much for Una, as Rochester, a seventeenth-century libertine of the highest order, was rather more interested in the Vulgar form of Cupid than the Divine.

Bacchus was a suitable god for Rochester. That was his Roman name; he was Dionysus to the Greeks. They said he came from the East: exotic and destabilising, bringing the gift – or curse – of wine along with him. He is twice born because he appeared, kicking and screaming, from his mother's womb at the exact moment that Zeus manifested in his full glory (since his mother Semele had asked for it); Zeus rescued the baby, and, in what is possibly the world's first intensive care procedure, incubated him in his own thigh.

*Dionysus*, said Una, *sounds dangerous.*

He is. Watch out for his followers, the Maenads, who go rampaging about, tearing animals and humans apart in a frenzied ecstasy. Their name is linked to 'mania'. Getting out of yourself – ecstatic – was a very important part of Bacchic ritual. Hedonists at raves come very close to achieving a similar state.

I once visited Jerash, in Jordan, an almost perfectly preserved Roman city. White colonnades stretch out in front of you; the desert is in sight. I was alone, and it was very early in the morning. I entered the temple of Bacchus and, there being nobody around, began the Bacchic cry: 'Io! Io!' It echoed around, and I did it again. In the stillness of the hour it felt as if I was only a sliver away from conjuring up the god himself. I heard a stone fall nearby. Was that a goat bleating? Could it be? 'Io, io!' I cried out once more. Only for a stream of German tourists in their sensible walking gear to emerge from round the corner, hoping for a re-enactment of a Dionysiac ritual. They were very disappointed when they saw, not some scantily clad maidens, but me in my jumper and cords. I scrabbled for my satchel and snuck away.

*Bacchae*, a play by Euripides, shows what happens if you refuse to believe in the god: when Bacchus comes a-calling to

Thebes, demanding worship, King Pentheus thinks he's a fraud. A disguised Bacchus sends him out to spy on the Maenads, who include his mother and aunt. They, in the throes of ecstasy, discover him and dismember him, and his mother, in one of the most striking scenes in all of Greek tragedy, brings his head back to the palace, under the impression that it's a lion.

More than any other god, Bacchus represents the idea of something absolutely other. He's on the edge of things. He rides big cats! He flies! He enjoys the theatre! He is, in short, the coolest god in town. And you don't want to mess with him.

Scholars now believe he was not an interloper, but an Ancient Greek god, whose name is found on archaic lists. His wildness didn't mesh with the Greeks' own idea of measured, reasonable Greekness, and so they pretended he came from elsewhere.

Understanding him is vital to grasping the ancient world: that undertone of danger and mystery, set against the apparent austerity and purity of the other gods. He is a god for our times, rocking the boat, confounding expectations. He doesn't fit in with received ideas about classical morality: and that's why he's so interesting.

Imagine the scene on Olympus. Dionysus rocks up, all glamorous and a bit drunk, having been to a lovely party, wearing a panther-skin. He stumbles over a spear his older sister, Athena, is carrying. She looks on disapprovingly, tutting. I imagine Athena as tutting most of the time. She was a mighty goddess; the head-sprung (and headstrong) Athena, always shown fully armed and almost always with her terrifying *aegis*.

*Her terrifying what?*

Aegis. The *Oxford Classical Dictionary* explains: 'a large all-round bib with scales, fringed with snakes' heads and usually bearing the head of the gorgon.'

*It's just…*

What?

*Bib. It's not a very frightening word, is it?*

You wouldn't say that if you saw her wearing it. Her provinces were crafts and war.

*How do those two go together?*

A maiden girl would spend a lot of time weaving, whilst a woman who never gave birth, like Athena (and her hunt-mad sister Artemis), was a 'masculine' woman, and a potential warrior. Ancient writers were fascinated with female warriors, as seen in the myths of Penthesilea and Hippolyta, both queens of the fearsome, legendary tribe of women known as the Amazons.

In the *Iliad*, Athena lays down her dress and dons the tunic of Zeus so she can get stuck into the fighting.

She's the only goddess whose name is explicitly linked to a city – Athens. Her Roman name, Minerva, has been bestowed upon a beloved character in J.K. Rowling's Harry Potter series, the wise witch Minerva McGonagall, who also proves herself useful in a battle.

You can see how important war was for the ancients, since there was another major war god, Ares, always rather bombastic, and nobody really liked him. Where Athena is head girl, member of the chess club, captain of the fencing team and can do the Rubik's cube in under a minute, Ares pours beer on his head and sometimes walks into glass doors; where she embodies strategy, he is brute force.

She is the general atop a charger, calm and reasonable during battle, issuing orders; he is the tank, crushing all in his path. There's a curious part in the *Iliad* where the hero Diomedes fights the gods. He manages to stab Aphrodite, and she patters off the battlefield, squealing; and then he wounds Ares, who scuttles shamefacedly back to Olympus to moan to his father, Zeus. 'Daaaad!'

Ares, for the Greeks, was an ambivalent being: war was necessary, but destructive. You needed Athena – strategy – to help defend yourself, alongside him. His Roman counterpart Mars had other facets, some of which associate him with vegetation and forests; he was exceptionally important to the Romans in his warlike aspect, and the Roman forces would exercise on the Campus Martius. He has, alas, nothing to do with Mars bars, which were named after the Mars family of confectioners.§

Mars was the father of Romulus and Remus, the legendary twins whose conflict resulted in the foundation of Rome. They had war, quite literally, in their blood; as well, of course, as being suckled by wolves. The milk of human kindness it is not.

If you'd only met Dionysus and Ares, you might be forgiven for thinking that the Greek gods were rather a brutal lot. Fortunately, there is Apollo to counter that. Apollo is the only god whose name is the same for both Romans and Greeks; he, with his twin sister Artemis, are both virgin gods. Apollo was traditionally associated with the sun (displacing the Titan Helios), and Artemis the moon (ditto Selene). The dishiest of all the gods, Apollo was associated with music, light and archery; he was also known as Apollo Smintheus, the mouse god.

*Was he... worshipped by mice?* Una, who had been nosing about a fascinating bit of fish and chip wrapping, glanced up.

No. He oversaw plagues, which were borne by rodents – that's why he's at the beginning of the *Iliad*, being invoked by a priest to bring down sickness on the Achaean army. One of

---

§   Mars is a variant of the surname Marr.

Apollo's titles is 'the far-shooter', and his arrow was sacred. His sister, Artemis, we have met before.

Una made a bow of obeisance. *I will catch a squirrel in her honour later*, she said.

Excellent. Apollo once had his bow stolen by Hermes. I have always had a special fondness for Hermes. This youthful god was a trickster even when he was in short trousers: carrying messages for the gods (like Iris), he also guided the souls of the dead to the Underworld, which earned him the title of Psychopomp.

In Roman myth he is Mercury, also known as quicksilver, and those are his qualities – glancing, mobile. He was the bearer of a staff with two snakes twined around it, called the caduceus; this has been incorrectly appropriated by the US Army Medical Corps. The staff of Asclepius (Apollo's son), who was the healing god, has only one snake.

Now, who's left? I galloped through the major pantheon in my mind, hoping that I'd not forgotten anyone. Ah yes. And finally, Hephaestus. We've seen how he was created through a process of virgin birth; you will also see how remarkably un-Christlike he is. He was Vulcan to the Romans, and married off to Aphrodite (much to her chagrin; she had rather more of an eye for ephebic⁹ youths like Adonis or sinewy warriors such as Ares). A smith god, and also a fire deity, his lameness means he is no threat. His limping about is a source of much amusement to the other gods. And he's also the originator of various immortal bronze dogs, and the first robots.

*Robots?*

Yes, he's got walking, talking bronze handmaidens. Robots!

---

⁹ An *ephebe* was an adolescent male, often shown on vases.

I stopped to catch my breath. Una was staring into the distance, thinking about bronze dogs, or squirrels. We'd left the bench behind some time ago, and were now in the woody zone of Regent's Park, where it feels fairly close to being in the countryside.

At least, if it were not for the office workers playing Frisbee, and the picnicking family with their overexcited toddler, I could almost imagine a faun slinking away through the trees; or a dryad stretching out her hand and tapping you on the shoulder, only to vanish in a whisper of murmuring leaves.

## DIVINITIES: THE SECOND ELEVEN

**Meliads** – ash tree nymphs. Ancient. Also sprang from the blood of Uranus' castrated genitals.
**Dryads** – tree nymphs of a more general kind.
**Hamadryads** – linked to the actual tree.
**Alseids** – nymphs of groves and glens. Enjoy whisky.
**Oreads** – mountain nymphs. Hearty.
**Naiads** – water nymphs. Likely to abduct beautiful boys.
**Hydriads** – also water nymphs. Also keen on beautiful boys.
**Nereids** – sea nymphs. Talk like pirates.
**Oceanids** – ocean nymphs. Mysterious.
**Leimoniads** – meadow nymphs. Like flowers.
**Psammeads** – sand nymphs. But only in E. Nesbit.

A Frisbee plonked down at my feet. Una snatched it up and went zooming round and round. It took a little while to extricate Frisbee from jaw; the missile was returned, with apologies, to the workers. We carried on.

In charge of these numerous lesser divinities was the great god Pan, whose name means 'All'. Often depicted with the legs of a goat, he has much in common with the satyrs and thus with Dionysus. He was the spirit of woods and wildness, not an Olympian. Although he's technically under the control of Zeus, Pan is very much his own being, a reminder of the bestial and the unpredictable.

*Is Peter Pan named after him?* Una is rather fond of the book, because of the role that the dog Nana plays in looking after the Darling children, although Una thinks she would do it rather better. I have yet to test this theory with my own child, though animals did seem to feature rather as nurses in the ancient world. We've seen wolves and goats acting as wet nurses, and you also find deer, horses, pigs and cows in the same role; the healing god Asclepius is supposed to have been suckled by a sheepdog.

*Maybe my ancestor!* said Una.

Barrie was very much working in the classical tradition. King Midas was nourished by ants, which is rather surprising; less so is the story that Zeus was fed honey by bees as a baby. The animal world was never far away.

The god Pan certainly gave his name to J.M. Barrie's creation, and the Edwardians had a real craze for him. Peter Pan has more in common with Ganymede, kept eternally youthful, particularly when you note that St Peter has the keys to heaven – as, of course, does Ganymede.

The first edition of Kenneth Grahame's *The Wind in the Willows* sports a picture of Pan on the cover, referring to a scene where Ratty, in search of a lost baby otter,** finds him in the charge of the great god Pan. Here he undergoes a quasi-religious experience. Pan could induce a condition called pano-lepsy – effectively, being possessed by the god. Sometimes Una pricks up her ears like antennae when there's nothing obviously interesting about, and I wonder whether she's picking up signals from Pan.

Pan was also the only god said to have died. There is a moment in the *Iliad* where we learn that Ares was once tied up and kept for ages in a bronze jar, and almost did pop his clogs. But the crucial thing here is that he *almost* dies; he's still immortal.

Plutarch tells us that a sailor, passing an island, heard a divine voice announcing that 'The great god Pan is dead.' This was associated with the beginnings of Christianity and the clearing out of old ways of thinking.

You could hardly move for gods in the ancient world: we're probably sitting within a few feet of some Hampsteadian nature spirit as we speak, possibly the goddess of quinoa. Not to forget the actual goddess of the sewer, Cloacina, a most important one in London, as she was in Rome.

*Were there no dog gods?*

Try saying that several times quickly. Hecate, who was a dark goddess (and not counted amongst the Olympians, though she seems to have begun as an aspect of Apollo), had a special relationship with dogs. So much so that sometimes she's shown with dogs instead of feet.

*Weird.*

---

** The words 'otter' and '*hydra*' are related to each other, both stemming from the same word for water.

Yeah, I guess so; though the sea monster Scylla's lower half is also made up of dogs. Hecate sometimes has one head, but also sometimes three, one of which was that of a dog. (The others varied, but could be a horse or a snake.) The number three was associated with power – that's why in tradition Cerberus settled with three heads, as opposed to the fifty that we are also told about. This, as you know, Una, was one of Heracles' labours – he had to drag the poor beast back as proof. And there is plenty of evidence for dog sacrifices, I'm afraid.

Una whimpered.

The Roman poet Ovid notes that celebrants offered up the entrails of a sacrificial dog at the festival of the Robigalia in April. It had to be a red dog: they were praying to Robigus, the god of wheat rust. There was also the *Augurium canarium*, where reddish bitches were sacrificed to dim the fierceness of the dog star. I'm afraid also – I wanted to tread delicately – that Hecate used to accept sacrifices of puppies.

Una looked horrified. It was in bad taste. I had made an error. I moved on, swiftly.

Pliny's *Natural History* notes that dogs were forbidden in Heracles' temple in Rome – maybe he developed a lifelong hatred of them.

*How could you hate dogs?*

I could tell that this was what Una was thinking, from the way her tail had gone between her legs. She was wounded. First puppy killings, then this.

Well. I hurriedly tried to think of something to distract her. In the same book, Pliny writes that he relieves his headaches by tying a woman's bra to his head.

*Gosh!*

# A Doggodly Digest

I think we can forgive Heracles his hatred of dogs – he did have to drag back Cerberus, after all, who must have been heavy, even for him.

Artemis, as you know, was frequently depicted with dogs, which is unsurprising since she was hot on hunting; whilst Asclepius, the doctor god, was also chummy with them because of the healing properties of dog saliva (and his upbringing). Plutarch tells us a guard-dog at Asclepius' temple even went sprinting after a thief and brought him back to meet his just deserts.

Returning to the dogs, I mean gods. Una, by a fluke you've hit upon the thinking of the philosopher Xenophanes. He suggested that if cattle, horses and lions had hands, and were able to paint, then horses would paint gods in the image of horses, cattle of cattle, and so on.

That's why the Olympians (which we'll call them, even though some, like Poseidon and Hades, didn't live on the mountain), look, act and think like humans, and yet at the same time are powerful deities or even expressions of abstractions.

As Barbara Graziosi shows in her *The Gods of Olympus: A History*, Xenophanes was only talking about representational images; the ancients were perfectly able to worship 'a basic piece of wood' and revere it as Artemis. The gods didn't have to look like humans.

Once Zeus was installed on his throne, everything became fairly stable – but not entirely so. He did face attacks from the Titans, and a many-headed monster called Typhoeus. Tim Whitmarsh plausibly argues that the Titans, who are also descended from Uranus, are rival claimants for the throne, and symbolise the aristocracy; Typhoeus is the clamorous mob. Both are representations of forces that might topple a king.

Once he's defeated them, there is a hierarchy in place: each part of the world has been allotted to a particular god. The Titans are safely locked up, deep in Tartarus, no more troublesome than minor heartburn.

Zeus, however, made pretty damn sure he would never be usurped. His family were always trying to upend him in one way or another, but were never strong enough to manage it.

Whenever he fancied someone (which was constantly), and there was a prophecy that the son would be mightier than the father (which was also constantly), he quickly postponed his lustful desires.

Because of such a prophecy, Zeus forced the nymph Thetis to marry a mortal, the hero Peleus. Their child was Achilles, the greatest, most beautiful warrior of the Greeks.

When Achilles receives his god-designed armour from Thetis, he shines with a golden aura sent from the heavens. He is the aristocratic ideal, the supreme incarnation of the warrior-hero, which is probably why they got Brad Pitt to play him in *Troy*, the 2004 film that also starred Orlando Bloom as Paris.

This marriage is a major focal point, as without it there would have been no Trojan War. Cat—

I instantly regretted it.

It was too late. The hated syllable had been uttered. Una's head snapped round.

Una! Don't worry, I'm not talking about cats...

*Really?* She relaxed.

No! I'm talking about the Roman poet Catullus, who produced a scintillating long poem about myth. He began with Peleus' first sight of Thetis from the deck of the *Argo*, moved on to Theseus, Ariadne and the Minotaur, took in the birth of Achilles, and ended with the three Fates spinning.

You can see that at least two heroes, as well as later families in history, liked to claim descent from gods. This is not uncommon.

Our own Queen Elizabeth II is, through the Anglo-Saxon kings, descended from the Norse god Odin. The ravens living in the Tower of London have the resonance of Norse myth. A princely Italian family, the Massimo, whose scions are alive and well today, were descended from the ancient Roman Quintus Fabius Maximus Verrucosus Cunctator (yes, Verrucosus, which means 'warty' – we'll talk about names later).

Quintus Fabius' family, the Fabii, claimed descent from Heracles. You may well have met one of the actual descendants of a demigod. A member of the Massimo family recently climbed Everest – so they are still achieving heroic feats.

*Did the ancients actually believe in these gods and myths?*

The gods were a vital part of daily life, as we've seen. And there was a great deal of thinking and talking about the gods and what they might mean.

Some tried to rationalise them, explaining that the stories were based on actual events. A girl falls off a cliff in a strong wind, say, and someone says: Boreas took her! Then the story goes round the houses: did you hear? Boreas raped that girl?

*That doesn't sound very convincing.*

No, it doesn't really, does it? Others claimed the gods did not exist, or even that there was only one single god (prefiguring Christianity).

Plato didn't have much truck with myths, and would have banned poets from his city (with tears, he admits, thankfully). The ideal city that he constructs in his *Republic* sounds like an absolutely appalling place to live.

*Why's that?*

It was totalitarian. The worst of it is that he didn't want any poets in there.

*No poets!*

No, because they told lies. But he does say, through the mouth of Socrates, that a dog is a true philosopher.

*Really?*

Yes – because dogs are gentle to those they know, and the opposite with those they don't; their decision is based on knowing and not knowing.

Many philosophers discounted belief in the gods: my philosopher pin-up, Lucretius, whose long poem *De Rerum Natura* discusses atomic theory, amongst other things, believed that the gods did exist, but that they had nothing to do with human life; and that in contemplating them and their carefree lives, we should aim to emulate their existence. Which sounds like just the ticket to me.

There were as many complex systems of belief and non-belief amongst the ancients at play as there are today. Many heroes, such as Heracles, were deified, and the Roman emperors often became gods after they died, and were even given the same kinds of cult-offerings when alive by some non-Roman cities.

## PHILOSOPHERS, AND HOW TO SPOT THEM

**Thales** – thought the fundamental basis of everything was water. Predicted eclipses.

**Anaximander** – argued that the elements couldn't be the basis for everything. Instead, the basis for everything was an indefinite substance he called 'apeiron'.

**Xenophanes** – thought events had natural, not divine origins. He was right.

**Pythagoras** – a mystic who believed everything was mathematical. Vegetarian.

**Heraclitus** – thought there was no stable element; 'panta rhei' – everything flows.

**Socrates** – taught in Athens, using a questioning method. The grandfather of philosophy, encouraging an examination of good and evil. Didn't leave behind any writings. Was made to drink hemlock by the Athenians, on a charge of corrupting the youth.

**Plato** – the pupil of Socrates. Who was Socrates' busiest student? The one with a lot on his plate-o. His dialogues, presented as spoken by Socrates and his friends, are hugely influential. Into metaphysics; his Theory of Forms argues that there's a permanent reality beyond ours, where perfection exists.

**Aristotle** – the pupil of Plato. Didn't believe in the Forms, but thought matter and form belonged to each individual thing. Taught Alexander the Great.

Which brings us neatly to the heroes and demigods, who straddle the divine and the mortal, and to what we might call the second phase of myth. Phase Two, if you will.

All the heroes are related to each other, since most of them descend from gods. In this category you'll find the proper heroes. They go on quests, usually because they've annoyed somebody, or somebody wants to kill them. They fight monsters, often without any help.

They resemble your thick-necked rugger-bugger, and could crush your forearm with their little finger. Whilst carrying an ox. Two. Their closest descendant today is Geralt of Rivia, in Andrzej Sapkowski's fantasy series *The Witcher*, a mutant muscleman who travels about slaying monsters for cash.

### A (VERY) ROUGH CHRONOLOGY OF MYTH

| | |
|---|---|
| CREATION | Reign of Uranus. |
| | Castration of Uranus. |
| | Cronus takes his place. |
| GOLDEN AGE | Zeus deposes Cronus. |
| | The Titanomachy: Titans attack; |
| | Zeus wins. |
| SILVER AGE | Not much happens. 'Men obey their mothers.' |
| BRONZE or HEROIC AGE | Prometheus steals fire from heaven. |
| | Pandora opens her box and releases all the ills of the world. |
| | Flood. Deucalion and Pyrrha survive. |
| | Pentheus refuses to believe in Bacchus and is murdered. |
| 1300–1200 BC | Perseus is born. |

Heracles does his labours. Jason sets out with the Argonauts and is helped by Medea. Theseus kills the Minotaur.

Oedipus kills his father, beats the Sphinx and marries his mother.

Orpheus rescues, or rather doesn't rescue, Eurydice.

Antigone buries her brother. Theseus marries Phaedra.

Helen, Clytemnestra, Paris, Odysseus and Achilles are born.

Paris makes his Judgement. The Trojan War starts.

Odysseus travels; Agamemnon returns home and dies. Aeneas sets sail.

Electra and Orestes murder Clytemnestra and Aegisthus. Aeneas reaches Italy.

Odysseus returns home. Orestes is absolved.

IRON AGE

800 BC  Homer is written down.

776 BC  Traditional date of founding of Olympic Games.

753 BC  Traditional date of foundation of Rome.

Perseus is the greatest of the early lot. He demonstrates both cunning and bravery: to get information from the Graiae (three ancient sisters who share an eye and a tooth), he steals their eye; he slays the gorgon Medusa, who turned people into stone, and rescues the Ethiopian princess Andromeda from a sea monster, before settling, ruling, and fathering many children to populate Greece.

Some genealogies show Perseus as the grandfather of Heracles, which gives you an idea of the generations, though it's difficult to be exact about the timings.

*Well, they're not real, are they?*

I suppose you're right. A *tiny* part of me wishes that there really was a strongman called Heracles whose deeds were magnified and memorialised.

In this next generation, alongside Heracles, you'll find Theseus and the half-bull, half-man Minotaur; and Jason with his band of Argonauts, called so because of their ship, the *Argo*.

The Argonauts consisted of an all-star gaggle of heroes, including the singer Orpheus, whose music was so wonderful it could charm beasts and move rocks.

Their quest is pure swashbuckle: assemble some heroes, head to Colchis, grab the Golden Fleece from a tree guarded by a dragon, and along the way meet gods and monsters. Huzzah!

There is an inbuilt sense of decline to Greek myth: the further away you get from the first heroes, the weedier you become. Later generations felt somewhat in their shadows.

Heracles is a brute, with his club and his lion-skin. His adventures usually involve slaying a beast, or fetching a magical object; one of them, in which he must retrieve the golden apples of the Hesperides in the West from a tree guarded by a dragon, very closely resembles Jason's quest to the East to fetch a golden fleece ...

*From a tree guarded by a dragon,* filled in Una.

Exactly. The two stories are in essence the same: they are descendants of the same archetype, although which came first isn't clear. Heracles is on the *Argo*, but he's usually jettisoned before the heroes get to Colchis in order to avoid things being too similar.

Both are to do with reaching a magical land – the daughters of the West, the Hesperides, are closely linked to the afterlife.

The number of Heracles' labours, by the way, is a bone of contention.

*Bone? Where?*

No, Una ... I mean, nobody's really certain how many labours there were; most agree on a dozen, but it's unclear what counts as a labour and what doesn't.

We get our idea of the twelve labours of Heracles from the Temple of Zeus at Olympia. Other sources give only five; still others ten.[††]

## THE ~~FIVE~~ ~~TEN~~ ~~TWELVE~~ MANY LABOURS OF HERACLES

The Nemean Lion * The Lernean Hydra * The Cerynitian (or Ceryneian) Hind * The Erymanthian Boar * The Augean Stables * The Stymphalian Birds * The Cretan Bull * The Flesh-eating Mares of

---

†† Alastair Blanshard, *Hercules: A Heroic Life.*

Diomedes * The Girdle of Hippolyta * The Cattle of Geryon * The Apples of the Hesperides * The Guard Dog of the Underworld * The Battle with Cycnus the son of Ares…

Heracles' influence on popular culture is larger than his, quite frankly, enormous pectorals. Any image of a strongman will be a direct reference to him.

Heracles became a god; Theseus and Jason did not. Theseus finds his way into tragedies, including *Hippolytus* by Euripides, which is later used by Racine in his *Phèdre*. In 1486, a version by the Roman writer Seneca was the first ancient play put on in Rome since its fall. Theseus pops up in *A Midsummer Night's Dream*, as a Renaissance duke married to the Amazon Hippolyta.

Jason, having returned triumphant with the Golden Fleece, if you can call a return triumphant that saw his new wife scattering the limbs of her own brother across the sea in order to deflect her pursuers, finds himself at the centre of a battle between duty and love in *Medea* by Euripides.

The myths of the heroes provide material for playwrights to mould into tragedies. These tend to revolve around the two great royal houses of Atreus and Cadmus, whose offspring provide the lifeblood (in some cases, quite literally) for most ancient literature. Comedy drew its characters from life; though the comic playwright Aristophanes was not above including gods and heroes in his burlesques, and in *The Frogs* he gleefully pokes fun at both Dionysus and Heracles.

Let's start with Tantalus, the progenitor of the House of Atreus, as it really is his bloody fault.

*Ahem,* said Una.

So wicked was Tantalus, incidentally, that he once asked somebody to nick the bronze dog that guarded Zeus when he was a baby.

*Blimey!* Una was scandalised.

And that's not the worst of it. Tantalus started off being chummy with the gods, and, as you do, invited them round for dinner. Talk about social climbing. He wanted to test their divinity, and so he killed his own son, Pelops, dismembered him and put him in the stew. Which was really not just beyond the pale, but out of sight of it.

*That is about the five hundredth time you've mentioned dismemberment.*

Don't look at me, I didn't come up with the things. Anyway, Demeter, whose mind was distracted because her daughter Persephone was missing (remember, she was snatched away by Hades), took a bite out of Pelops' shoulder.

You may have seen those cartoons by H.M. Bateman: somebody commits a social howler, as the crowds look on aghast. Imagine the scene.

Up until now there has been general chatter about the problems one has with finding reliable nymphs, or obtaining the right kind of axle grease for a golden chariot. And as for feeding the peacocks – my dear, the expense!

Demeter, hardly listening as Hera rabbits on about a fabulous little satyr she's found, who can provide peacock feed for only a handful of ambrosia, nibbles on a hunk of meat.

She chokes. It's not what she was expecting. It doesn't taste like beef. Realisation dawns. Divine spoons would have been dropped; regal brows would have clouded.

The other gods quickly realised what had happened. Fortunately, they were able to reassemble Pelops, and bring him back to life.

*Did he go around without a shoulder?*

Nope, the gods made one for him, out of ivory.

Tantalus was swiftly rusticated to Tartarus, where he was doomed to stand in a pool of water that he could never bend to drink from, with some delicious food just out of his reach, and I can never think of this nursery rhyme without remembering him: 'Doctor Foster/Went to Gloucester/In a Shower of Rain./ He stepped in a puddle/Right up to his middle/and never came out again.'

Pelops went on to become a great hero and gave his name to the Peloponnese, the enormous peninsula that forms most of modern Greece (bar the islands).

Apart from his ivory shoulder, he was mostly distinguished by cursing everybody or being cursed, and therefore being the main cause of Greek tragedy, which, in the parlance of Sellar and Yeatman, is either a Good or a Bad Thing.

He had three sons: Atreus, Thyestes and Chrysippus, who was so drop-dead gorgeous that everybody fancied him (including Poseidon). Atreus and Thyestes, being of a jealous cast of mind, tried to drown their brother, and so Pelops cursed his own family. Mistake number one.

There's a moment here where the two great families come into contact with each other: Laius, the father of Oedipus, from the House of Cadmus, came to visit Pelops and fell hook, line and sinker for Chrysippus and, it seeming the most sensible thing to do at the time, abducted him.

Pelops then cursed him as well. Mistake number two. This led to the monstrous Sphinx, which devastated Thebes, and so to the rest of Oedipus' troubles. Sometimes the Sphinx is referred to as a '*kuon*', or dog, and even as having a dog body rather than a lion one. Somehow, Una, a dog with the face of a woman lacks the grandeur of a lion-bodied woman.

*I disagree*, replied Una. *In fact*, she said, *I strongly disagree.*

There was yet another curse in play at the same time: Pelops cheated in a chariot race, in which he was competing to win the hand of a princess called Hippodameia, and failed to honour a bargain with the charioteer he'd bribed.

You'd have thought that Pelops, being so au fait with maledictions, would have considered what happened next. Oh no, he had to go and kill him, with the result that the dying charioteer cursed Pelops and all his descendants. Mistake number three, though it was this chariot race that was commemorated by the Olympian Games, from which our own Olympic Games descend.

The story of Pelops' sons, the murderous brothers Atreus and Thyestes, is particularly repugnant, and yet has been replayed many times. I won't go into all the literally gory details, but put it like this: Atreus murders his brother's children. Then, continuing the human consumption theme, he bakes them into a pie, which he serves up to his brother to eat, presumably on the equivalent of a silver platter.

Thyestes does, and is then, reasonably enough, rather put out by the fact.

*Gosh.*

Exactly. The story pops up in Shakespeare's fabulously enjoyable early play *Titus Andronicus*, where Titus bakes Tamora the Goth Queen's sons into a pie; and it's also resurfaced more recently in the television series *Game of Thrones*, where Arya Stark delivers her enemy's sons to him in exactly the same kind of pastry offering. That show owes plenty of its themes to Greek myth, including the sacrifice of Stannis Baratheon's royal daughter to appease a god.

At least there wasn't any more kin-eating in the next generation, though there was kin-slaying.

*Well, it's a start.*

Atreus' son Agamemnon was the leader of the Greeks at Troy. He came to a particularly ghastly end, because his wife Clytemnestra bumped him off in the bath when he returned home victorious.

*Why on earth would she do something like that?*

He'd ordered the death of their own daughter, Iphigenia, as a sacrifice to Artemis so that the Greek fleet could sail. And that death, like a falling domino, set off a whole sequence of other deaths, beginning with Agamemnon's, and then Clytemnestra's, who is done in by her own son, the returning Orestes. Note here that Menelaus, Agamemnon's brother, was not subject to the curse of the House of Atreus: he died, we assume, happily in his bed.

*Why?*

He didn't do anything really bad himself. How Odysseus and Agamemnon must have resented Menelaus! If only Agamemnon hadn't killed Iphigenia, then, we can assume, he would have been safe. The Greek fleet wouldn't have sailed; so no Trojan War, no return of Helen, and the tragedians would have had to look somewhere else for their stories.

Since there's nobody left to take revenge on Orestes, he was then chased by the Furies (sometimes called '*kunes*', or dogs) until he reached Athens, where he was finally absolved of his crimes, and purified. In the *Odyssey*, Orestes is commended as a hero for taking his revenge. It's the tragedies that grapple with the terrible idea of matricide.

Some even say that Iphigenia was alive all the time, acting as a priestess in Tauris, and there's a play by Euripides that deals with that particular story. Rather annoying for Agamemnon, though, if it had turned out to be the case.

*So that was the House of Atreus. What about the other one?*

We sweep across the Peloponnese to Thebes of the seven gates, the mighty city of Cadmus.

Cadmus was searching for his sister Europa, who'd been snatched away by Zeus in the form of a bull.

*She was a bull?*

No, he took the form of a bull. Cadmus couldn't find his sister, and instead was instructed by the Delphic oracle to found a city in the place where a certain cow lay down.[‡‡] This became Thebes, and its inhabitants sprang from the teeth of a dragon sown into the ground.

## INTERESTING USES FOR BODY PARTS

Founding a city – teeth
Creating men for your city – teeth
As a snack – Pelops' shoulder
As a bargaining chip – the single eye of the Graiae
As a record player – the severed singing head of Orpheus
As a warning – the tongue and hands of Cicero

---

‡‡ Given the number of stories about cities founded where animals lay down (viz., Aeneas), one imagines the ancient world to be full of people trailing cows, sheep… any passing beast will do.

We find, in Homer's *Odyssey*, Cadmus' descendant Oedipus. *Oediwhat?* Una's ears had pricked up.

It's not a cat. '*Pus*' means 'foot' in Greek, and the first part, some people think, means 'swollen', possibly referring to the legend that Oedipus' feet were pinned together when he was abandoned as a baby.

*If you say so.* Still she looked around, nostrils quivering, in case there were any members of the feline persuasion within sight.

In the version told in the *Odyssey*, Oedipus killed his father unknowingly and then married his mother (called Epicaste rather than the Jocasta of Sophocles). The gods reveal the truth, and Epicaste hangs herself, whilst Oedipus continues to reign, not exactly blithely, but subject to the tortures of the Furies.

This isn't quite the familiar story that had such an impact on psychology and thought in the twentieth century, in which Oedipus, after learning the appalling truth, blinds himself. Sophocles fashioned out of these bare materials the ironic, gorgeously constructed *Oedipus Rex*.

*Rex? Is he a dog?*

No, I admitted. It's the Latin form of *Tyrannos*, meaning 'Oedipus the King'. And we'll talk about the play later on.

Oedipus' two sons, Eteocles and Polynices, end up fighting over who gets to rule Thebes; and then kill each other, with Polynices left to the dogs and birds – unburied. This is why his sister, Antigone, wanted to bury him properly. Note too that the god Dionysus' mother Semele was a member of the House of Cadmus. The family descends, via Harmonia, from the union of Aphrodite and Ares; and ultimately from Zeus and Io, who, poor thing, was turned into a cow.

There's a lot of cows in the House of Cadmus, I mused.

*Don't say it.*

In fact, you could call it the House of Cudmus?

Una sprinted away to make a lap of an oak tree.

When she returned, trotting beautifully by my side like a little deer, unabashed I continued my theme.

Alongside these two great families, a host of others occupied the ranks. You would need a *Who's Who* of the heroes in order to understand them and their connections. They were obsessed with lineage: in the palaces of Greece, they talked of little else.

There was the family of Odysseus, known by the Romans as Ulysses, the famed hero of his own poem, whose ancestor Cephalus, as you'll remember, was so keen on Laelaps.

*I've heard of Ulysses,* said Una.

You have?

*I have. There's a book with that name on your shelf.*

Oh yes. Well, Ulysses is the Latin name for Odysseus.

Una continued to look perplexed.

*I don't really see how they're the same.*

There were many other forms of Odysseus' name – such as Olusseus or Olutteos. The Latins took their tradition from the Olusseus version, and so called him Ulysses.

*You'd have thought,* said Una, *that they could have had a meeting and decided on everything being the same.*

Do you want to write them a letter?

*I haven't got any hands,* said Una.

Right. I continued. Odysseus' son was Telemachus; his wife was Penelope, who waited so patiently for her husband to return from his long travels.

Penelope and Helen were cousins, whilst Helen and Clytemnestra were sisters; their brothers were the demigod twins Castor and Polydeuces/Pollux. Helen and her siblings were born from an egg: their father was Zeus, disguised as a swan; their mother, Leda.

We often forget about the Trojans, keeping our beady eyes on the Greek families, but there is a rich mythological tradition around the city of Troy, beginning with its founder, Tros, whose son Ganymede was snatched up to heaven to be Zeus' cup-bearer because of his exceptional beauty. James Davidson, in his wonderful, comprehensive study *The Greeks and Greek Love*, which looks into same-sex relations across the Ancient Greek world, explains that whilst many believed there was a salacious aspect to this, it was actually a way of showing that the Trojans had a member of their family on Olympus itself: the absolute apotheosis of a mortal. They could claim to be top dog in the divine stakes.

King Priam himself, who reigned during the Trojan War, had fifty sons; whether all of these were borne by his wife, Hecuba, is unclear. There is a link between the royal houses of Troy and Greece: Priam's sister, Hesione, married Achilles' uncle. Which brings an added poignancy to the destruction of Troy.

Tithonus, King Priam's brother, married the dawn goddess.

*Wasn't she the one who lusted after Cephalus?*

She was. In Homer, she is 'rosy-fingered Dawn'. Say it without the hyphen. Tithonus was granted eternal life; without, however, the vital ingredient of eternal youthfulness; and so he ended up as dry and husky as a cricket.

*That wasn't very clever*, said Una.

Well I think his mind was probably on other things. So there was one Trojan who was ever youthful; and another who was eternally ancient. Whether there was one eternally in the grip of a midlife crisis is unrecorded.

Now, as I am guiding you, Una, on this mythological tour, a special mention must go to the guides and the prophets.

Cassandra was a Trojan princess, daughter of King Priam, who was taken home as a slave by Agamemnon. She wouldn't give herself up to Apollo, and so he cursed her: she would have true sight, but nobody would believe her.

Like Cassandra, Teiresias the blind seer can see the future clearly, as well as the events of the past, and warns everybody all the time. Nobody listens, of course.

Being a prophet was a tough gig. The urge to say 'I told you so!' must have been very strong.

The sibyl was a prophetess in Rome who took the hero Aeneas through the Underworld, much as I am now taking you, Una, from the fog of your ignorance into the light of truth.

*If you say so…*

Ahem. And I also want to mention the Muses, since they are so important to us scribblers. There were nine of them. And there's an easy way of remembering all nine. Simply imagine that a Geordie chap is on the golf course with his friend Mick and asking him to take a putt. 'Mec! Tec! Put!'

MEC

TEC

PUT

They are: Melpomene, whose province was tragedy; Erato, who was in charge of lyric poetry; Calliope, who gave inspiration to the epic poets; Terpsichore is much called upon in dance lessons, whilst Euterpe is the name on musicians' lips.

When historians dry up, they send an invocation to Clio. Those who write sacred poetry sing to Polyhymnia; astronomers send their wishes to Urania; and I imagine Stephen Fry, before he goes onstage to talk amusingly about Greek myths, brings to mind Thalia, the Muse of comedy.

At this point, I had to stop by a water fountain, whilst Una waited patiently beside me. We'd been walking for quite some time, and my feet were beginning to ache like Sisyphus' shoulders.

Those are the main figures of myth: we will meet many of them as we go along. The gods were objects of veneration; yet they were also remarkably human. The heroes were much admired, yet they were also faulty, and their faults provided the subject for poetry and tragedies. The myths seek to explain the world on every level. There is the greatest: cosmology. The idea that from Chaos sprang the Earth is not all that different from our scientific explanation of the Big Bang. Then there are the aetiologies, looking for explanations for the origins of constellations, mountains, cities, families. And they also explore every aspect of emotion, from love to hatred to friendship to revenge.

*It's a lot to take in*, said Una. *How do you start learning about these things?*

Through language, I answered. And now, I think it's time to head home.

We wandered back through the streets, and as we went by the chicken shop and the betting shop, the boarded-up windows and the cracked windowpanes, I tipped my hat to all the deities of north London.

There, in the teenage boy holding hands with his girlfriend, was Aphrodite; Hermes, fleet-footed, was bringing news from phone to iPad to laptop; and in the minds of each of us, the Minotaurs, the gorgons, the chimeras that we face up to and defeat every day.

## Chapter 4

# LATRO, LATRAS, LATRAT
## A Note on Language

It was a Tuesday morning, somewhere towards the middle of September, and I'd been working since 6a.m. Laying down my pen, as I imagine Achilles might lay down his sword after a particularly pleasing bout of fighting, I glanced at Una.

There was no need to say anything; she understood my intention, and soon she and I were heading up to the Heath by a different route, pottering through the car-jammed streets of Kentish Town and then via the slightly more salubrious Tufnell Park. I say it's slightly more salubrious because if you buy a coffee, some bread and a bit of ham for your lunch here, you'll have to remortgage your house.

I was mentally noting the makes of cars and, under my breath, because I don't want to look too much like a weirdo, translating those that look like Latin. This is an unfortunate habit that afflicts many classicists. It can pop up at embarrassing moments.

Audi – listen!
Volvo – I roll.
Mercedes – wealth.
Transit – he crosses.

Uber – teat.

*Teat?* said Una.

Yup.

*Like, nipple?*

Yup.

*So do you actually speak Latin, then?*

It's funny how often I get asked this, usually accompanied by a look that suggests I've forgotten to put my trousers on.

From the age of nine to thirteen I boarded at a countryside prep school, nestled on the banks of the River Arun in West Sussex.

If you wanted to get rid of something, like a conker or a bit of string, you'd shout '*Quis!*', which means 'Who?' Whoever answered '*Ego*' first would win the prize. Saying '*Pax*' would stop an argument. '*Cave*' was a warning that a teacher was approaching, though that had fallen out of fashion by my time.

You'd find pupils saying these things in hundreds of schools of all types, wherever Latin is or was taught. One commenter remembers using '*Quis*' to offload overripe fruit in South Africa in the 1970s. Don't underestimate how many people have studied Latin, in thousands of different kinds of situations, across the world, and over the centuries. Latin is not the preserve of the privileged, although sadly it has become associated with cruel Victorian masters and boys in boaters.

I don't really speak Latin, though, or Ancient Greek. I have a fantasy, which I hope one day to turn into a novel. No, Una, not *that* kind of fantasy. A rift occurs in the fabric of time, and a cohort of legionaries, led by the Emperor Augustus himself, is hurtled into twenty-first-century Britain.

Unperturbed by modernity, with ruthless, violent efficiency Augustus wrests control of London.

Soon the eagle standard flutters above Buckingham Palace, and the country becomes flooded with Romans, for whom Jupiter set no bounds in space or time. *Roma Aeterna* indeed.

Who would get the nod? Who would be hurled from mouldy obscurity into positions of prominence? The call would go out, from book-lined study to muddy playing-field, from red-brick university to windswept tower.

At last! Here come the Latin teachers, marching into Whitehall with our tattered grammar books under our arms and our heads full of Virgil. Our hour will come!

The way that Una was looking at me suggested that this was not very likely to happen.

Well, I can but dream.

When I was at Oxford, there was a Speaking Latin party, run by a formidable philologist, who would pounce on anyone not actually speaking the language with a brisk '*Haec non Latina est!*'

The truth is that when put on the spot many of us would have trouble forming long sentences in Latin; and, when reading, would encounter words we do not know, or constructions requiring idiomatic translations.

In the Monty Python film *Life of Brian*, Brian, an insurrectionary Jew, is graffitiing the sentence ROMANES EUNT DOMUS. He thinks he's written 'Romans go home'.

A centurion nobbles him. Expecting to be punished, Brian is instead treated to a lecture in which the centurion systematically destroys his grammar, even going as far as to correct it himself with the paintbrush. He suggests that Brian should use what he calls the locative case, '*domum*'. (The locative is a particular form of a noun that indicates place: 'at home'.)

'Centurion: Now, write it out a hundred times.

Brian: Yes, sir. Thank you, sir. Hail Caesar, sir.

Centurion: Hail Caesar! And if it's not done by sunrise, I'll cut your balls off.'

This is a lovely parody of a certain kind of Latin teacher (and indeed, for many of us, a fantasy of what Latin teachers ought to be able to say to reluctant charges).

The only thing here is that the centurion is wrong – '*domum*' is not the locative; it's a different form, which suggests 'towards home'. The locative is '*domi*'. Even Latin speakers, or pretend Latin speakers, can get it wrong. Although the Pythons may have been poking fun at the kind of pedant who likes to correct other people and gets it wrong themselves.

People make mistakes: the Supreme Court judge Baroness Hale, when she was awarded her coat of arms, chose for her motto '*Omnia Feminae Aequissimae*'. The translation given in the press coverage was 'Women are equal to all things'. The only problem is, that's not what it means. It could, just about, mean: 'Women are very equal with respect to everything', but that's bad Latin. If I saw that in a piece of prose, I'd translate it as 'All things of a most equal woman', which doesn't make much sense at all.

Translating out of Latin and Greek is done, at first, painstakingly. It is a long and sometimes frustrating process. You look up words in a dictionary, note their grammatical function, and then puzzle out the sentence.

Even looking up a word can be difficult, as sometimes parts of Latin words don't resemble their root forms. The past tense of the verb '*rego*', which means 'I rule', is '*rexi*'. If you see '*rexi*' you might be tempted to look up '*rexi*' in the dictionary, only you'd find nothing, because Latin dictionaries don't like to be helpful. You might also be forgiven for thinking that the past tense of *'fero'*, 'I bring', might be something along those lines, like *'fexi'*; only it isn't.

*What is it?*

*'Tuli'*. There's plenty of that sort of thing.

With Ancient Greek you're in even stickier trouble, particularly as so many words look so similar to each other. And that's not even considering the irregular verbs, which are fiendish enough to cause trouble even to the brainiest. It's almost as if generations of sadistic schoolmasters have engineered the whole thing simply to frustrate their charges.

This can be off-putting for many young acolytes of the languages, who become lost in a tangle of obscure forms.

I was speaking to a fellow novelist the other day, who also happens to be a classicist. He said that there seemed to be two types of Classics teacher. You either got the incredibly charismatic eccentric kind, who inspired and charmed; or you got an uber-strict, dry Victorian. There doesn't seem to be anything in between, and if you get the latter kind, it can put you off.

*What kind are you?*

Er... Let's move on. There wasn't ever a Golden Age when all schoolchildren lapped up Latin and were able to compose instantly in fluent, Ciceronic prose. A piece in *The Times* of 1887 shows exactly what young Tommy thinks of Latin:

*'Latinam linguam (admitto) cordialiter odi'*

which translates as 'I admit I cordially detest the Latin language.'

It's all to do with perseverance. You begin to realise why you were sent out on six-mile runs in the rain. The odder forms soon become second nature. Well, they do after you've spent hours and hours sweating over them. Eventually, I promise.

In my second year at university I began to be able to read confidently in both languages; that was a wonderful time. In my third year, about four days before my finals, I could have read and translated pretty much anything put in front of me.

I could never, however, put myself on a par with the protagonists of Donna Tartt's novel *The Secret History*, in which an elite group of American Classics students are able to converse in Ancient Greek when they've only just begun learning it. They then go on to murder someone, so perhaps that's a good thing.

If you don't practise a language constantly, it tends to vanish. It's a muscle that needs to be exercised, like running scales up and down a piano. Even a couple of weeks away from translating can mean that you lose the knack. This seems to be particularly the case with Ancient Greek. My own personal theory is that it's to do with the different alphabet.

Since there's not as much call for teaching Ancient Greek as there is for Latin, it's this that slipped away from my own brain first; and three years after leaving university, when called upon to teach Homer for the first time, I found myself staring in terrified apprehension at symbols that looked as if they'd been written down by aliens.

However, like a faithful hound, it comes back.

Una preened.

These days, I can read most Latin of the first centuries BC and AD fairly breezily.

With Greek, Homer becomes easy, because the nature of the poems means there are many repetitive structures, such as epithets ('Hector of the flashing helmet', for example), or set pieces, such as sacrificing or putting out to sea.

Similarly so for Sophocles, whose sentences suddenly fall into place like beautiful blocks of marble. Aeschylus, however, can be more difficult; and Aristophanes, which is brimming with idioms and puns, can puzzle. It all depends on the author. Once you've got the hang of an author, the intellectual delight is boundless.

This process is aided by the Loeb Library series, which presents readers with a facing translation in English.

Most classicists will have a shelf full of Loebs, the green covers for Ancient Greek, the scarlet for Latin, and both looking terribly smart.

I spoke recently to Jeffrey Henderson, the general editor of the Loeb Classical Library; he explained that the legend is that 'green' was for 'Greek' and 'red' for 'Roman'. He added that the first dummy volumes were red for no recorded reason, and so Loeb may simply have carried on using those colours.

My own association is that the warlike Romans suit red, like the scarlet coats of soldiers all serried in rows, or the planet Mars; whereas the Greeks fit the more pensive green.

The Library has a fan club:

'The Loeb Library... came as a gift of freedom... The existence of the amateur was recognised by the publication of this Library, and to a great extent made respectable... The difficulty of Greek is not sufficiently dwelt upon, chiefly perhaps because the sirens who lure us to these perilous waters are generally scholars [who] have forgotten... what those difficulties are. But for the ordinary amateur they are very real and very great; and we shall do well to recognise the fact and to make up our minds that we shall never be independent of our Loeb.' This was Virginia Woolf, writing in *The Times Literary Supplement* in 1917.

With a Loeb, I'll read a few lines in the Ancient Greek or Latin, and then if I come across an unfamiliar word or phrase, I'll check the English.

It's piecemeal, but I get a great thrill when it all flows together.

Loeb wanted the books to fit into your pocket – and many of mine are battered and torn from being lugged around the world. My Aeschylus has travelled with me to Canada; my Homer, to Spain; and it's acutely pleasurable to think of these authors hopping all over the world. On the same trip to Canada, I brought with me a compact edition of Edward Gibbon's *Decline and Fall of the Roman Empire*. The lady who picked me up at the airport looked at it with interest. 'What is that,' she asked, 'a thriller?'

In many ways, she was right. We'll talk about the Empire later.

Translating from English into Latin or Greek comes with its own problems. Just, whatever you do, Una, don't use Google, like some hapless Cambridge inhabitants did when trying to protest against a building development. Make sure you employ your own magnificent brain.

I had been feeding her a lot of fish recently, in the hope that, Jeeves-like, it might increase her mental ability.

*What were you saying about Cambridge?*

Some new houses there were spray-painted with the words '*Locus in Domos Loci Populum!*' If you type 'local homes for local people' into Google Translate – I did so, for Una's benefit – that is what it churns out. But strung together like this, these words are meaningless: 'the place into the houses of the place with respect to the people.' If you're going to use Latin, make sure you get an actual classicist to do it for you. (Which is not a pitch for work, by the way…)

So what is Latin? It's the language spoken by the Latin tribe, which spread throughout the Italian peninsula, pushing out other languages (such as Oscan and Umbrian, from which we only have remaining a few inscriptions or place names, like the name of the town of Pompeii. That's what I call a dead language.)

Latin is an Indo-European language; this is the term for a family of languages including many tongues that, like Dobermanns and pugs, at first glance appear to have absolutely nothing to do with each other. However, also like Dobermanns and pugs, they are intimately related.

Its similarities to Ancient Greek are fairly clear, even to the non-linguist. The words for mother and father are effectively the same:

English: mother/father

Latin: mater/pater

Greek: mēter/pater

Note too the similarity with the English words – the 'p', thanks to a process first described by the Brothers Grimm,[*] no less, became an 'f' in Germanic languages. 'Piscis' and 'fish', for example, also demonstrate this, and if you say a 'p' and an 'f' quickly after each other, you'll see for yourself how similar the sounds are.

Ancient Greek was not particularly fertile. Its only descendant is Modern Greek, which seems rather sad.

To a student of the language, a trip to modern Greece is wondrous, since so many of the words are exactly the same, though pronounced differently.

Modern Greeks find English classicists rather bizarre. My wife and I went for part of our honeymoon to Athens (not a research trip, I hasten to add). '*Metaphores!*' I would shout, with glee, when a removal lorry went by (since that is what removal

---

[*] You won't find this in their fairy tales, however, but in their extensive works on philology.

lorries are called). '*Desma!*' when I saw some graffiti about chains. Every time I read out a sign our guide would look at me as if I had left my brain behind in England. Yes, she seemed to be saying. We know you can read.

A friend was on holiday in Greece, trying to find a ferry. She met a fisherman on the beach and in her best Ancient Greek – written down because the modern accent is so different – she composed the equivalent of 'Hail Mariner, whence does the trireme set sail?' The fisherman got the giggles, but he understood, and she found her boat.

That is why if you learn the Ancient Greek word '*oinos*', pronounced '*oy-nos*', and ask for that in Greece, you'll get funny looks; though the word is written in the same way, it's pronounced 'ee-nos'. In linguistic terms, '*oinos*' and 'wine' are essentially the same word, since there used to be a 'w' sound before the 'oi', also seen in Latin 'vinum' – 'v' in Latin is pronounced 'w'.

Tons of Ancient Greek words have been absorbed into English.

The word '*metropolis*', for example, which literally means 'mother city'. It's one of the peculiarities of language that the 'metro' part of it is synonymous with 'city' – think of the London newspaper *Metro*, or metro stations, or Bertie Wooster pootling up to the 'metrop'.

Although once you know it means 'mother', it feels strange to say you're 'taking the metro to work'. The word 'police' derives ultimately from '*polis*' – so if you're talking about the Metropolitan Police, you're really talking about the 'mother-cityish city'.

*Weird*, said Una.

I know. Latin, like King Priam of Troy, had many sons and daughters.

*My name is a Latin word, isn't it?* Una twitched her nose, pattering to catch up.

It certainly is, I answered. It means 'the one'. And it also means 'together'.

*Una – together? That feels very doggy.*

The Latin word for dog is '*canis*', which you'll remember from the constellations (Canis Major and Minor); it is very closely related to the Greek '*kuon*'. The link to one of our own words for dog is harder to see. There is much evidence showing that 'hound' is directly related to a previous word for dog that began with a 'k' sound. Over time, this sound weakened from a 'k' to a 'ch', and then to 'h'. So '*canis*' and 'hound' are actually close cousins.

At this point, as we came to a wooded part of the Heath, Una stiffened.

A terrier was in the vicinity.

Whenever Una sees one, particularly the yappy, beribboned kind that looks as if it ought to belong in a toyshop, she has to restrain herself and remember her dignity.

She did, however, let out a bark – enough to send the terrier squealing away, and its owner scurrying to the rescue.

We trotted onwards.

We describe the sounds that dogs make as 'bark' or 'woof'. Compare this to the French – Dogmatix, the little hound in the Asterix books, says 'Ouah!'

When you learn Latin, your first encounter is usually the present tense of the first conjugation verb, [†] *amo*, I love. The jingly sounds of '*Amo, amas, amat*' are familiar across the

---

[†] Verbs are grouped in 'conjugations'; nouns in 'declensions'. Nouns, like the Roman Empire, decline.

centuries. How odd it would sound to any passing Roman, to hear a roomful of children shouting 'I love, you love, he loves...'

The Latin verb, like the Greek, is made up of a stem and an ending; the stem gives you the 'dictionary' meaning of the word, and the ending provides the tense (i.e., whether it's present, past or future), person (first, second or third) and number (singular or plural). So '*am-o*' means 'love-I', or in English, 'I love.'

In Ancient Greek, the first verb you learn tends to be '*luo*', which means 'I set free': '*luo, lueis, luei*' is much less familiar in popular culture than the Latin. This runs on exactly the same principles, with the ending telling you who's 'doing' the verb. No innuendo please, now, Una.

The first Latin noun table is '*mensa*', which means 'a table'.

This kind of thing makes us Latin teachers, in the words of the immortal fictional schoolboy Nigel Molesworth, 'fall about larfing'.

Nouns, as well as verbs, also hold information in their endings, which alerts you to their grammatical position in the sentence: these endings are called 'cases'. Sometimes I tell my pupils they're called cases because they're packed with information, but that never seems to go down as well as I'd hope.‡

Declining *mensa* did cause Winston Churchill to wonder why he had to learn the vocative case (used for addressing people, viz., 'O Una!'):

---

‡   There are six proper cases in Latin, memorised since time immemorial with the mnemonic Naughty Victoria Always Goes Downstairs Awkwardly, for the nominative, vocative, accusative, genitive, dative and ablative cases. Each of these has its own function.

'But,' I repeated, 'what does it mean?'

'*Mensa* means a table,' he answered.

'Then why does *mensa* also mean O table,' I enquired, 'and what does O table mean?'...

'O table – you would use that in addressing a table, in invoking a table.'...

'But I never do,' I blurted out in honest amazement.

I wonder, though, if Churchill had ever stubbed his toe. 'Bloody table...'

These days beginners are more likely to learn '*puella*', which means 'girl', and of course, there are many more reasons why you would want to address a girl than a table. I should hope so, at any rate.

## LATIN CASES

Naughty – Nominative. Used for the 'subject' of the sentence. e.g. **Una** gnaws a bone.

Victoria – Vocative. Used for addressing. e.g. **Una**, drop that!

Always – Accusative. Used for the 'object' of a sentence. e.g. I patted **Una**.

Goes – Genitive. The possessive case. Not in a stalkery way. e.g. **Una's** tail wagged.

Downstairs – Dative. The giving case. Lovely stuff. e.g. I gave a treat **to Una**.

Awkwardly – Ablative. The taking-away case. e.g. I took an old kebab **from Una**.

If I were teaching you Latin, Una, I would choose for your first lesson '*latro*', the verb that means 'I bark'. *Latro, latras, latrat…* 'I bark, you bark, he barks…'

*Latro*, barked Una. *I like that.* She tried it out, causing some consternation in a passing shih-tzu.

**THE FIRST CONJUGATION**

Latro – I bark
Latras – You (s.) bark
Latrat – He, she, or it barks
Latramus – We bark
Latratis – You (pl) bark
Latrant – They bark

The process by which Latin became several other languages happened, gradually, over many centuries.

Whilst, say, French was developing, monks and scholars were still writing in Latin. There must have been a point when the spoken language diverged enough from the written to become a separate entity: a point where, as a scribe in a monastery, you say to your novice, '*au jour d'hui*' to emphasise that you want him to sharpen your quills 'today'; but when you're writing about it later in your chronicles, you carefully ink in the Latin word '*hodie*'.

Anyone who's studied or spoken French alongside either Spanish, Portuguese or Italian will be alive to the similarities between these tongues; they are all direct descendants of Latin, thanks in large part to the Roman Empire's extent across Europe.

Fewer are aware, however, that Latin, or a much bastardised version of it, is still in use in Romania – and that the very name of the country refers to the Romans, a vestige of the ancient Empire. There is also Aromanian, a dialect form, which is the language of the Vlachs, whose similarities to Latin are almost spooky. (Imagine if there were a lost tribe of Romans who'd been living deep in the forests of Romania for centuries!)

Long study of both Latin and Greek will result in a preference. My own, fickle as the western breeze, switches from one to the other. Sometimes it's the sensuous, gorgeous tones of Latin I find most alluring. There's something about Virgil, vivid and plangent, that is incomparable.

At other times, it's the stark purity of someone like Sophocles, or the ancient complexity of Aeschylus.

Both languages are inflected.

*What does that mean?*

Their words can in put whatever like they order.

*What?*

Sorry. It means they can put their words in whatever order they like. Doesn't work in English, you see. At least, unless Yoda you are. Although we do have words whose endings contain information about the meaning of the word – such as the difference between he and him – order still matters.

Latin word order is trickier; but that is its beauty and power, because a word in Latin can cast a shadow over the rest of the sentence through its grammatical nature. It's as if there are invisible links between the words, conducting energy between them.

Latin can achieve effects in style that would be impossible in English. In Philip Pullman's novel *Northern Lights*, every human being has a daemon (based on the Greek word *daimon*, meaning 'spirit'), an external, living manifestation of his or her soul.

The heroine, Lyra, has a pine marten called Pantalaimon. Unusually, the two can separate over long distances, but still sense each other: this is how I think of the way that Latin words, though apart from their grammatical fellows, are still linked together, each sensing and influencing the other.

*Latro!* said Una. She dashed towards an overeager Alsatian, and I had to step in to separate them.

Both Latin and Greek are worth the blood, sweat and toil of learning. Not because many words in English derive from them, or because you want to be a doctor or a lawyer, or because they are the foundations of European languages, or because it 'trains your brain'.

Because in learning them you will be able to read the ancients, to savour their words, and enter into their minds.

It will be as if you yourself are sitting on a warm night, in the shade of a fig tree, in a courtyard, with the sun low, and the pine torches just beginning to flicker, as Homer begins to sing his tale.

# Chapter 5

# DOGFACE!
## Homer's *Iliad*

It was about a week or so later, towards the end of September. Una and I had been spending a few days pottering about in the countryside.

At least, I had been pottering about; she had embarked upon a killing spree, neutralising two plump squirrels and one unfortunate shrew.

Now we were back in London. It was around the time of the morning when I start to feel hungry again, that is, about 11:30a.m., and Una was waiting, patiently it must be said, at the door, as I stumbled about in search of her lead, then my wallet, then my keys, then her lead, which I had put down somewhere and now couldn't find.

She has a way of putting her head slightly on one side, and fixing me with her black eyes, ears alert.

*We've talked about language,* said Una. But what about the literature? I blinked. Yes, I'd promised that we were going to talk about Homer, the poet of the *Iliad* and the *Odyssey*. We find Homer popping up everywhere: notably, for example, in a short story by Jorge Luis Borges, where he appears as an immortal – a nice comment on his literary longevity, although in the story the poet has all but forgotten his identity.

The importance of the *Iliad*, I began, stepping confidently out into the street, Una trotting smartly beside me, cannot be overstated.

For centuries, the poem provided the mainstay of Western education. People learned whole passages by heart, if not the entire thing. When out campaigning, Alexander the Great bedded down with a copy of it snuggled under his pillow.

Although not for the same reason that I slept with it under mine whilst taking my final examinations.

*Why did you do that?*

I was hoping to absorb it by osmosis. Newsflash: it didn't work.

*Alexander the Great was a good dog man. Did he carry it because of all the dogs in the poem?*

No, he believed he was an incarnation of the warrior Achilles. You're right, though; there are many dogs in the *Iliad*. At the very beginning, tons of them die of the plague, along with the horses, and not a few of the soldiers. 'Dog-face' is used quite liberally as an insult. Which, Una, I think is a bit rude myself.

There's also always a worry that the bodies of the slain might be left unburied, to the predations of birds and dogs.

Una made a face. A dog-face. She did not appear to be in a jocund mood.

I tried to cheer her up. Dogs in the *Iliad* are pretty cool: they're usually hunters, pets or guards, as you would expect.[*] They can also be scavengers; and in the similes they're very proud and fierce.

---

[*]  Margaret Graver, 'Dog-Helen and Homeric Insult'.

Her tail was now up, like a white flag wiggling in the breeze. Although perhaps, being a dog, she had simply already forgotten.

We sauntered through the square garden, the air cool on my cheeks. I kicked through a pile of browning leaves.

Falling leaves are a motif in Homer. They mark the generations of mankind. We watched them drifting, curling at the edges.

*When did you first read Homer?* asked Una.

It was a good question, because you usually encounter the idea of Homer before you encounter Homer in the flesh, as it were.

I had my first experience of the *Iliad* aged about ten,[†] curled up on my downstairs bunkbed in my dormitory, which was called, with a certain suitability, Champions. I had begun learning Latin that year.

I had been attracted to the language, to a sense, stirred partly by reading the works of E. Nesbit, whose child characters were steeped in Latin and Greek, that I would be entering the realm of something eternal.

And so I had bought a paperback translation of the *Iliad*, snatching it from under the nose of a school prefect who'd wanted it for himself.

I'd begun reading it in full enthusiasm. But now – though I didn't want to admit it, at least to my headmaster, who taught us Latin – I'd become lost in the prose Penguin translation by E.V. Rieu, whom we've met before, which is simply heaving with words like 'doughty'.

---

† Heinrich Schliemann, the first excavator of Troy, was captivated by Homer at the age of eight. So luckily I came to it late, then, or WHO KNOWS what might have happened.

*Doughty?* Una raised a doggy eyebrow.

Well indeed, I answered. I had a vague idea that it might have something to do with cakes. I didn't know it meant 'steadfast'.

I'd expected a version of the children's myths that so obsessed me. There'd be a brawny chap, who'd drunk too many protein shakes and was pretty handy with a sword. Gods would float around knowingly, materialising at opportune moments with helpful magical objects.

The chap would battle with someone who was demonstrably a villain, or even a monster that would, for reasons unclear, have several heads, one of which was invariably a goat.

The monster would be slain, the girl would be retrieved and married, the chap would get some treasure and/or a kingdom, and everyone would go home happy and feast whilst guzzling from large drinking vessels. Huzzah! I slapped my thigh and struck what I hoped was a heroic pose.

Una emitted a slightly embarrassed yelp.

*What would they feast on?* she asked, changing the subject. She is ever interested in food, and started licking her elegant chops.

In the *Iliad* the *plat du jour* is only ever roast meat, despite the fact that they are right next to a river and the sea. The culinary arts were somewhat lacking amongst the tents of the Achaeans. No Anatole in the kitchens, concocting delicacies for the heroes' weary palates: Sylphides à la Troy. Chickens did not appear in Europe until later on. As for vegetables – well. There is mention of an onion, but it's used as a relish for a drink, because that's what real heroes do.

*I dare you next time you go to the pub to ask for an onion in your wine.*

I demurred.

# Dogface!

When I first picked up that Penguin Classic, which I still have, though it's almost not so much well-thumbed as pawed to death, I was not prepared for the grandeur and the glory of Homer's *Iliad*. Nor was I ready for the sheer strangeness of it, from my child's point of view and, as I later discovered, from many adults' perspectives too.

The main action hangs on the hero, Achilles, withdrawing from battle and not only sulking, but playing the lyre, and crying. A lot. Ancient mythographers kept a list of people who bore the name Achilles. It concludes: 'plus another fourteen, two of whom were dogs'. It was a name given to racehorses, and 'would have been an obvious enough name for a hunting dog'.[‡]

Una liked the comparison, I could tell, because she dashed off to a clump of trees several hundred yards away, scrambled up a trunk as fast as she could, bobbed up and down a few times in pursuit of a glimpse of squirrel fur, and then came zooming back.

*How could the hero spend most of the time sitting down?* she said, between pants, her long pink tongue hanging out over her bottom jaw.

Exactly. I continued on. I knew the poem concerned a siege. But it isn't simply relentless fighting, though there are many brutal passages of very specific violence involving eyeballs and swords piercing through bones. There's the whole galaxy of emotions. When the Trojan hero Hector returns from battle, he meets his wife Andromache and son Astyanax, and the little boy cries at the sight of his father's helmet. His parents laugh, involving us in a tender, moving family scene. And there is the sublime

‡ Alan Cameron, *Greek Mythography in the Roman World.*

climactic moment when King Priam goes under cover of night, led by a god, to retrieve the corpse of his best-beloved son.

Now don't come running to me mewling about spoilers – a lot of the emotional heft derives from the knowledge that many will die and the city will fall.

The poem portrays a realistic world, which for the audience was in the past. Yet it also brims with fantastical elements.

In the *Iliad* anybody might turn out to be a god or goddess in disguise. Aphrodite, pretending to be a handmaiden, brings a chair for Helen to sit down on. The gods also manifest in all their cosmic glory. There is a wonderful scene where Poseidon decides he wants to get his hands dirty in the battle, and leaps for miles across the land to fetch his horses and golden chariot.

The gods intervene at the drop of a helmet, snatching favourites away from the battlefield or sending mists to shroud the action. When Zeus' son, the Trojan ally Sarpedon, is killed, his heavenly father makes the sky pour down black rain, and Sleep and Death themselves sweep down to bear the body away.

In one of the most poignant moments, Achilles' horses (who are immortal) are given the gift of speech, and weep when they see the future. Achilles himself battles the River Scamander, not personified in the form of a god, but as the elemental being itself.

There are many other things about the poem that appear strange to modern readers. They are all essential features of the epic style. One of the most important is the heroic code, or how the heroes conduct themselves. We see this in two heroes from opposing sides, the Greek Diomedes and the Trojan ally Glaucus, when they pause mid-battle to discuss mythology and lineage before cheerfully agreeing to avoid each other's spears.

Another essential part of epic style is the epithets: everyone is referred to by an adjective – *grey-eyed* Athena, *swift-footed*

Achilles, *horse-taming* Hector; and, related to these, the long, elaborate similes that illuminate the action. And finally, the formulaic elements, with many scenes, such as sacrifices, being almost exact repetitions of previous ones.

There are no outright heroes or villains, but there are different characteristics to both sides: overall the Trojans are more glamorous. They wear panther-skins and gold; they're the kids you'd want to hang out with, undisciplined and lounging about the dance floor. Paris, despite his many faults, is still someone you'd want to come to your party. The Greeks, on the other hand, are – on the whole – more serious and better led, though Agamemnon is hardly the most effective overlord.

Fighting is a matter of honour, and they have to get on with it and plunder treasure and prizes from the outlying cities, until they manage to break the siege, cause Troy to fall and return Helen to Sparta. Then everyone can go home too and carry on stealing cattle and boasting like they did before.

*But they must like fighting?* Una was puzzled. *Isn't that what they're for, the heroes?*

Oh, absolutely. They love fighting, and they love talking about fighting, and they especially love winning the spoils of war, which, tastelessly to our sensibilities, but crucially for the plot, include slave girls. Christopher Logue's *War Music* is a sequence of poems based on the *Iliad*: one of the sections is called 'All Day Permanent Red'. I thought this was a brilliant way of conveying the terror and bloodiness of battle, even when someone pointed out that he half-inched it from a L'Oréal advert for lipstick.

The original audience would have loved listening to the fighting scenes, in ways that we perhaps will never be able to grasp, in the same way that they would have loved the Catalogue of

Ships, where Homer describes, in a very long list, all the tribes taking part. A little bit, perhaps, like an MC doing a shout-out?

Una looked away in embarrassment. She tried to change the subject. *So why is it called the* Iliad? *Why not the Troy-iad?*

It's the story, or part of the story, of the holy and magnificent city of Ilion, or Ilium, also known as Troy.

The Greeks are not called the Greeks, and would not have thought of themselves as Greeks. '*Graecia*' was used much later by the Romans, and the besieging armies here are a loose collection of peoples, all led, if that is the right word, by King Agamemnon of Argos. These soldiers are collectively labelled Achaeans.

Contemporary Greece is Hellas; in the *Iliad*, only the Myrmidons, the Thessalian tribe of Achilles, are called Hellenes. And, given the importance of Athens in later Greek thought and history, it's notable that only two Athenian leaders are listed in the Catalogue of Ships.

**THINGS THE GREEKS ARE CALLED IN THE *ILIAD***

Danaans (*Danaoi*, after Danaus, father of the fifty Danaids, forty-nine of whom killed their husbands on their wedding night)

Achaeans (*Achaioi*, after a region of the Peloponnese in the north-east, in Thessaly)

Argives (*Argeioi*, after the city of Argos in southern Greece)

**THINGS THE TROJANS ARE CALLED IN THE** *ILIAD*

Dardans (*Dardanioi*, after the founder of a city near Troy)
Trojans

**THINGS THE GREEKS ARE NOT CALLED IN THE** *ILIAD*

Greeks

*So the Trojans are called Dardans and the Greeks are called Danaans?*

That's right, I answered. And that's why the tag in the *Aeneid* is '*timeo Danaos et dona ferentes*' – I fear the Danaans, or rather the Greeks, even when they bear gifts.

There are other challenges with names. Paris is also known as Alexander. There are two Greek heroes called Ajax (the Greater and the Lesser); and characters are often referred to by what's called a patronymic. Agamemnon is the son of Atreus, or Atreides; Achilles the son of Peleus, or Peleides; and so on, much as the pop singer Björk's surname is Guðmundsdóttir, or daughter of Guðmun.

Or Prince Harry's son, whose middle name, Harrison, might be termed a patronymic. These were ways of referring to male aristocrats. The only non-toff in the *Iliad*, Thersites, definitely doesn't have a patronymic. Nor does he have a particularly good time of it, getting bashed about by Odysseus for being chippy.

*What about women?*

Women have only one name, which is often a version of their father's name: such as Chriseis, the daughter of the priest Chryses. Like Nigel Lawson calling his daughter Nigella.

We had reached the top of Parliament Hill and were looking out across the city of London, at its bright glass-and-steel buildings, at the endlessly moving streams of people and vehicles.

Troy itself, or rather its citadel, sat on top of a hill, and was contained within walls, as London once was.

*Was it a real place?*

We don't know, although there is compelling archaeological evidence. Heinrich Schliemann, the merchant prince-cum-amateur archaeologist, deserves full credit for excavating a mound at present-day Hissarlik in Turkey, and uncovering many layers of ruins.

The further down he dug, the further back in time he went, to the remains of an ancient settlement that existed in about 3000 BC, known as Troy I. Each layer represents a settlement that was destroyed and then built upon again. The latest is Troy IX, which fell in c. AD 500. A Trojan layer cake would be a great theme for a chef to tackle.

If there really was a Trojan War, it happened in around 1200 BC. The ruins from this era hardly suggest a great, noble city as described in the poem, and certainly not extended warfare. War was synonymous with, say, raiding a whole load of cattle from your neighbour. The *Iliad* is probably rendering heroic what was a fairly mundane event, if it happened at all.

*Which layer do they think was the Troy in the poem?*

The most likely candidate is Troy VIIIa; but as M.I. Finley says in *The World of Odysseus*, this is 'a pitiful poverty-stricken little place, with no treasure, without even any large and imposing buildings, with nothing remotely resembling a palace.'

Schliemann was determined that he had found the Troy of legend, and so when he unearthed many ornate objects, he excitedly named them 'Priam's Treasure'; unfortunately these came from a much older layer of the city. He's also accused of 'salting' the earth with finds from elsewhere. He was, in short, a bit of a charlatan, but he also— Hey Una, I said. Ask me what job I do.

*What job do you do?*

I'm an archaeologist.

*How's business?*

Groundbreaking.

Una had the grace to look away. Schliemann was also an innovative archaeologist.

Laying aside the historical veracity of the poem, the next thing to grasp about the *Iliad* is nobody's really certain who composed it.

*I get the feeling,* said Una, *that there's a lot of uncertainty involved in Classics.*

We are dealing with things that were written or composed so long ago that they appear almost without context. For the Greeks, Homer was 'the poet'. As Theocritus said, 'Who would listen to any other poet? Homer is enough for everyone.'

Yet we know absolutely nothing about Homer. There is no biography to draw on, no letters, no memoirs by friends or relatives. We have no *Homer as I Knew Him*, by his nephew, no jealous family carefully moulding his image. What we call 'Homer' is, very possibly, a construct, an idealised version of a wandering poet, singing his song from memory in the feasting halls of aristocrats to earn his hunk of beef and skinful of wine.

In tradition, Homer is blind, his bardic abilities awarded to him in compensation for his loss of sight, affording him true visions of the gods. The ancients delighted in making up stories about him, and where he got his material from, even suggesting that he had adapted his verses from the oracles of the daughter of the prophet Teiresias.

The poem's not even in the Classical Greek that you learn at the start of a course, but is a mixture of different dialects.

How the poem was constructed bothered scholars for years. According to an American academic, Milman Parry[§], it was composed orally, sometime in the 800s BC, and written down later. Parry visited the hills of Serbia and found bards there able to memorise, and 'compose' apparently off the cuff, very long poems.[¶]

Parry concluded that the formulaic elements – the epithets, the repeated scenes – were the building blocks of the poem. So important was his theory to the field of classics that he's been called 'the Darwin of Homeric studies'. He suggested that a bard would memorise the whole thing in pieces, and then use the formulae as a way to kickstart his memory into a particular scene. When the drunken audience bayed for 'the death of Patroclus', you'd know exactly where to start. And would thus, presumably, both earn your supper and avoid being pelted with onions.

The *Iliad* is far too long to be recited all at once, and we don't know whether the ancient Greeks ever felt the need to binge-listen to the entire twenty-four books, although there is a reference

---

§   Adam Parry, *The Making of Homeric Verse*.
¶   Although it has been noted that the literary content of these poems is not the highest.

to bards singing the whole shebang in relays at the festival of the Great Panathenaea in Athens.

It is an epic poem, in more ways than one.

*Epic? As in, that was an epic squirrel chase?*

It's not a word that's much used properly these days, but then, what is? Epic, as distinct from the other genres of the ancient world – that is tragedy, comedy, and so on – means, essentially, a really long poem in hexameters that dealt with mighty subjects. It comes from the Greek word '*epos*', which means simply 'word'.

At some point, this orally composed poem was written down, and was split up into twenty-four 'books', which are about the length of chapters, each labelled with a letter (alpha, beta, and so on, from the Greek alphabet).

The version we have, and which seems so stable and unchanging, is an edited transcript. This brings up various questions of authorship: was it composed by one person? Or by many? Some scholars think it's a hodgepodge, with bits and pieces added at different times; others think there is enough internal evidence to suggest a unified whole.

The very first line evokes the poem's theme:

*Menin, aeide, thea, Peleiadeo Achileos...*

Translated, in the same order, to give you an idea of the way that Ancient Greek works:

*The wrath, sing, o goddess!, of the Peleid Achileos...*

Or:

'Sing, goddess, the anger of Achilles, son of Peleus...'

Compare that Greek to the two translations we looked at back in August.

*It's very different, isn't it?* said Una. *That word,* menin – *it's so powerful!*

Yes, it forces you to listen, doesn't it? The 'goddess' is the Muse: the poet is making a strong statement. What follows springs from divinity; it is the truth.

There is a remnant of the sacred origins of epic poetry in this (and we will see something similar when we come to tragedy).

The engine of the poem is Achilles' anger.

*Why is he so angry?*

Because his honour is at stake. And that's a major problem. There's a plague devastating the Achaean camps, because Agamemnon – 'Old King Cock-of-the-Walk', as Seamus Heaney calls him – had taken Chriseis, the daughter of a priest of Apollo, as his slave girl. The priest comes on an embassy to retrieve her; Agamemnon, somewhat reluctantly, returns her.

This is a reflection on Agamemnon's own honour, so he wants, nay demands, another girl to take her place. These poor women are prizes, so interchangeable that even their names sound similar. Agamemnon's eye falls on his best fighter Achilles, and on his girl, Briseis. To take the girl from Achilles means that his honour will be slighted.

Whoever wrote the poem down, or composed it, had a gift for literary form: consider how it begins with the ransoming of Chriseis, and ends with Priam retrieving the dead body of his son.**

There are many such mirrorings within the poem, all of which point towards its being carefully constructed.

The whole cycle depends on the transfer of bodies, alive or dead, beginning with the forced marriage of Peleus to Thetis, and ending with the return of Iphigenia (or even, if you take it

---

** Ransoming was common in the ancient world. Priam himself was ransomed as a boy; his name even means 'ransomed'.

to the furthest possible end, to the marriage of Odysseus' son Telemachus).

Patterns are an important part of this literature. And the greatest pattern is fate. The world of the *Iliad* is a fateful one. Characters often refer to the future fall of Troy – even Hector, who is meant to be its greatest defender, talks about it as if it's a foregone thing. Everything happens within the ambit of the will of Zeus, known in the poem as '*Dios boule*'. Zeus' will and Fate have a difficult relationship. Close study of the poem leads some to believe Zeus himself is subject to fate; others think that he can override it. Either way, it suggests that the poem has a purpose, that everything in it is important, and that everything is meant to be.

The popular image of the *Iliad* is that it contains the whole narrative of the Trojan War, including the fall of the city, and the enduring image of the Trojan Horse dragged in by the unsuspecting Trojans. This isn't helped by films such as *Troy* that telescope the action into a short burst of sex and fighting.

I wrote a piece about Troy on my blog, and illustrated it with a picture of Brad Pitt as Achilles in the film. It was my most-read piece for months. Brilliant, I thought – until I saw the search analysis. Nobody was looking for Achilles; they were all looking for Brad Pitt.

The *Iliad* is only a tiny fragment of the vast cycle of stories around the city. I hope, Una, that somewhere in the sands of the desert, or perhaps in an underwater cave, or stopping up a bottle of ancient port in a monastery, we'll find the manuscripts of all the lost epics. I once mentioned this dream to a graduate student in Oxford. 'Oh heavens no,' she exclaimed. 'Think of the trouble of translating it all …'

The Trojan cycle begins with the marriage of the sea-goddess Thetis and the mortal Peleus. All the gods and nobility came to celebrate their wedding. They did not invite one particular goddess, Eris, the goddess of strife. Somebody has to do the job.

She snuck into the wedding, and hurled down a golden apple on which she'd inscribed the words, TO THE MOST BEAUTIFUL.

'For me?' said Aphrodite.

'I think you mean me,' said Hera.

'Well, I think the answer is perfectly obvious,' cut in Athena.

Zeus, with good reason, would not judge between the three goddesses, so he asked Paris, a Trojan shepherd as yet unaware he had been born a prince, to fill in for him. Delegate, delegate, delegate, as they say in managerial manuals.

Paris could hardly refuse. Each goddess promised a bribe to Paris if he chose her. Hera offered worldly power; Athena skill in war; but Paris chose Aphrodite's offering. This happened to be Helen, the most beautiful woman in the world; and so off he went, feeling rather perky, and by night stole her away – or seduced her, the stories vary – from her palace in Sparta.

Helen, because she was so beautiful, had been courted by all the Greek princes; so when Menelaus of Sparta won her hand, they were made to swear an oath to protect her if anybody ever harmed her.

When Helen was abducted, the entire body of the Greek aristocracy was called into action to fetch her back, some more willingly than others. Odysseus put up a fight, pretending to be mad; but they placed his baby son Telemachus in front of a plough he was pulling, and of course he stopped rather than run over him.

Achilles' mother disguised him as a girl and packed him off to an island full of nymphs, which might not have been exactly the best place to keep an adolescent boy secret; he was found out when the Greeks arrived with gifts, amongst which was a sword. Achilles was the only one who went for it, and he was nabbed.

So the Greeks assembled at Aulis. There was no wind, because Agamemnon had offended Artemis by killing a sacred hind. We heard earlier about Iphigenia.

How terrible it must have been. Agamemnon told her mother Clytemnestra that Iphigenia was to marry Achilles. They came to the Greek camp, full of hope for the future. When they arrived, they found no wedding ceremony. Instead, an altar, and a knife.

Iphigenia was sacrificed. Once more a girl is taken by a man, as Thetis was, as Helen was, as Briseis will be, and terrible consequences ensue.

The wind rose, and the Greek fleet sailed, leaving Clytemnestra behind, burning with the injustice of it. Note that plot point, as she returns to Argos to brood on her husband's conduct. On the way to Troy, the Greeks jettisoned the hero Philoctetes, because he had a smelly foot.

*That seems a bit... unfair?*

He was suffering bitterly from a festering wound, so was making a lot of noise, which is a problem. If you're noisy during a sacrifice, you have to perform the whole thing again. So they left him on an island, along with his special bow, which would prove essential to the eventual fall of the city. Silence remained essential for sacrifices, even down to the Romans, who would employ a flute-player to drown out any accidental sounds, which they considered bad omens. The Greeks would later have to return to the island to retrieve Philoctetes and his bow.

The forces of Agamemnon arrived at Troy, full of beans. It'll be over by Christmas (or whatever the equivalent was), they said to each other over their evening hunk of venison.

And... nothing happened. For years and years, they camped on the sand, building huts and putting up tents, and fought in skirmishes, and plundered local cities.

The *Iliad* covers a few weeks in the ninth year of the war.

*Only a few weeks?*

Yes, and though scholars disagree about exactly how many—

—*they seem to disagree about a lot*, interrupted Una.

It's probably about fifty days. The *Iliad* is a snapshot: a small section snipped out from a much greater tapestry. That is Homer's great art, to focus on the consequences of Achilles' anger, and fashion it into a metaphor for the whole. Achilles, though, doesn't die in the poem, as is popularly supposed.

*I thought he was shot by an arrow in his ankle? Achilles heel and all that?*

He is – but only later stories make him vulnerable in that place. In the poem, it's Hector who dies, slain by Achilles.

The retrieval of Hector's body also has a mirroring function: Priam, ancient, enters an enemy camp to get his son back, as his own young son Paris went amongst the Achaeans to steal away Helen. His recklessness is painfully contrasted with Priam's great dignity and pathos. Once the body is returned, the poem ends.

Eventually, Paris slew Achilles – with an arrow, you're right – and some say he was helped by Apollo.

The story of the Trojan Horse appears in Virgil's later Latin epic, the *Aeneid*, which alters the perspective from the attacking Greeks to the defeated Trojans.

Later playwrights and poets fill in the rest. There's a lot of mopping up to be done. In one of the most heart-wrenching moments, Hector's little son Astyanax – which means 'defender of the city' – is beaten to death. The captured Trojan women and girls must be distributed as slaves, and some of them even sacrificed: the ghost of Achilles, still murderous in the afterlife, demands the death of Priam's daughter Polyxena, because she'd been promised to him as a slave; a gruesome parallel to the earlier sacrifice of Iphigenia. See how the sympathies shift: are we to feel for the conquered, or the conquering, or both?

**THE POLYGRAPH TEST**

**Poly...xena**: Daughter of Priam. Sacrificed to Achilles.
**Poly...dorus**: Son of Priam. Murdered by his keepers and found by Hecuba.
**Poly...mestor**: The king who murders Polydorus.
**Poly...deuces**: Brother of Castor, Helen and Clytemnestra. Also known as Pollux.
**Poly...phemus**: One-eyed Cyclops, son of Poseidon. Angry.
**Poly...nices**: The son of Oedipus. Brother of Antigone and Eteocles.
**Poly...dectes**: King who sent Perseus after Medusa.
**Poly...filla**: A kind of paste used for filling in holes.

The Greek heroes must all get home, in what are known as the *Nostoi*, or homecomings. Odysseus' journey is the most famous (and the most elaborate).

We were coming down the other side of Parliament Hill. Una was looking thoughtful. *So it's a pretty supreme effort of art, to get all of that into one poem without detracting from the story?* she said.

It is indeed. Not all of it is referred to in the poem, of course; but listeners would be aware of the whole.

To return to the *Iliad* itself:

Homer sometimes follows a particular hero, such as Diomedes, or Patroclus, and then, at greatest extent, Achilles, throughout the battle, as if he were a camera lens focused on one particular person.

This narrative technique, in which the fighter is shown at his best, is known as an *aristeia*. Each warrior was burning to win not only spoils, but also renown, the word for which was '*kleos*': it was most important that deeds were known about, and sung about by bards, for eternity (and look how right they were). *Kleos* is a fascinating concept. It's almost elemental, like fire or water.

It's also exceptionally pressing for your spoils of war to be kept with you: you can see what happened when Achilles' were taken away. The mere fact of having plenty of rich objects is part of what makes an aristocrat an aristocrat: you have wealth, and so you must fight for your people.

I mentioned that Diomedes and Glaucus stop mid-battle to chat at length. Diomedes, who is in the middle of his *aristeia*, has just wounded both Aphrodite and Ares. He challenges Glaucus, saying he'll only fight him if he's mortal. The heroes have their limits: though they are often called 'godlike', they can't be too much like one.

Glaucus answers with one of the most poignant images in the poem: as some leaves are scattered by the wind, and others grow on trees in the spring, so one generation thrives whilst another passes away. Man's life is fragile and brief, and that is why your deeds matter so much.

He then tells of his lineage: he descends from Bellerophon (in the Homeric Greek he is Bellerophontes, but I'll use the more common form); Bellerophon's father was another Glaucus, and his father Sisyphus (he who rolls the stone up a hill for ever in the Underworld).

Glaucus almost becomes a bard himself, telling a myth to Diomedes, and Diomedes takes the place of the listener.

Picture the scene: all around the pair spears are hurtling, bronze sword clashes against ox-hide shield, their companions are dying; and they pause.

Glaucus' story is substantially different from the childish Usborne version I'd known. The gods love Bellerophon, and bestow upon him beauty and strength.

Anteia, King Proetus'[††] wife, lusted after Bellerophon, but was unable to seduce him. She then lied to her husband.

*What did she say?* asked Una.

'Kill yourself, or Bellerophon.' You can imagine the king was a bit surprised at this. 'Why, my dear?' he might have said. 'Because,' she replied, 'Bellerophon tried to rape me.' You will find echoes of this in Euripides' *Hippolytus*, where Phaedra lies about the same thing, for broadly the same reason.

Proetus didn't kill our hero, but set him on the route to certain death. Bellerophon was sent to Lycia, bearing a letter ordering his own death. This is the only place in the *Iliad* that

---

†† Don't confuse with Proteus.

shows knowledge of writing, a memory of the Linear B alphabet, surviving from the Mycenaean age.[‡‡]

In Lycia, the king feasted Bellerophon for nine days – he was a royal visitor, after all, and deserving of such attention. But then business had to be attended to, and I imagine the King of Lycia perused the contents of the letter in private.

He decided to send Bellerophon off to slay the monstrous chimera, the fire-breathing lion-goat-serpent. Pegasus, alas, is not mentioned here.

Bellerophon succeeded, and was then sent to fight the Solymi (whom many ancient writers identified as the Jews); and then the Amazons (the warrior women); he is glorious in all he does.

The king recognised his power, and offered him his daughter and half his kingdom.

*That sounds like a fairy tale.*

It does. But the story does not finish there, with triumph, as you would expect a fairy tale to do.

Instead, we have that peculiarly Iliadic, fateful worldview. Bellerophon, mysteriously, becomes hated by the gods, and three of his children are killed; but one survived, and he was Glaucus' father.

Homer doesn't explain why Bellerophon suffered this fate (note: it's slightly different from the canonical version). There is a theory that the reason the gods hated him was because he killed his brother unknowingly, and shared in the same blood guilt as Orestes; only in his world, there's no possibility of purification, and he must wander for ever, alone.

---

‡‡ Writing had been lost in the twelfth century BC, when disaster struck the Mycenaean civilisation; it reappeared in about 850 BC, when the Greeks started using the Phoenician alphabet.

*That's sad.*

Glaucus finishes with a statement of the heroic code:
'Hippolochus begot me, and I say I was sprung from him.
He sent me to Troy, and ordered me many times to be
the best and excel above all others, and not to bring shame
on the people of his fathers, who were by far the best men
in Ephyre and in broad Lycia.'

After this speech, Diomedes plants his spear in the ground –
a highly symbolic gesture – and says, well, in that case, let's not
fight, since my ancestor hosted Bellerophon for twenty days,
and they exchanged gifts: Oeneus gave him a smashing purple
belt, and Bellerophon gave a gold cup in return, which is still in
my palace.

They then clasp hands, and swap armour, Glaucus exchanging his fancy golden armour for Diomedes' bronze armour, causing the poet to step in and say that he had gone a bit crazy, since Diomedes' armour was worth a lot less than Glaucus'. Remember how the Trojans are a bit more glamorous than the Greeks? Here's a good example.

What do we make of this scene? As a child, I found it puzzling. Glaucus' story has the same structure as a folk tale: the hero performs three tasks, and then he's rewarded with the hand of the king's daughter and half the kingdom. You may think that the *Iliad* would be simply swimming with mythical beasts, but in fact the chimera's a lonely one: he's the sole composite animal in the poem (bar the centaurs, who are not described in physical terms).

## COMPOSITE ANIMALS NOT FOUND IN THE *ILIAD*

**Satyrs** – rough types. Not to be trusted around girls. Or boys. Or other satyrs. Or anyone. They have goatish legs sometimes, or horse tails. They like drinking.

**Harpies** – half-bird, half-woman. They'll swoop down on your food like seagulls on Brighton beach.

**Griffin** – part lion, part eagle. Borrowed from Eastern mythology; these were meant to guard gold deposits in Asia.

**Sphinx** – part lion (or dog), part woman. The curse of Thebes; all travellers would have to solve her riddle or be eaten. Died from embarrassment when Oedipus solved it.

The exchange between Glaucus and Diomedes demonstrates the system of guest-friendship, known as *xenia*. This was a mainstay of ancient society, in which a guest is entertained by a stranger (in Greek the word '*xenos*' means both 'guest' and 'host'). This sort of relationship was remembered throughout the generations, the gifts themselves being physical reminders of it. The *Odyssey* is more concerned with this than the *Iliad*, since Odysseus visits such a lot of people, but it's so central to this heroic society that it appears even amid the fighting, and trumps the hostility between Greeks and Trojans.

It is as if we are watching in miniature the first meeting between Trojan and Greek, which might well have been a courtly occasion, with heralds announcing the impressive and divine lineages of their kings. It is a reminder, mid-carnage, of what is at stake here: on both sides, power and glory, the golden armour itself being a fine prize. And it expresses the things that are most important in this society of fighters.

*I see. It is a bit like what we dogs do, when we greet each other in ceremonial fashion in the park.*

You mean when you sniff a poodle's bottom?

*So you said something about epithets and similes?*

Ah yes. You can have plenty of fun thinking about how an epic might work today, and what epithets the players would have. Orange-haired Trump, perhaps?

In the *Iliad*, the major question is whether the epithets are there for a specific poetic reason, or whether they give us more general information. 'She could be as lovely as golden Aphrodite and skilful as Athene of the Flashing Eyes' (Rieu translates), says Achilles when he's refusing the offer of a new concubine from Agamemnon. But why does he use 'golden' and 'Flashing Eyes' for the goddesses? Are they stock phrases, which tell us about what Aphrodite and Athene were like; or do they throw particular light on the way that Achilles is thinking and talking here? Plenty of heroes are 'swift', though only Achilles is 'swift-footed'; many of them are 'godlike' or 'godborn'; women are usually 'lovely-cheeked' or 'white-armed' or 'ox-eyed'.

*Ox-eyed?*

Er, yes. Don't ask me why.

*OK. Oooh! I've heard an epithet before. Like 'the wine-dark sea'?*

Well that, Una, is how it's translated, mostly. But the epithet itself means something more like 'wine-faced'; so we're still not clear as to what exact colour it refers to. Jasper Griffin suggests it has to do with the movement of the waves, as Greek wine was full of bubbles.

Griffin, in his study *Homer on Life and Death*, remembers that as a 'sixth-form boy' he was able to see how Achilles and Agamemnon were 'contrasted with each other', simply by their epithets: 'Elegantly and suggestively, in the very first naming of the two: 1.7, "the son of Atreus, king of men, and godlike Achilles" – the one identified by his titles and rank, the other by his personal quality.'

The Trojans are often called 'horse-taming'; and the Achaeans are 'those with the hollow ships', which suggests the poet was thinking in a general sense about how to categorise both armies.

When Hector dies, he is called '*koruthaiolos*' – Hector of the flashing helmet. This is an essential part of his character as a soldier, and particularly relevant to this scene because it has been no help to him against Achilles. It reminds us also of his son, Astyanax, afraid of his father's helmet. It appears to be perfectly chosen for the occasion. A few lines earlier, when Hector is fighting, he is '*poimena laon*' – shepherd of men. This seems not to be appropriate to the scene; but it does tell us that Hector is an aristocrat, and that his actions are significant.

*I see.*

The similes are another feature of the epic style. The poet embarks on lengthy comparisons, quite often mid-battle. These are 'drawn overwhelmingly from the world of nature: beasts, trees and plants, and scenes from inanimate nature (mountains, sun, moon, stars, fire, clouds, sea, snow, etc.)'.§§ There is much the same argument over the similes as there is about the

---

§§ Carroll Moulton, 'Similes in the *Iliad*'.

epithets: do they portray character and theme in a systematic way or not? Iris, when she descends to meet Thetis, is compared to a bit of lead used by an angler thrown into the sea: there will be deadly consequences for the fish. Here we can see that the simile intensifies the sense of mounting danger, but Iris isn't going to kill anyone. Hector, Diomedes and Achilles – fighters from both sides – are all compared to the dog star when fighting, emphasising their almost supernatural qualities and the parity of excellence between them all.

The similes both relieve and add tension and suspense, casting new light upon characters, such as the famous simile where Achilles compares Patroclus to a little girl pulling at her mother's skirt; the implication is that Achilles is the mother. It seems particularly unwarlike, and makes us reconsider the hero. Through the similes, the narrator offers us a fleeting glimpse into the world of the audience.

Now, we can't talk about the *Iliad* without discussing Achilles, the most beautiful and the best of the Greeks, pouting and pretty as he was.

*Steady on there.*

Sorry. Students often say to me: why isn't he happy with another girl? Why does he sulk? Why doesn't he just carry on fighting?

The answer to that is the same I give when talking about Shakespeare: if Macbeth were the king's nephew in *Hamlet*, then Claudius would have been pushing up daisies soon after his wedding, if not before; and if the Dane had been transported to Scotland, he would have entered into a philosophical discussion with the witches and, three hours later, would have still been humming and hawing whilst the weird sisters looked at their watches. 'I think I left the cauldron on …'

Achilles does these things because he is Achilles: because honour (*kleos*) matters to him, and the decision that he made, to lead a short life full of glory, really matters to him.

I mentioned earlier that Achilles, when he's away from battle, takes up the lyre. Here he sings of the '*klea andron*' – the fame of men. A critic points out the delicious paradox: in the very act of withdrawing from the fighting, Achilles will end up having a part in the acts of famous men.

Achilles is an extraordinary character in many other ways, too: his anger is so great that it causes the gods to get involved on both sides; his withdrawal from fighting means that the Trojans storm through to the ships of the Greeks; and it also, and here lies the tragedy of his anger, leads to the death of Patroclus, his closest friend.

Much ink has been spattered on the exact relationship between Achilles and his companion Patroclus, his older boyhood friend. Were they lovers? Or did they just express their admiration for each other in the homoerotic terms that men sometimes use when they are being manly after a few pints? ('I love you, man. No really, I really, really love you.')

The answer is not entirely clear: James Davidson suggests they were not only lovers, but were in a great line of same-sex relationships that has its roots in ancient Indo-European tradition; other critics say that they were bound to each other by deep ties of friendship and war.

Patroclus loves Achilles enough to don his armour and fight in his place, and embarks on a powerful *aristeia*.

But it's no good. However much he looks like Achilles, he can't match up to him. He is eventually slain, but it takes the god Apollo to stop him.

# Dogface!

Achilles' reaction is, as you would expect, not an unquiet one. He throws dust over his head and face and clothes; he tears his hair, and groans. He begs his mother to allow him to die, before deciding to re-enter the fray, and clambers up to the battle lines. His shout alone is enough to terrify the Trojans, twelve of whom drop dead on the spot.

He builds a funeral pyre, and offers up two dogs, his own companions, out of the nine he has at his table – pet dogs, designed to be shown off, and which he fed himself from his own meat – to be placed on it. That is a great honour indeed.

*Quite so*, said Una.

Achilles must enter battle once more, to take revenge on the Trojans. Since Patroclus died wearing Achilles' armour, the hero needs a new set. This provides an opportunity to emphasise Achilles' divine ancestry, again setting his mortality and his heroism into relief. Thetis, who flits between the mortal and immortal worlds, visits Hephaestus to ask him to forge it.

This isn't any old armour, and the poet devotes a long section to describing Achilles' shield, which is decorated with many beautiful images.

*What are the images?* asked Una. *Are they of noble warriors and poignant death scenes?*

You would think so, but surprisingly, they're not. There is a besieged city, which is obviously appropriate. Most are of peaceful, even joyful things, such as dancing, vineyards, sheep pastures and hunting scenes; the whole encircled by the great ocean that surrounds the world. Agamemnon's shield, on the other hand, sports a terrifying picture of the gorgon.

*Why's that?* said Una.

That is exactly the question that bothers Homer specialists. Was it based on an artefact given in guest-friendship? The kind that Schliemann longed to find? This is highly unlikely. As Oliver Taplin says, it's a shield made by a god – so it is supposed to be wondrous.[¶¶] It shows the whole universe, and reminds us of what life is like outside of war.

Achilles arms, and fights. His fighting terrifies the Trojans, and he embarks on the greatest *aristeia* in the poem. This is a brutal, highly tense sequence, which climaxes by becoming a duel between Achilles and Hector. Here, Achilles is compared to the dog star, a harbinger of danger.

Hector flees, Achilles chasing him – those swift feet come in handy. Three times round the city he pursues him. The fourth time, he catches up, and Hector, the pride of the Trojans, sensible, loving, is slaughtered beneath the walls of his own city.

It is a moment full of terror and of pathos. We don't triumph over the death of an enemy, but witness the human consequences of rage and war.

Achilles has not finished. What he does next is shocking. He defiles Hector's body, pierces the ankles, ties it to his chariot and drags it around the walls of Troy.

Here is Achilles' excessive nature. It's tempting to impose our own terminology onto the behaviour of ancient characters, and we must be wary of doing so, but I see in this a compulsive, ritualistic behaviour, an impulse of deep-seated psychological trauma, as he drags the corpse round and round in an endless circle. There is no way out, is the message. Troy has been girdled with death.

Achilles' action galvanises the emotional climax of the poem. King Priam, devastated by the death of his best son, rails at his other sons: they are weak fops; Hector was the only good one

---

¶¶ Oliver Taplin, 'The Shield of Achilles within the *Iliad*'.

amongst them. He tears at his clothes and rolls in the dung: the royal head of the royal city of Troy is entirely debased by grief.

When it has abated slightly, and after Iris has told him not to worry, the god Hermes comes to him with instructions.

At night, Hermes leads him right into the centre of the Greek camp.

*He goes amongst his enemies? An old man, unarmed?*

He does. It is a different kind of heroism: the bold act of a devastated man. This is the emotional heart of the poem. Priam enters the tent of Achilles, and throws himself on his mercy.

There are many moments when Achilles reminds Priam that he could kill him.

Had it been another kind of poem, Achilles would have done so, and Troy would have fallen.

But instead Achilles, reminded of his own father, weeps; Priam joins him, and kisses the hands of the man who slew his son, the 'man-slaying hands'. United in grief, they cease for a moment to be warrior and king, and become simply men.

Here we confront life and death, war and peace, and what it means to be a human under the gods. Both are to die soon: Achilles at the hands of Priam's son Paris, the Trojan who loves to dance; and Priam at the hands of Achilles' own son, Neoptolemus. I do not think that the choice of their killers was left to chance.

We were silent for a minute or two, Una and I.

One final word. The poem finishes with the phrase: 'Hector, tamer of horses'. This epithet throws an image at us. We see Hector before he was a fighter, in peace time, breaking in horses on the plains of Troy.

In elegant, subtle fashion, it also foreshadows the fall of the whole city.

We look forward to a different kind of horse, built from wood, and left at the city gates.

That was an idea that came from the mind of the most cunning of all the Greeks – Odysseus, a master of technological skills.

We were back in Kentish Town; it was time for the midday chow-down, and I was remarkably hungry. It is amazing how hungry-making talking about the *Iliad* is.

I think it's time for some roast beef, don't you? I said to Una. There was a cold joint in the fridge at home. Una has never been known to refuse roast beef. That she has in common with the heroes, amongst other things. She agreed.

Let's go. We talk about relevance: here is a poem from the earliest reaches of time, whose characters and incidents inform everything that came after them. Any besieged city is Troy; as we'll see, any city could become Troy. It tells us how precarious things are: might can be overthrown, the best can die, but nobility can exist amongst the savagery. Zeus, says the poem, has two jars; from one he sends good fortune, and from the other bad. Some men receive only bad fortune; others a mixture of good and bad. But nobody receives only good.

*You were talking about roast beef.*

So I was. Come on then, Una. And tomorrow, we will meet Argus, and look at the most touching doggy scene in all literature.

# Chapter 6

# ARGUS THE DOG
## Homer's *Odyssey*

It was raining, again, in titanic downpours, as if a whole river had decided to unburden itself onto the London streets, each massive drop almost the size of a hailstone. I could almost imagine, amongst the floating plastic bottles, that a boat might drift by, a man standing in the stern, wild-eyed and hungry...

*Sometimes*, said Una, *you do let your imagination run away with you.*

It was eleven o'clock in the morning, and as usual I had various bits of work to do, all due the day before yesterday. My life, day to day, very closely resembles Heracles' battle with the Hydra: chop one head off, and two more grow in its place. I had resolved the issue by ignoring everything, slamming the door on the avalanche of papers and books in my study and retreating to the sitting room, where I was curled in my armchair, a book open on my lap, gazing out of the window.

Una was poking her nose in at me from the corridor.

It's wet, isn't it, I said.

*Is it as if Scamander himself had burst his banks?* she said.

You're catching on, I replied, tickled that Una had remembered the Trojan river. Shall we save a walk till later, as I don't feel particularly like Achilles today?

Una looked a weeny bit put out, but she padded in, and flowed up the sofa, settling into her favourite circular shape, her eyes peeking out at me from under her long lashes.

*So you were going to tell me about the* Odyssey?

Before we get on to that, I want to say a few words about Helen, because of her supreme importance in both poems. In the *Iliad*, she's aware of herself, much more so than the other characters. She talks about Troy as a subject for future poets, and weaves tapestries of the events of the war – a nice touch, as it is essentially a model of the art of the poet.

Weaving is what women did, especially aristocratic ones, and you'll see how Penelope, the wife of Odysseus, is always at her loom (although for a different reason). Helen also helps Priam to identify the heroes, standing on the battlements at Troy, in a scene known as the *Teichoskopia* – which has caused much kerfuffle amongst literary critics.

*Why?*

It's meant to be the tenth year of the war, so it's odd that she's only telling him now.

Una thought a little bit.

*Well – isn't he an old man?*

He is.

*So he might need reminding. And when people watch rugby matches, they quite often ask, 'Isn't that so and so?' even if they know who it is, because they can't see or they're just trying to make conversation.*

That is also true.

*So what's the big deal?*

Well quite. In a fascinating essay on Helen, Margaret Graver notes that in the *Iliad* she is the only person who insults herself – and you can guess what term she uses!

Una snuffled.

You're right. 'A dog', and our favourite, 'dog-face'. Graver explains it has associations with both shame and hunger. But nobody ever calls Helen this: so it's almost as if she's looking outside of the poem, at the audience, daring us to call her that.

Helen reappears in the *Odyssey*, reinstated in Sparta, as a powerful queen with arcane knowledge from Egypt. Menelaus rather bumbles beside her. The *Odyssey* is, as I was going to say, the other great poem generally agreed to be by Homer.

*Generally?*

It almost certainly was composed after the *Iliad*, and shows its influence; but there is some argument about whether it was composed by the same poet.

And some of that debate, remarkably, has to do with dogs.

Una lifted her head.

You remember that in the *Iliad* dogs are scavengers, or a word used to insult somebody, although there are proud and ferocious dogs in the similes?

*I do.*

In the *Odyssey*, some suggest there is a greater love of dogs, which means that the same person can't possibly have written both poems. Presumably, the author of the *Iliad* was a cat person.

Una shuddered.

Although, in fact, this is wrong. 'Dog' is used as an insult just as much in the *Odyssey*, and there are Achilles' pet dogs in the *Iliad*, as we saw.

Other things make people think the two poems were written by different people. There are even suggestions that, given the amount of clothes-washing, and the many women characters, the author might have been a woman.[*] When Odysseus washes up in the land of the Phaeacians, he meets the princess Nausicaa, who sends him to the palace and tells him to talk to her mother, not her father – it's the queen in this land who has the real power.

Una looked approving. She is very much the queen of the house.

The witch Circe; the nymph Calypso; the old nurse Eurycleia, who eventually recognises Odysseus, and Penelope herself are all developed and sophisticated characters. Attention is paid to female servants, even to an old woman grinding corn at the mill. As Jasper Griffin points out, though, 'it is rather naïve to think that an interest in women necessarily suggests feminine authorship.'[†]

Though for centuries the *Iliad* was admired and loved above all else, I'd wager a shilling or two that the *Odyssey* is more popular today. Its landscape of nymphs, monsters and wrecks, as well as its more episodic nature, lends itself very easily to summary and anthologising, as opposed to the *Iliad*, and particularly so for children's entertainment. It's concerned with identity, much more so than the *Iliad*; and identity is very much the subject of our times.

I paused. The rain was turning into something less biblical, and a bit more like a gentle Religious Studies lesson, and it seemed we might soon have an opportunity to set out.

---

[*] This was a theory of the nineteenth-century writer Samuel Butler.

[†] Jasper Griffin, *Homer*.

But it was so comfortable in the sitting room, by the fire, and Una showed no sign of wanting to leave.

Stories about the gruesome, one-eyed, man-eating Cyclops, and the sea nymph sirens who sing unwary sailors to their doom, remain enduringly accessible.[‡] Although it is a curious thing, Una, that we now have police sirens, warning us away rather than luring us onwards.

It's a wide-ranging quest, as opposed to the narrow setting of the *Iliad*. Whenever people think of a long, difficult journey, the first word that springs to their lips is 'odyssey'. You may have no knowledge of the poem at all, and still understand the word, which is not so much the case with its sister poem. When soldiers endure a war, they don't talk of an Iliad. So what is the *Odyssey*?

*An epic poem, like the* Iliad? answered Una, who had definitely been paying attention, and I acknowledged her suggestion with a nod, and reached over to scratch her under the chin. She stretched out her paws in blissful appreciation, giving out a groan of pleasure, before returning to chewing her current favourite, a bit of dried goat's ear.

You'd think that was true. Many of the features are similar – the high-flown diction, the epithets, the mostly aristocratic characters (though it has a greater social range than the *Iliad*) and the machinery of the gods.

Again, we have a question of unity, and we also have a question of subject matter. A lot of the central part of the poem is fantastical – as opposed to the *Iliad* – and plenty of it happens not on the battlefield, but in domestic situations. There's even a

---

‡ Although it's often forgotten that the hero Orpheus went past the sirens first, with the Argonauts.

famous simile where the hero is described as a sizzling sausage!

*No!* said Una. Then, *Sausage?*

There is!

Una licked her chops.

It points to problems with Odysseus. How can he be compared to something so mundane?

*I don't think sausages are mundane. I think they're rather wonderful.*

Thank you, Una. Is he really a hero? Later, when he finally reaches his home island of Ithaca, Odysseus even degrades himself by disguising himself as a peasant. Does this sound like epic to you?

*You said it was normally about war and noble people, and truth. So no, it doesn't.*

We still have the invocation to the divine Muse. Where the *Iliad* asked the Muse to sing of the wrath of Achilles, the poet of the *Odyssey* needs inspiration to sing of 'Andra' – the man, given the epithet *polutropon*, meaning, literally, 'much-turned', and therefore much-travelled, and so, by degrees, to shifty and wily. It's a word often used of Hermes. We can translate it as 'resourceful' or 'versatile'. Here's the first line:

'*Andra moi ennepe, Mousa, polutropon, hos mala polla …*'

'Tell me, Muse, of the resourceful man …'

Note the emphasis is on the man himself: on his travels and his mental abilities.

Because of all this, we can think of the poem as a 'romance' – that is, as a very early ancestor of the novel. These are very often associated with the sea, with long journeys, separated royal families and wondrous happenings. 'Romance' in this sense has nothing to do with Mills and Boon. It's no good trying to plot Odysseus' journey on a map; you might as well, goes the ancient saying, try to find the man who made the bag of winds. People aren't even sure whether the island that's currently called Ithaca is the Ithaca of Odysseus.

Whereas the *Iliad* seems raw and stark (though of course it is not: it is full of little ironies and literary touches, and plainly did not burst into existence out of nowhere), and you can count the jokes on one hand, many light moments dot the texture of the *Odyssey*, as when Odysseus appears, naked but for a couple of branches, in front of the princess Nausicaa. The *Odyssey* is much more aware of itself as a story, like Helen weaving herself into her tapestries. It's not quite 'breaking the fourth wall' but we're clear that this is a world full of bards and stories. There's a lovely moment when, disguised, Odysseus listens to a poem about himself and his quarrel with Achilles: everybody else enjoys it, but he covers his head with his cloak and weeps, affected at once by truth and artifice.

Even Menelaus – not known in the *Iliad* for very much at all, really, which is odd given that it's his wife they're there to get – spins a yarn about how the daughter of Proteus got him off an Egyptian island by disguising him and his shipmates as seals.

*Why would she do that?*

So that he can grab her shape-shifting father, who, like Thetis, can turn into all sorts of creatures, including a snake, a leopard and a tree, which he does. I'm not sure why it should be so difficult to hold on to a tree; though it is a tree that kills Pentheus in the *Bacchae*.

The seal-disguise also foreshadows Odysseus' escape from the Cyclops' cave by clinging to the underside of some sheep. It helps to set up the fantastical atmosphere, and prepares us for the later, taller tales that Odysseus spins.

Writers were never quite sure about Odysseus' guile and quick thinking. In Sophocles' *Philoctetes*, Odysseus is the villain of the piece; his ancestor Autolycus was known for being a thief; other genealogies made him descend from that prince of stinkers, Sisyphus. Sisyphus' eternal punishment was to heave a boulder up a hill in the Underworld; when he got to the top, it would, as stones do in such situations, roll down again, and he'd have to start once more.

*Ouch. What did he do to deserve such a thing?*

Don't make me digress, Una.

*You can't remember, can you?*

It's not exactly burned into my memory.

*Well, can't you find out?*

I disappeared to my study for a few seconds, and found the relevant info, reappearing before Una had had a chance to lick her more intimate parts.

He was a trickster, I said to Una, triumphantly. Much like Odysseus in fact, although, it must be said, rather worse.

## SINNERS PUNISHED IN THE UNDERWORLD

**Sisyphus** – founder of Corinth. Punished for being a cad. **Punishment:** to keep rolling a rock up the same hill for eternity.

**Ixion** – a king of Thessaly. The first person to knock off his own father-in-law, then tried to rape an actual honest-to-god goddess. Epic Fail for Ixion. **Punishment:** to be tied to a fiery wheel for ever.

**Tantalus** – tried to dish up his son Pelops to the gods for dinner. In a stew. **Punishment:** to stand in a pool, with grapes just out of his reach, and be thirsty and hungry for ever.

**The Danaids** – remember them? Yes, the ones the Danaans are named after. They killed their husbands on their wedding night. **Punishment:** to carry water in a sieve.

Odysseus' heroism is markedly different from that of the Iliadic heroes. In the first four books of the *Odyssey*, he's not present at all.

*What?*

Yes, it's true.

*I'm seeing a pattern.*

How so?

*Achilles isn't in the* Iliad *for ages either.*

Yes – but the *Odyssey* has two separate narrative threads. In the first, we meet Telemachus, Odysseus' only son, who in his father's lengthy absence – twenty years, no less – is fending off suitors to his mother, Penelope. They've infested his house. When he goes to address them he is followed, you will be pleased to hear, Una, by two dogs, which is a little flourish of the kind that makes Homer so alive. These dogs often accompany him, and suggest a country landowner going about his business, thinking of hunting and horses.

The suitors are consuming Odysseus' stores with all the rapaciousness of the weasels when they take over Toad Hall (Kenneth Grahame based the episode on this very story), and gulping down his wine, and Telemachus has had enough.

The position of the suitors is a tad unclear: sometimes it seems as if whoever marries Penelope will win the kingship of Ithaca, bypassing Telemachus, which was not the custom of the Greeks. There's also the problem of Laertes, Odysseus' father, who is still alive and tending to his gardens. We never learn why the kingship passed down from him. It may simply be that 'kingship' was a much more flexible idea than our notion of a hereditary monarchy.

Telemachus' mother and his palace are in danger, and he needs to know if his father is still alive. Nobody's heard anything about him.

The goddess Athena (in disguise, natch) instructs him to seek out news of Odysseus. This mission takes up four books. The books of the *Odyssey* number, like the *Iliad*, twenty-four, each also labelled with a letter of the Greek alphabet.

These first few sections are, for this reason, sometimes called 'the Telemachy'. They comprise a mini-journey, in which Telemachus voyages out to meet first the old warrior Nestor and then on to Menelaus and Helen. Menelaus is referred to as '*xanthos*' – yellow-headed. Or so it's often translated; but the definition is a lot broader, including shades from auburn to brown. So it's unclear really what colour hair he had.

Una lifted her tail up and down a couple of times to beat the cushion. I understood what she meant. Get on with it!

I cleared my throat.

These two heroes have managed to make it home alive and well and also to take back control of their kingdoms: they are examples of what Odysseus should be doing.

The Telemachy's major theme concerns revenge on the suitors. Orestes, they say in the *Odyssey*, did the right thing when he killed Aegisthus. Clytemnestra is hardly mentioned; we suppose that the later Athenian dramatists chose to emphasise the mother-killing aspects of Orestes' actions for their own purposes. The Telemachy introduces homecoming and travel as a prelude to the main event.

*Which is?*

Odysseus himself, of course. He doesn't have to excel in an *aristeia*. He has to survive. He needs his guile, his ability to think, as it were, outside the box. This is part of what makes him a hero.

*Ouch.*

I'm sorry. You know what I mean. Blue-sky thinking… that sort of thing. Except the ancients wouldn't have called the sky blue. Oh dear, I'm doing it again, sorry.

*Don't worry, carry on.* Una can be magnanimous when she wants to be.

We first meet Odysseus properly when he's feeling exceptionally sorry for himself, trapped on the island of the nymph Calypso, whose very name suggests concealment, coming, as it does, from the verb '*kaluptein*', to hide.

Una looked thoughtful. *She's a nymph, right? Are nymphs more powerful than mortals? How is she trapping him?*

Well, she, er, makes him sleep with her.

*Oh.*

Anyway, Odysseus isn't enjoying it very much, as he loves his wife, and really, really wants to get home – so in a rare intervention, Zeus sends Hermes down to talk to Calypso and get her to set him on his way.

As Segal points out in his book *Singers, Heroes and Gods in the Odyssey*, the contrast with the poem's predecessor is evident even in the way that Hermes 'lingers admiringly over the landscape'. Despite the fact that he's a 'frequent flyer', he notices things. Setting, landscape and geography, an outward movement, are important here, as opposed to the stark, limited purviews of Troy.

Here, also, we see the poem's interest in civilisation and friendship writ clear: Calypso entertains Hermes (as, in the first four books, both Menelaus and Nestor entertain Telemachus); she doesn't really want Odysseus to leave, so after Hermes has skedaddled back to Olympus, she offers him immortality.

*And he refuses?*

He does. We all know what happens when mortals become immortal: it can go horribly wrong, as with Tithonus. An immortal Odysseus would be no subject for a poem, as his struggles would then have no relevance. We need him to get back to Penelope, and to die, happily, an old man, alongside her.

From here, Odysseus is thrown upon the land of the Phaeacians. He has suffered most of his trials; now he's ready to go home. He emerges, completely starkers, from a bush – which marks an important moment of rebirth – providing a startling sight for the princess Nausicaa, who's playing volleyball with her friends whilst waiting for her clothes to dry.

Una's eyebrows formed interrogation marks.

Well, no, you're right, she's not really playing volleyball – but she is enjoying a kind of ball game, and they've just finished doing the washing for the palace. Even the daughter of the king gets involved in this kind of activity.

At first sight, the Phaeacians appear to be normal. Unlike the gigantic, cannibalistic Laestrygonians, they're not going to try to eat you; and unlike the Lotus-Eaters, they're not going to drug you so you stay in a blissful slumber for ever.

## THE TRIALS OF ODYSSEUS

**The Cicones** – the inhabitants of a city attacked by Odysseus on his way back from Troy. Their allies then send him packing. No relation to Madonna.

**The Lotus-Eaters** – the original caners, zonked out on herbs.

**The Cyclops** – one-eyed son of Poseidon. Good with sheep. Likes eating cheeses and people.

**Aeolus** – King of the Winds. Gives Odysseus a bag full of winds, which his men then later release. Fail for Odysseus' men. Note to those who want to plan out exactly where Odysseus sailed: you'll find his route when you find the man who stitched the bag for the winds.

**Laestrygonians** – unpleasant people. Also cannibals.

**Circe** – an enchantress with her own special way of dealing with visitors, turning them into beasts.

**The Underworld** – visited by Odysseus, largely so he can say he's been there. Early version of extreme tourism.

**The Sirens** – what they sang was the subject of much debate in antiquity, especially since nobody who'd heard them survived (apart from Odysseus, natch, and Orpheus). It was one of the Emperor Tiberius' favourite questions.

**Charybdis & Scylla** – the former is a terrifying whirlpool; the latter, a monster who snatches sailors for her supper. Odysseus must find a way between them.

**The Cattle of Helios** – eaten by Odysseus' crew. Big mistake. Straight to Jail, do not pass Go.

**Calypso** – not an ice lolly. A nymph who detains Odysseus for her own sexual pleasure.

**The Phaeacians** – very affable people who send Odysseus on his way home.

**The Suitors** – Odysseus' final challenge. Massacred. Odysseus wins!

The Phaeacians are a staging post on the way back home to Ithaca, a transition zone between the world of the monstrous and the world of the mundane.

They live far from mankind; they used to be near neighbours to the Cyclopses, but were always being raided, so upped sticks. This puts them off the map – quite literally. They also live in abundance – it's like the hall of a fairy king, where food and drink are limitless. They even have those magical bronze dogs I was telling you about, which guard their palace. Just as today dogs match their owners, these extraordinary creatures are fitting to the utopian Phaeacians.

*Huh*, said Una. *I'd like to see those.* But I knew from her proudly wagging tail that she was really thinking that she was better than any bronze dog.

Which, of course, she is.

I would have liked the Phaeacians.

*Why so?*

Their king says they love banquets, music, dancing, changing clothes, warm baths and sitting down. The good life. They were not impartial to a night on the tiles – much like the sons of Priam in the *Iliad*, who enjoy a shimmy on the dance floor. They love hanging about not doing very much, and even play a sophisticated kind of dancing game with a purple ball.

*Sounds like the kind of thing you enjoy.*

Exactly. I resettled in my armchair. Sitting down in a comfortable armchair is one of the greatest pleasures that civilisation has yet to produce and I defy anyone to come up with better.

The rain was still heavy, and I could see a figure in one of those fearsomely waterproof anoraks struggling against the wind. Poor, much-enduring soul, I thought, giving a guilty glance at Una, who hadn't yet seemed much perturbed at not going out.

Odysseus gets settled in, as according to the rules of *xenia*, a host mustn't ask a guest any questions until he's eaten properly.

Only then does he tell his story. This part forms the bulk of what most people know about the poem.

It's an inset narrative: a story within a story, an extension of the kinds of myths and stories that the heroes in the *Iliad* told each other (remember Glaucus and Diomedes?). The poet is being supremely tactful: the more fantastical elements of the poem are told through the voice of one of the characters; therefore their 'truth' is at one remove.

There have been many attempts, since literary criticism began, to read meaning into Odysseus' adventures. Here is a sailor, an everyman, who battles different kinds of monsters, all ripe for interpretation as allegory or, later on, as elements in a psychological journey.

There is the fearsome, one-eyed Cyclops. He's brutish, but is civilised enough to be able to make cheese and wine. His hospitality is not exactly of the sort that one would expect in the best houses. Having trapped Odysseus and his crew, he polishes them off, two by two. I once saw a dog swallow a duckling whole as it waddled past in a line with its fellows; that's how I imagine the Cyclops picking off the men.

This is rather a predicament. Odysseus can't use his strength, because the Cyclops is too big. The stone across the entrance to the cave is impossible to move. Wit and intelligence are needed: Odysseus decides to get him drunk, and blind him. Which really points to the evolutionary usefulness of having two eyes.

*Why did they think that the Cyclopses had one eye? Is that even possible?*

Robert Graves has an answer: he thought that the Cyclopses were originally a guild of bronze-smiths, with concentric rings tattooed on their foreheads – hence the name, from '*cyclos*'/'*kuklos*', circle, and '*ops*', eye: 'ring-eyed.' He also mentions that smiths sometimes shaded one of their eyes with patches.

*Is he right?*

I'm not sure that it's entirely persuasive. This Cyclops doesn't have anything to do with smithing; though Hephaestus does have Cyclopses as helpers.

What Odysseus does to beat the Cyclops highlights the poem's interest in identity. He claims that his name is 'No one'– which, in the Greek, is *Outis*. Notice how close it is to the first two syllables of his name, 'Odyss', almost as if the idea occurred to him as he spoke.

Segal also notes the echoes in his name of 'pain' – *odunai*, and 'hatred' – *odussesthai*, as well as a lurking pun. In Greek, there are two negatives, *ou* and *me*; *outis* is equivalent to *metis*, which also means 'cunning.' So he is, at one and the same time, both Cunning and Nobody – a pun almost impossible to recreate in English.

*Can you try?*

I had a think. Well you could just about do it: if he called himself 'Knowin' – My name is 'Knowin/No one.'

*Fair play.*

Up to this point, Odysseus has been your average Iliadic hero; after this episode, he's set to be the canny and crafty new hero that his circumstances demand.

After the Cyclops, Odysseus and his men pitch up on the island of the witch Circe – Medea's aunt. You can visit the island today: Monte Circeo. Whether she's still there or not, I don't know, and I'm not sure I'd like to find out. Circe is an archetypal enchantress, and an ambiguous character. She promptly transforms most of his men into pigs, because, you know, why not.

*Why does she?*

To show her power, and to remind the audience how close we are to beasts. Compare her house to that of the nymph Calypso, and you'll see that although she is ostensibly civilised, she has an edge of wildness.

The beasts that have been men – which include lions – fawn over Odysseus rather pathetically, even wagging their tails like dogs. Odysseus, however, is protected from Circe's magic because Hermes warns him, giving him a herb called moly (the name of the love-inducing flower Puck uses in *A Midsummer Night's Dream*, and nothing to do, sadly, with the phrase 'holy moly').

Circe does have a more than merely decorative or delaying function within the plot. She sends Odysseus off on a strange trip to the edge of the world of the dead to garner a prophecy from the seer Teiresias.

It's important for heroes to visit the Underworld.

## GOING UNDERGROUND: HEROES IN THE UNDERWORLD

1. Heracles – twice: first to get Theseus. Lucky Theseus. And then to fetch the dog Cerberus. Heracles zooms up the ladder to an unassailable number one.

2. Aeneas – to meet the ghost of his father, Anchises, and see the future heroes of Rome. Does the job, but not as exciting as Heracles.

3. Odysseus – to talk to the prophet Teiresias. Doesn't really count because no one's sure whether he quite made it into the actual Underworld.

4. Theseus – to abduct Persephone. He failed. Theseus falls several places down the hero

> ladder. Literally. He was accompanied by some-
> one called Pirithoos whom nobody ever
> remembers. Poor Pirithoos.
> 5. Orpheus – to retrieve, unsuccessfully, his wife,
>    Eurydice, who had died because of a snakebite.
>    Orpheus is too mystical even to be on the ladder.

It makes you a special kind of hero to have contact with the world of the dead and come out alive. Even if, like Theseus, you get stuck there until someone else comes to rescue you. This kind of journey is known as a *katabasis*.

Going to the Underworld allows Homer to have some fun with the ghosts that he meets, including Agamemnon and Achilles.

*What does Achilles say? Something about being really glad he's had a life so packed with glory?*

Odysseus says to him, don't be sad that you're dead, because you're a king amongst the ghosts. And Achilles replies that actually, he'd rather, if he so had the choice, live again as a landless man and work for someone else. He'd prefer to be at the bottom of the pile just so that he can be alive.

Una twitched her nose. *Interesting*, she said. *So that kind of undercuts the whole 'kleos'/glory thing doesn't it?*

You have been listening. Yes, it does. Another example of the ironic complexity of these poems. And so, on to Teiresias. He says to Odysseus that he will die, away from the sea, when he's old and prosperous, and must go to a place where the oar he carries is mistaken for a winnowing fan.

*That's nice.*

It is. Eventually, Odysseus lands in Ithaca, and you might think that he would complete his *nostos* immediately, having used his *noos*, or resourcefulness, and it would all be fine and dandy.

*But I'm guessing that's not the case*, said Una.

Things aren't over yet for him. Segal sees this latter part of the poem as the third trial in Odysseus' life. The first was a boar hunt, where he gained a scar that proves significant later on, so pay attention. There he was initiated into adulthood. The second was his journey back home from Troy; the third is taking back control of his house and lands, and returning to his wife's side.

Before he does that, he runs into some hounds: they are keeping guard over all of Odysseus' swine – that is, all the swine that have not yet been consumed by the predations of the suitors. They are 'like wild beasts'. As soon as they spot Odysseus, they bark, with the excellent word '*hulakomoroi*' describing their noise.

*Hulakomoroi*, said Una. She enjoyed the sound of it.

The dogs approach. Remember, these would have been the large Molossian hounds, bred to defend their territory. Their teeth are bared. They move in a tight pack, ready to pounce on this intruder. Our hero Odysseus sits down. You might think that unheroic, but then I don't know what else you might be expected to do. He drops his staff.

There is a moment here when he might have been torn to pieces, when the whole purpose of his return would have been cruelly extinguished, if it weren't for the quick thinking of the swineherd Eumaeus.

He steps in. The dogs know him, and obey him. They are brought to heel. The returning prince is saved, and Eumaeus at this point is entirely unaware of whose death he has prevented.

# Argus the Dog

We read here an ominous foreshadowing of Odysseus' encounter with the suitors. Eumaeus, too, has a literary function, as he was born a prince but was taken into slavery; he provides a foil to the disguised Odysseus, a Homeric mirroring of the type we saw in the *Iliad*.

Odysseus spends a long time with Eumaeus; many critics (and readers) think rather too long a time. As a result, it's a fair few books before Odysseus finally approaches the palace, still disguised as a beggar. And what does the poet choose to emphasise?

He walks past his old dog, Argus, who lifts his head and pricks up his ears.

Una preened. Dogs do preen, much like birds. She then returned to gnawing on the large bone remnant she'd been very keen on for the past few days, which had displaced the goat's ear in her affections.

The vignette of Argus bursts with lively, poignant detail. I absolutely love that dogginess and dogs are so clearly and neatly embedded into the heart of this poem. Argus wasn't just any old hound. Odysseus himself bred him. But he was forced to go to Troy, and so could not enjoy him – and that is, effectively, the word that the poet uses, suggesting the complex and ancient relationship between humans and dogs. It's wonderful that one of the reasons why Odysseus didn't want to join the expedition (aside from having to leave his wife and child) is that he didn't want to abandon his puppy.

Argus was a hunting dog; but, since his master has been gone for so long, he lies, distraught, in the dung of mules and cattle, full of ticks.

*That's awful*, said Una.

It's a reminder of what is lost because of war, that the apparently small things can also be loaded with significance.

When Odysseus nears him, Argus wags his tail and drops his ears. He recognises his master: the first point of recognition in this poem about recognitions. A dog cannot lie.

Odysseus recognises him in turn, and charmingly wipes away a tear, and asks about him. Was such a dog, he says, ever a swift hunter, or was he only kept for show? Eumaeus replies that this is Odysseus' dog – which is another example of the poet's keen sense of irony, as of course Odysseus knows this – and that he is unsurpassed in speed and strength.

But nobody looks after him, and Odysseus, he thinks, is dead.

I can imagine that Odysseus wanted to linger, give the old dog a scratch on the withers, to commune with Argus for a few moments in the way we do with our dog friends. Perhaps he wanted to tell him all he'd been through, and give him a bone, and a wash, and let him lie on a soft rug at his feet for the rest of his days.

But he can't, I surmise, as that would give too much away, and he is still disguised as a beggar. So they pass on.

As they enter the halls of Odysseus, Argus dies. Odysseus' reaction is not recorded. But we can imagine his grief at the passing of an old, loyal companion.

Una gave a little bow of respect.

I took a moment to call her over to my side, and give her an extra-special scratch around the ears.

It's not hard to see in Argus a parallel with the house Odysseus returns to, which is now infested by tick-like suitors.

The dog also represents Odysseus. Can he, now older and beggar-like, really be strong enough to defeat what's coming to him?

Una, I noticed, had left off chewing. *I should hope so*, she said.

There's also a simile that occurs as the disguised Odysseus lies down to sleep in the porch of his own house. He sees the maidservants enjoying themselves. Not a problem, you might think, except these are the ones who have been sleeping with the suitors.

The sight of them stirs his spirt, and his heart growls, like a bitch protecting her puppies. Odysseus wishes he could protect his family against these strangers. Again, as with the simile of Patroclus as a little girl in the *Iliad*, we see Odysseus through a different lens.

When Odysseus enters the palace, he has a long conversation with Penelope. 'I've seen Odysseus,' he says.

'Well then,' replies Penelope, hardly betraying her interest; 'what was he wearing?'

Odysseus describes a beautiful purple cloak, held together by a brooch. On the brooch is a marvellous design: a hound, clutching a dappled fawn as it writhes.

*Another hound!* said Una.

Again, see how dogginess is so central to the *Odyssey*.

You could almost call it the…

*Don't*, said Una.

*Dogyssey*, I continued.

*Fair play*, said Una.

The human moment of recognition comes when Penelope tells the old nurse Eurycleia to wash the feet of the disguised Odysseus. The feet of this man, says the nurse, are probably in the same condition as those of Odysseus himself.

With perfect dramatic irony, the nurse launches into a speech in which she addresses the absent Odysseus, little knowing that the man himself is sitting right in front of her. She chatters on about the awful suitors. 'I've never seen anyone so like Odysseus,' she says, and washes him.

Almost at once she recognises the scar he gained from a boar's tusk.

This causes a long digression, which we mentioned before: the boar hunt that forms the first part of Odysseus' trials. The scene is beautiful and moving, brimming with hounds, spears and a huge wild boar with eyes that flash fire. Odysseus gained his scar at the same moment as he killed it: in fulfilling this heroic function, he receives a permanent mark.

There's debate about whether Penelope recognises Odysseus here or not. The nurse tries to catch her attention, but Athena turns Penelope's thoughts away.

Some argue that from now on, Penelope does know, but chooses not to make this apparent, which adds another layer of delicious irony to the poem. Either way, the stage is now set for Odysseus to wrest back control of his lands, to become once more the kind of king we saw in the rural similes of the *Iliad* or on the shield of Achilles: settled, with his wife and son, amongst fertile lands, at peace.

*And with lots of dogs.*

Indeed. He has a way to go yet, though. For many readers, the final few books of the *Odyssey* present problems, of a sort that has led critics to question the unity of the poem.

The first of these is the violence. It seems unnecessary that not only the suitors but also the maids are slaughtered. Odysseus becomes a towering figure, first shooting his arrows at the suitors and then, armed, fighting them one by one.

He spares the bard Phemius; but the maidservants who slept with the suitors – thus dishonouring Telemachus and his mother – are summarily hanged, their feet twitching as they die, whilst Melanthius, who threw a stool at Odysseus when he was disguised, has his nose, ears, genitals, feet and hands cut off; his genitals are thrown to the dogs to eat.

*Yuck*, said Una, wrinkling her nose.

Odysseus' violence must be seen in the context of what he has endured. Annihilation of the suitors is the only option: since they are all local aristocrats, he can't have them hanging about alive, causing more trouble. The maidservants are necessary collateral damage: if one had been impregnated, the resulting child would be another threat. This kind of ruthlessness is something modern readers shrink from.

Penelope at last recognises Odysseus. She welcomes him, and re-consummates their marriage, on a bed that only Odysseus knew about (because it's carved from a living tree). He tells her the story of his travels – a mini-*Odyssey*.

*Is that the end?*

Not quite. Odysseus' position is still precarious until this point: the homecoming could just as easily have ended with Odysseus dead like Agamemnon – and the final book, 24, begins with the ghosts of the suitors meeting those of Agamemnon and Achilles in the Underworld – also a neat reference back to the *Iliad*. Odysseus visits his father Laertes, and is then confronted by the people of Ithaca, who accuse him, reasonably enough, of slaying two generations of Ithacans (the first being his men at Troy and on the boats; the second, the suitors); it takes Athena to shimmy down from heaven to bring peace.

And she has to do so: because otherwise, the relatives of the suitors would all want revenge. The divine interference prevents it; and the two sides make peace, and all is well.

The movement of the *Odyssey* is towards restoration; so it could not have finished with him dead, or with any threat hanging over him.

And there it does end: though Odysseus has still to go on his journey into the furthest interior of the land.

I took a deep breath, and paused. So those are the Homeric poems, Una.

You couldn't read everything that had been written on Homer, even if you wanted to. I expect that once you'd finished, there would already be another hundred volumes. We are fleeting; the poems are not. We are shadows; they endure. In a thousand years' time, when there are colonies on Mars or on the moons of Jupiter, those first pioneers will have with them copies of Homer, and they will talk of a new Odysseus who sails out into the stars.

There was a slight reduction in the amount of rain. It was time to embark on our own little odyssey around the streets and parks of north London, where the only danger was the siren call of the pub.

## Chapter 7

# SUCKLED BY WOLVES
## Virgil's *Aeneid*

Wednesday morning. A helicopter was buzzing across the sky.

Una and I were on the Heath once more, standing at the top of Parliament Hill, looking across at the city. At least, given the general haziness and heaviness of the air, I was looking at it. Una was otherwise engaged.

London, I said, turning to Una, who was worrying at a patch of grass where, she hoped, there might be a small, furry animal, or an interesting bit of discarded clothing. London, when it tried to prove to the rest of the world that it was a Proper City, decided that a Trojan had washed up on British soil.

Una's black eyes blinked at me. *Oh yes! We were going to talk about the— What did you call it?*

The *Aeneid*, Virgil's poem about Aeneas, a nephew of King Priam of Troy. Geoffrey of Monmouth in the twelfth century AD told of a fellow called Brutus, meant to be the son of Aeneas, who then, says Geoffrey, founded a city on the banks of the River Thames. The city we are in now.

*Did he follow a pig or something?*

Ooh, I'm not sure about that. I don't think so. It's not historically true; there was no Brutus (of that sort, anyway). Much as

I would like to imagine that there really was a king called something like Agamemnon, who laid siege to a city in what is now Turkey, we cannot at all be sure about the historical truth of the *Iliad*. We are equally unsure about Aeneas and his relationship to Italy. But the influence of Troy is great: so many lay claim to it as an ancestor.

Troy is a universal city, a place that new cities strive to be. Which is odd, really, when you think about it.

*Why?*

Since it came to such a bad end.

*So we're the descendants of Trojans?*

Certainly in the literary sense. All writers are in the shadows of Achilles and Hector, Andromache and Helen. But it is entirely possible that in a genetic sense we are too.

*Go on. You're having a laugh. I know who my mother and father were, and even right up to my grandfather.*

Una is very proud of her grandmother on her father's side, who was the head sheepdog at Blenheim Palace, and she's quite happy name-dropping about that. As I am too, of course.

Ancestors were supremely important to the Romans: they were a literal presence. Death masks representing them hung on the walls of their houses. The more noble the house, the more masks it would have. You would feel the weight of their gaze upon you as you went about your business, giving them a very hearty pip-pip as you went by. The effect in the gloom, I imagine, would be rather startling, and no doubt intended to keep young Roman wastrels and scallywags firmly in their places.

The grander families, such as the Julii or the Claudii, could claim generals, senators and warriors in their lines. The senatorial families had special privileges – including the right to wear purple stripes on their togas, and red shoes.

*Fancy!*

Yes – a privilege that the office of the Pope took on. You could see them peeking out from Benedict XVI's vestments (though the current Pope, Francis, has eschewed them). Rather wonderful to think that the streets of Rome were trodden by pairs of red shoes for centuries.

The Romans' ancestors stretched back into the hazy origins of the Roman tribes. Before Romulus and Remus, who were their local heroic ancestors, they decided they had sprung from the Trojans.

*Romulus and Remus – they were twins, suckled by a wolf, weren't they?* Una had a half-remembered memory about it, passed down through her own family, who were ultimately wolves.

The story of Romulus and Remus is bizarre. Romulus, I imagine, is a diminutive of Romus; the twins' names are so similar as to suggest that they are essentially aspects of each other. When they were engaged in building the city, Remus made a point of jumping over the defensive wall Romulus had erected, to show how ineffective it was. Romulus, whose nose had been whacked out of joint, hurled his toys out of the pram, and killed his brother on the spot.

*He killed his own brother?*

He did.

*That's a strange thing to have as your founding story.*

The Romans were aware of this. It feels uncomfortably like saying you've established a society built on civil strife. Which isn't really a good look. And that's why they were just as, if not more so, interested in the figure of Aeneas, whose heroism was more straightforward. There were many odd things in early Roman mythology: the goddess Acca Larentia, for example, who was meant to be a prostitute who left all her goods to the

Romans; others thought she was Romulus' adopted mother. This all hangs on the word *lupa*, which means both 'female wolf' and 'prostitute'.

Julius Caesar's family claimed to derive from the semi-divine Aeneas, whose mother was the goddess Venus. He appears in the *Iliad*, but he's not a particularly interesting hero there; he is snatched away by his mother from the fighting in a mist.

The Julian claim, like many such, requires a bit of sideways thinking. Aeneas had a son, Ascanius, whom the Romans renamed Iulus/Julus, and whom the Julians nominated as a forebear.

Iulus didn't have any children; so any descendants had to come via Aeneas' other son, Silvius. The Julian family were not the only Romans who believed they were Trojan descendants. Something like fifty aristocratic families boasted a bit of the old Trojan in their blood. It's as if the Duke of Westminster suddenly put King Arthur or Old King Cole at the top of his pedigree, and the rest of the peerage followed suit, until you were nobody unless you could claim Lady Godiva or the Queen of Hearts as your great-grandmother.

The Julians were proud of their name, however tenuous the link might have been.

*Their names are all very similar, aren't they? How did it work?*

These days, we tend to have a first name, a middle name or two and a surname. We also don't really think about what our names actually mean. Philip means something like 'one who tends to horses', and is Greek in origin, whilst Womack is Anglo-Saxon, and means, essentially, 'stomach'.

*So your name is 'One Who Tends to Horses Stomach'?*

Er, yes. And luckily there isn't an apostrophe after horses, or, by nominal determinism, I should have been a vet. Since the 'ph' sound in Greek was originally more like a 'p', my name is actually Pilip Womack. Try getting your chops round that.

Una tried, and was not successful. She coughed, delicately, and resumed padding beside me as we began our walk down Parliament Hill. It was cold, and I blew on my hands to keep them warm.

But my surname is a way into the Roman naming system, since Womack was originally bestowed, in about the fourteenth century, on someone who was either very fat or, given the English sense of humour, very thin. Womack can be translated into Latin as *Venter*, 'stomach'; or possibly *Obesus* (fat) or *Crassus* (stout). So my Latin name could be Philippus Venter.

*You must be pleased you're not a Roman.*

I am. A Roman male's full designation would have looked like this:

M. Tullius M. f. Cor. Cicero

which means: Marcus Tullius Cicero son of Marcus from the tribe of Cornelia. Your name could include your grandfather's: C. Iulius C. f. C. n. Caesar: which meant Gaius Julius son of Gaius grandson of Gaius Caesar. Your name was therefore a way of commanding huge respect. In the days when double-barrelling surnames meant a joining of two dynasties, there would have been a similar effect.

Roman men – at least, the higher-class ones – had three names, for example Gaius Julius Caesar. Gaius was the first name, or *praenomen*, equivalent to Philip. There were only a few of these in circulation. If you shouted 'Gaius' in the forum of a morning, several dozen heads would pop up.

Julius was the *gens* name, or family name – the wider clan, usually ending in 'ius'; and *Caesar* the *cognomen*, which was the specific family.

## SOME ROMAN COGNOMENS

**Naso** – nose. Big nose. Publius Ovidius Naso, notable poet.

**Cicero** – chickpea; possibly a wart. Marcus Tullius Cicero, notable orator.

**Rufus** – redhead. Marcus Caelius Rufus, notable playboy.

**Bibulus** – thirsty. Marcus Calpurnius Bibulus, unnotable consul. Whoever the first Bibulus was must have been a good person to know.

We don't really have an equivalent to the gens name. The cognomen was usually a nickname that was then inherited through the generations, like baldness or a liking for boiled sweets.

You were lucky if your ancestor was a hero; less lucky if he was someone who had a big wart on his nose. Of course, all of this started to change towards the latter end of the first century AD; but we won't worry ourselves with that today.

We sometimes call Romans by their cognomens (strictly, in Latin, cognomina, but I don't mind about that sort of thing).

*What do you mean?*

You know how some people call octopuses 'octopi'? Well, they're wrong for a start, as it's actually a Greek word, and should be something like octopods. These are the sort of people who call stadiums 'stadia', or a single piece of information a 'datum' rather than data.

Una nodded.

A Latin word co-opted into English should, generally speaking, act as such, and be pluralised normally, since we're not actually speaking Latin. So cognomens it is. Anyway.

We call Cicero by his cognomen. His full name was Marcus Tullius Cicero (he's quite often called 'Tully' in medieval literature). Sometimes we know people by their *nomen* – such as the poet Ovid, whose full name is Publius Ovidius Naso.

This is largely due to tradition. Sometimes Romans don't have cognomens, such as Mark Antony, whose full name was Marcus Antonius.

*Why didn't he have one?*

His family was the plebeian branch of an ancient noble family, the Antonii.

There was also the *agnomen*, bestowed on you if you won a great military victory. Publius Cornelius Scipio, after he defeated the Carthaginian general Hannibal near Zama in Africa, in 202 BC, was awarded the agnomen Africanus. The Duke of Wellington gaining the title Prince of Waterloo by the Dutch is a similar idea.

*I am glad*, said Una, *that I only have one name. But you say these cognomens often meant something. What does Caesar mean?*

If you read Robert Graves' *I, Claudius*, you'll find the traditional interpretation is something like 'hairy'. Caesar himself endorsed the idea that it was linked, somehow, to a mysterious Carthaginian word for elephant, thereby suggesting that his ancestor was a mighty killer of war-elephants.

Nicholas Ostler, in his book about the development of the Latin language, more plausibly suggests a link with the Etruscan city Caere – so the first person to take on the nickname was 'that chap from Caere', which is a tiny little bit less glamorous than an elephant-killer, even if it might be someone who took or conquered Caere.

It's another linguistic quirk that this nickname has become synonymous with our word for emperor, bestowed upon the German Kaisers and the Russian Tsars.

We are lucky, Una, that Marcus Junius Brutus, after assassinating Caesar, never felt a pressing need to spawn a dynasty and pass down his cognomen as a title, or we might have seen a First World War started by a Brute.

*I don't see anything wrong with that*, said Una.

She had a point.

*What about women?*

I'm afraid that women were only known by the feminised version of their gens name. So if your father was Marcus Sempronius Afer, you would be Sempronia f. Afer.

*What if you had sisters?*

Then they would be Sempronia Minor, followed by Tertia, Quarta, etc. There were also diminutives, so you might be Sempronilla. And I'm sure, although I have no proof, that families would have their own nicknames for their daughters. It's often thought that if you were called Quintus or Sextus, then you were the fifth or sixth son; in fact, it referred to the date on which you were born. This perception isn't helped by the Victorians, who often did name their fifth, sixth or seventh sons by number, presumably having run out of names.

Slaves, when freed, would take the nomen and cognomen of their master. The poet Quintus Horatius Flaccus' father was a freed slave, who had been a member of the household of the famous Horatii, whose ancestor, Horatius Cocles, defended the city single-handedly.

*You were talking*, she suggested, *about Virgil.*

So I was. In many ways the *Aeneid* is a totally different beast from the *Iliad* and the *Odyssey*. Homer has a throbbing sense of rawness, depicting a world of wolfskin-wearing heroes, straight from the smoking fires. The *Aeneid* is very obviously a supreme work of self-conscious art.

The Romans felt oppressed by Greek literature. They lacked their own literary tradition, and were keener than mustard to show they were as sophisticated as their now subjugated friends, the Greeks.

Readers and writers like the orator Cicero knew of old Roman epics, but these had been lost; for our sakes, rather fortunately. Other than that, all they'd produced were tables of laws.

*A fun read, I expect,* said Una.

The first chap who brought literature to the Romans was an ex-slave, Livius Andronicus, who happened to be of Greek birth. Around 220 BC, he translated the tragedies and the *Odyssey* into Latin. We only have a few fragments.

This is Andronicus' version of the *Odyssey*'s first line:

*'Virum mihi, Camena, insece versutum'.*

*Virum* means 'man', and *insece* means, broadly, something like 'tell', whereas *Camena* is more like 'Spirit of song'. *Versutum* doesn't quite achieve the complexities of the Homeric *polutropon*.

You see how difficult it was, even for the ancients, to get the exact flavour of things, as much as it is for us. Cicero was mightily sniffy about Andronicus, sneering that his plays were not worth reading more than once, and that his version of the *Odyssey* was like some primitive sculpture.

An account of Roman history (as far as it went) by Ennius came barrelling in next; it was bombastic and alliterative. There is a saying: 'When Virgil was reading Ennius and someone asked him what he was doing, he replied, "I'm looking for gold on a dunghill."'

Virgil first properly dragged the benighted Romans into the dazzling lights of literary accomplishment (although the poet Catullus was active just before him, writing in imitation of the Greeks, and creating something entirely Roman in nature. Lucretius, also around this time, produced an extraordinary philosophical poem about atomic theory called *De Rerum Natura*).

Virgil's first poems were the *Eclogues*, in which various shepherds sing about how much they love each other.

One of his poems talks of a 'saviour'. Although some think he meant Augustus, or even Mark Antony, or the son of his patron, medieval readers took it to mean Jesus, and saw in Virgil a pagan saint (which is partly why he leads Dante through the Inferno in the *Divine Comedy*. Some even thought he was a wizard, with some truly bizarre legends about him. Apparently he once animated two copper dogs and made them bite to death all the dishonest people in Rome\*). The *Eclogues* were swiftly followed by the *Georgics*, a masterful long poem about …

I paused.

*About what?* said Una.

About the best ways to farm.

*Really?*

Yes, it is mainly about farming. It is good, I promise you, and in a long tradition of didactic poetry.

*I'll take your word for it.*

After this, Virgil composed his *pièce de résistance*, the epic poem, the *Aeneid*.

---

\*    Andrew Lang, *The Violet Fairy Book*.

It was an immediate success. And it somewhat vexed the Greeks:

'It is a poem greater than any that had been produced in Greek for several centuries past; but the Greeks, not unnaturally, refused to notice. It was bad enough to have been conquered, oppressed, and looted by these Roman barbarians. To be expected to take seriously a poem in their uncouth language: that, for a Hellene of any culture, was altogether too much to ask,' notes Jasper Griffin.[†]

I feel for Virgil. Although it is a delicious irony to note that, through the extraordinary passage of time, the Greeks now use the word *Romiosyne* to describe Greekness.

*How's that?*

Thanks to the Byzantines. It means Roman-ness; they, being the eastern part of the Roman Empire, used it to mean patriotic; so when modern Greeks want to talk about their patriotism, they call themselves Romans. I think Virgil would have been amused.

Much like Homer, the verses were recited. We know of a performance before the Emperor Augustus, his wife Livia and his sister Octavia, during which the latter fainted.

*Why?*

Her son, Marcellus, the hope and flower of the Empire, had died young. Virgil mentions him when Aeneas visits the Underworld, his description so powerful it had a measurable emotional effect: '*ostendent terris hunc tantum fata/nec ultra esse sinent.*' The Fates will only show him to Earth; they will not let him stay there long.

To understand the *Aeneid*, we must know that Virgil was trying to surpass both the *Iliad* and the *Odyssey*.

---

[†]   Jasper Griffin, 'Greek epic', in *The Cambridge Companion to the Epic*.

Virgil wrote in hexameters, in direct imitation of the epics, and used many of the same features, such as epithets. Any reader in the Latin will soon become well acquainted with the phrase '*pius* Aeneas', variously translated as 'pious' or 'dutiful'; extended similes; and a divine framework, with gods getting their divine mitts involved in the action at many levels. Virgil pulls out every stop imaginable.

You will remember that the *Iliad* had no composite beasts; the *Odyssey* has a few, but only in the tales that Odysseus tells the Phaeacians. The *Aeneid* positively teems with them, not only encountered by Aeneas and his companions in his travels across the Mediterranean, but also in the Underworld. The full panoply of myth and legend is brought to bear for one single purpose: building a literary foundation for Rome.

Whereas we know very little about Homer – and indeed, though romantics like me imagine that he really did exist, it's fairly probable he is a construct – we do know some things about Virgil, or Publius Vergilius Maro, to give him his full name. (Some call him Vergil, just to confuse matters.)

Virgil, by the way, wasn't a Roman.

*What?* said Una.

We think of the 'Romans' as synonymous with Italians, but Virgil was born in the provinces, in what is now Mantua. Many of the greatest poets of the Roman Empire were not from the city itself, which perhaps, as outsiders, gave them more insight into the workings of the great capital.

There is something else in the mix here too, an extra spice in the stew.

We don't know if Homer was trying to make a political point about kings of Sparta or Troy, bar being slightly more broadly in favour of the Achaeans; as far as we know, he was telling a bloody good story.

It's possible, given that the world of the Mycenaean kings depicted in the *Iliad* was not contemporaneous with Homer, that there was some implied or even overt comparison with their own systems of kingship; but the answer is that we don't know and, as far as I'm concerned, it doesn't matter.

With Virgil, however, there absolutely is a political element. He had a very powerful aesthetic motive, to compose something that could better what had gone before him. He died before the poem was completely finished, and urged his friends to burn the manuscript, such a perfectionist was he. Fortunately for us, they didn't.

Alongside this, and unlike Homer, there is a very strong political strand, which comes in the unmistakeable form of a celebration of the Emperor Augustus – the first emperor. This marked the end of years of the proud tradition of the Roman Republic.

The Romans, since they had chucked out Tarquinius Superbus, their last king, were very suspicious of such autocratic institutions.

*They had kings?*

They believed they had seven kings, but they couldn't quite match up the kings to the years in between the legendary date of the founding of Rome, at a convenient crossing point on the River Tiber, which is 753 BC, and the start of the Roman Republic, some time in the sixth century BC.

Even the most long-lived of kings couldn't have stretched across that time period, if you only have seven.

What we mean by a king – a monarch, decked out in all the regalia of previous centuries – is not exactly what they meant. A '*rex*' would have been more like a warlord or a chieftain, much like the 'kings' in the Homeric armies; and these kings were not always Roman, nor even aristocratic.

After Tarquinius Superbus – known as Tarquin the Proud, a tyrannical king whose forebears came from the Greek city of Corinth – was given the heave-ho, the Romans began to elect two consuls a year to rule, along with the Senate, and so instituting the great Republic of Rome: SPQR, *Senatus Populusque Romanorum* – the Senate and the People of the Romans. Which you still see on manhole covers in Rome.

## THE SEVEN(ISH) ANCIENT (POSSIBLY LEGENDARY) KINGS OF ROME

**Romulus** – suckled by a wolf. Murdered his brother.
**Numa Pompilius** – a Sabine. Meant to have set up the basics of Roman religion. No fun at parties.
**Tullus Hostilius** – warlike, as his name suggests. Son of an ally of Romulus.
**Ancus Marcius** – also warlike. You sense a theme? Grandson of Numa.
**Lucius Tarquinius Priscus** – the first Tarquin. His Corinthian ancestors settled in Etruria. Moved to Rome and became king.
**Servius Tullius** – a slave, though the son of an enslaved Latin princess. His head caught fire so they thought he was divine.
**Tarquinius Superbus** – the one who got the heave-ho.
(See also: Titus Tatius, Mastarna.)

Nobody can ever remember the names of all seven canonical kings. If you fancy a party trick, this is how you do it. Imagine you are a general.

*OK*, said Una.

Now imagine that you're issuing orders: R, N, T, A, T, S, T. 'Royal Navy! Territorial Army! Tanks, Sailors, Tanks!'

After the kings, the Roman Republic lasted for centuries, the two consuls ruling, changing every year. The Senate, however, was considered supreme. These were times of war – locally, with tribes on the Italian mainland, and with the Carthaginians, amongst others; they were also times of huge Roman expansion.

It really was a big step – especially given how Julius Caesar was murdered for approximating a king – for Augustus to become an emperor. Which, by the time the *Aeneid* was being composed, he had very much become.

*What was he before?*

He was born Gaius Octavius, the great-nephew of Julius Caesar. Because he had no sons, Caesar adopted him and made him his heir. From then on Gaius Octavius, as was conventional, went by the name Gaius Julius Caesar, the same name as his adopted father.

*That is confusing.*

Octavianus was a nickname, probably to distinguish him from his great-uncle, but also a slightly snide reminder of his more humble origins. The elder Gaius Julius Caesar is the one we know as Julius Caesar, familiar from the *Asterix* books, with his laurel wreath and beaky nose.

*Didn't he come to Britain and say 'Veni, vidi, vici'? Only it's pronounced weeny, weedy and weaky, because that's what the Brits looked like?*

Una had heard this when I read *1066 and All That* to her.

Well, he did go to Britain, but he didn't conquer it. That was the Emperor Claudius, later on. Caesar actually said '*Veni, vidi, vici*' – I came, I saw, I conquered – at the battle of Zela in Asia, which is rather less renowned. The other thing he's supposed to have said is '*Alea iacta est*' – the die has been cast – when he crossed the Rubicon.

*The what?*

The River Rubicon. A highly significant moment, and another one that's entered into our general lexicon: it was the boundary between Italy and Cisalpine Gaul; anyone who crossed it with an army was breaking the law. This catalysed the civil war. What he actually said was '*iacta alea esto*' – let the die be cast. Which has a slightly different emphasis.

Anyway, on the assassination of Julius Caesar – you will be familiar, I am sure, with the way that he was killed…

Una looked at me.

*I'm not*, she replied.

He was done in by Marcus Junius Brutus, leading a group of senators. Brutus had his genealogy painted on the wall in his house, so every day he could see his connection to the Brutus who deposed Tarquinius Superbus.

*Why did they get rid of Tarquin?*

Tyranny; as shown by his attitude to Lucretia, the virtuous wife of one of his companions, whom he raped. She killed herself; and a group of her husband's friends vowed to expel him. One of these was Lucius Junius Brutus, the son of one of Tarquin's daughters. The later Brutus boasted both tyrant and liberator in his bloodline.

Many suggest that Julius Caesar wanted to become a king, and that's why the senators stopped him, in the cause of that most Roman of virtues, liberty. He was voted divine honours, given a golden throne and offered a golden crown; but when crowds shouted out 'King!' to him, he would reprimand them. Whether he wanted to be king or not, it is certain that his powers as a lifelong dictator were huge.

On the Ides of March, 44 BC, Caesar went, as he usually would, to meet the Senate.

*What are Ides? Is there such a thing as an Ide?*

It's part of the Roman calendar system – the name for a particular day in the month, usually the thirteenth, but in March, May, July and October, the fifteenth. It was supposed to be the day of the full moon.

On this day, at the Senate House, Caesar was confronted by a group of senators, including Marcus Junius Brutus; he was set upon, and stabbed to death. It would have been a bloody, confused scene, with senators getting injured by mistake.

That the dying Caesar said '*Et tu, Brute*', or 'You too, Brutus', is probably a legend. Some think that he uttered a Greek phrase, '*kai su, teknon*' – literally 'and you, my child', which would mean, effectively, 'Same to you, old chap.' But whatever he said or didn't say, it makes a good story, doesn't it?

Rome slipped once more into civil war. The key players were Octavian and Mark Antony. Mark Antony had been one of Julius Caesar's greatest supporters; the two came into conflict.

After much toing and froing, all you need to know is that our boy – and when I say boy, I mean boy, as he was barely eighteen years old when Julius Caesar died – Octavian defeated Mark Antony and Cleopatra in a sea-battle at Actium in 31 BC. Although, as Robin Lane Fox points out, there wasn't much fighting in the battle per se; as soon as they could, Cleopatra and her forces sailed away. (Lane Fox, by the way, was quite the hero when I was at university: he waived a consultant's fee so that he could lead a cavalry charge on the set of Oliver Stone's 2004 film *Alexander*, starring Colin Farrell as an Alexander with a decidedly dodgy haircut, let alone accent.)

*Cleopatra was in the battle? That Cleopatra?*

Yes, that Cleopatra. She appears in the *Aeneid,* accompanied by various gods, including Anubis, who, as the poet Dryden has it, barks, but barks in vain.

*Woof!* Una said, barking in vain, as there were no dogs nearby, nor even squirrels.

*What's the* Aeneid *about?*

It's the legendary story of the Trojan prince Aeneas. He escaped from Troy before it fell, with his son Ascanius, his father Anchises and a band of followers. The image of Aeneas carrying his father on his back, and leading his little son by the hand, is a powerful one (though much parodied too – there is a version where he has a dog's head).

The first line of the poem is

'*Arma virumque cano, Troiae qui primus ab oris*', which you can translate as: 'I sing of arms, and the man, who first from the shores of Troy…' Does that remind you of anything?

*It's a bit like the first line of the* Odyssey, *but with weapons too. So it's like both that and the* Iliad.

You're absolutely right, Una. And look how Virgil places Troy into the first line. The next begins with '*Italiam*'; that's in an accusative form, which suggests motion – the force of Aeneas' arrival is momentous, carrying over the poetic line. This is followed by '*fato profugus*', bringing out two other major themes, that of his fugitive status from Troy, and the theme of the controlling power of fate.

Aeneas is motivated by a strong sense of duty – known in the poem as *pietas*, which informs, but does not quite overlap with, our own word 'piety' – as he must fulfil his fate, which is to found a city for his people.

The *Aeneid* is in twelve books, a very elegant way for Virgil to pay homage to Homer's twenty-four. The first six books are the Odyssean half, since they follow the travels and travails of Aeneas as he zigzags across the Mediterranean. The second six are the Iliadic half, which deal with Aeneas arriving in Italy, settling, fighting, and attempting to marry a local Latin princess, Lavinia.

The even-numbered books are the most exciting: Book II tells the story of the Trojan War as described by Aeneas; IV is the passion and suicide of Dido, Queen of Carthage; VI, Aeneas' visit to the Underworld; VIII, a trip to the site of the future Rome; X, lots of fighting; and XII, the climactic duel between Aeneas and his enemy Turnus. The odd-numbered books have their charms, too. The *Aeneid* is powered by a system of complex oppositions: duty vs self-interest; rage vs rationality; the East vs the West. These are not cut-and-dried by any means, and quite often reflect and feed into each other.

We begin the whole epic with the hero *in medias res*, tossed on the waves thanks to a storm caused by Juno (Hera), who has a particular animus towards Aeneas, because he's a Trojan and she's still sore about Paris picking Venus.

*The gods have long memories.*

Well they don't have much else to do. He and his companions are washed up on the shores of Carthage, in north Africa. Whilst Odysseus had to be on his tod in order to be heroic – he had to jettison his men and return alone to Ithaca – Aeneas is very much the father of his people. You can't jumpstart a dynasty without your loyal and deserving followers. His heroism is also shown by the special attention paid to him by the gods, especially his mother, Venus.

*Why is Venus so important to the Romans? She doesn't seem particularly Roman.*

She was an ancient goddess from Lavinium – the city that Aeneas founds; she was then assimilated with Aphrodite. She's a link to the earliest history of the Romans.

Aeneas, the prime example of duty, is shipwrecked in Carthage, the domain of Dido, the queen. She is beautiful and powerful, and a parallel to Aeneas, having fled her lands in Phoenicia to found a new city for her people. Both are refugees, tossed about by fate, seeking anchorage and stability.

Aeneas and Dido are smitten (something Venus has a hand in, as she wants to make sure that Juno doesn't try to hurt Aeneas through Dido).

They go hunting together. Driven into a cave by a thunderstorm, they consummate their love, surrounded by shrieking nymphs. This scene would inevitably bring one of my Latin teachers into transports of delight. He was Scottish, and would gleefully accentuate the 'r' in 'shrieking'.

Aeneas, of course, cannot stay, and, motivated by his sense of duty and the fate that drives him, he abandons Dido. This conflict ignites much classroom discussion: it's akin to the decision that Jason makes when he decides to marry a young Corinthian princess in *Medea*, sidelining the titular heroine. Dido is so consumed with fiery passion that she kills herself, demonstrating the kind of excess that Aeneas must avoid. The dying Dido threatens to pursue Aeneas as if she were a doglike Fury, but Virgil also displays great sympathy for her and her noble passion.

Virgil makes a historical point, as Carthage was to become a great enemy of Rome, facing it across the Mediterranean, its leader Hannibal bringing war-elephants to the Italian mainland.

Dido is clearly envisaged as a forerunner of Cleopatra at the Battle of Actium.

The scene is a brilliant example of Virgil's artfulness. It's described on the divine armour given to Aeneas by Vulcan – again, a direct homage Virgil pays to Homer, as you will remember the shield of Achilles with its varied scenes of civilisation, farming, war, dancing and justice. ('Another?' we can imagine Vulcan saying, when Venus arrives with her request. 'I've only just finished the last one!')

The technical word for this is an *ekphrasis*, which we'll see later when we meet Catullus: a description of a work of art within a poem. Virgil invests it with so much power that you forget you're looking at a static image, and are hurled right into the action.

Virgil uses the shield as a means of displaying to his audience the glorious history and might of Rome. Aeneas is the heroic type, matched against Hercules whilst also being the direct forerunner of Augustus.

Aeneas has no idea of the import of the pictures he carries on his shield: images of the future. His descendants, listening to the poem, would have responded to it eagerly.

Here is everything that defines what it means to be Roman: Romulus and Remus, being licked by their wolf nurse; the rape of the Sabines (where the Romans, needing to expand their population, invited the Sabines to the city, then stole their wives); the expulsion of Tarquin the Proud; the heroism of Horatius Cocles and of Cloelia, who escaped from her prisoners, only to be sent back by the dutiful Romans; the attack of the Gauls, where Rome was saved by the hissing of the sacred geese; the wicked rebel Catiline, who threatened to overturn the state; and the austere law-giver Cato. Most of these are romanticised, to say the least; far from defeating the Gauls, Rome was actually overrun by them; and whether Catiline's rebellion was really so dangerous or just a way for Cicero to make political capital is hotly debated.

The big reveal, at the heart of the shield, is the battle of Actium – even if it is an exaggerated version of what actually happened.

Here a shining Augustus, aided by the gods, is followed by the Senate and the people. In opposition to them is Mark Antony, leading a ragtag troop of Egyptians, including Cleopatra. Monstrous gods surround her, like Anubis, who barks and causes chaos. The word '*latrator*' is used, which you will remember from your Latin lessons, Una.

*I do. It means* 'barker'. *I like the sound of Anubis*, said Una.

Yes, and I wish there were more such interactions between cultures in the poem, and in ancient literature in general.

Augustus, on the shield, demonstrates all the virtues of a great leader. He is dutiful, ordered, rational; and of course he wins the battle, as opposed to Mark Antony, glamorous, swashbuckling, daring. The triumph of Augustus is the triumph of reason; we are meant to draw a parallel with Aeneas deciding to abandon Dido in order to further his fate.

We then see Augustus entering the city of Rome in triumph. He pays honour to the gods and builds temples throughout the city. Augustus was consciously claiming to be bringing in a new Golden Age: an end to disorder and chaos and a new beginning for the might of Rome.

He was in reality ruling over a complicated, messy city of a million inhabitants: the biggest city in the world, until London eclipsed it in the early nineteenth century.

The final image is of the magnificent extent of the Roman Empire, with Augustus enthroned and watching the vanquished peoples passing in front of him. And so ends Book VIII.

I wonder what might have happened had Mark Antony won the battle. It's certainly one of those major cruxes in time. There would have been no Augustus, no Julio-Claudians, and who knows what else – perhaps even no Roman Empire and thus no Romance languages, no Charlemagne and no European Union?

Lane Fox gives us a more reasonable idea: 'Rome would have had a very special tie with Egypt and Alexandria … Thousands of barbarian lives might have been spared … a regeneration of the ravaged Greek cities could have been brought forward.' And instead of the *Aeneid*, we might have been given a poem about Dionysus, with whom Mark Antony was closely associated.[‡]

Since he also claimed his family descended from Anton, the son of Heracles, another critic claims we might have been treated to an epic about Heracles instead.

Things that seem inevitable are not; things that seem immutable are more often than not the result of happenstance and circumstance.

*Did the right side win?*

---

‡    There does exist the *Dionysiaca* by Nonnus, a Greek epic poem (and it is *really* long) from the fifth century AD.
*How many books is it?* asked Una. *Twelve? Twenty-four?*
Forty-eight.
*Jeepers.*
Virgil, one thinks, could have done a better job.

It wasn't like the Persians versus the Greeks, where quite clearly the freedom of the Greeks would have been seriously curtailed had they become an outpost of the Persian Empire. Was there much to choose between Octavian and Mark Antony? Certainly, if Antony had won, Rome might have been rather a jollier place; there wouldn't have been such a shed-load of laws on morality, for example, which Augustus was perhaps a little too keen on, especially given the scandalous behaviour of his own daughter, which we'll see when we talk about Ovid.

*But was Virgil really in thrall to Augustus?*

Plenty of readers discern a lot of what's called 'Anti-Augustanism' in the poem. It isn't pure propaganda, you see – when a song or a poem is too rigidly doctrinaire, too tub-thumping, it fails.

Virgil has vast amounts of sympathy for those destroyed in the process of the remorseless journey of Aeneas – Dido being one of them, of course.

And from this we can infer a major question: is Rome a force for civilisation and good? Or is it, and its newly minted empire, more ambiguous? Does Augustus really herald a new Golden Age? Or is he a harbinger of something authoritarian and troubling, that is in conflict with Roman ideas about liberty? Read the poem, Una, and you'll soon see just how ambivalent it can be about power.

*I can't read.*

Audible, then. Or I'll read it to you. We've seen how none of the questions about poetic unity trouble Virgil, since we know that he had a scheme and that he followed it carefully.

But there are questions about the poem's ending, and its aptness. How would you expect the *Aeneid* to end? I asked Una, who was greeting a passing chihuahua in the time-honoured fashion of a good sniff of its bottom.

*It's about the founding of Rome, and dynasties, so I guess it would end with Aeneas marrying Lavinia, and with the city being built?* offered Una. *I can imagine a big wedding ceremony, and maybe some significant building being constructed?*

That is exactly what you would expect, I replied. It doesn't, however. They don't reach the actual founding of Rome – which would be several hundred years later, in any case – because Aeneas himself only settles down in a city called Lavinium.

There are references, of course, to Romulus, in another of the poem's masterstrokes, in which Aeneas, in search of allies, visits the site of the future Rome, which gives the poet a chance to describe its coming glories.

There'd have to be a lot more tacked on to the end of the poem to get to Romulus – most of which was pretty hazy, even to the Romans.

The epic ends with Aeneas slaughtering his enemy Turnus, who is the leader of a local Italian tribe called the Rutulians. Turnus has plenty of beef with Aeneas.

*Why?*

Turnus was engaged to Lavinia. But, when our friend Aeneas turns up, her father Latinus instead betroths her to him.

Annoying for Turnus, wouldn't you think? Interestingly, I added as an aside to Una, Latinus is thought to be a descendant of Circe and Ulysses. Which would mean that the sorceress's blood ran in Julius Caesar's veins, too, as well as that of the cunning silver-tongued hero. Just about.

*That seems odd. Why would he let his daughter marry some random Trojan?*

Because of a prophecy.

*There are a lot of prophecies, aren't there?*

There are indeed, and it adds to the general sense that Aeneas is motivated by not only duty but by cosmic fate. Everything has to happen in this way so that Rome can exist.

Turnus and his allies are prime examples of the negative qualities we were discussing. Turnus' anger is excessive. Aeneas, too, displays some of these characteristics. The question arises: is he consumed by his own anger? Or is his anger in service of his piety and duty?

Like Achilles chasing Hector around the walls of Troy, Aeneas pursues Turnus. There is a simile describing him as a '*venator canis*' – a hunting dog. I looked up a translation by Theodore C. Williams, which you can find on the excellent Perseus website.

> As when a stag-hound drives the baffled roe
> to torrent's edge (or where the flaunting snare
> of crimson feathers fearfully confines)
> and with incessant barking swift pursues;
> while through the snared copse or embankment high
> the frightened creature by a thousand ways
> doubles and turns; but that keen Umbrian hound
> with wide jaws, undesisting, grasps his prey,
> or, thinking that he grasps it, snaps his teeth
> cracking together, and deludes his rage,
> devouring empty air: then peal on peal
> the cry of hunters bursts; the lake and shore
> reecho, and confusion fills the sky

Here there is a sense of frustrated desire: hunter and hunted shade into one another. Many scholarly articles have been written about this: how Aeneas and Turnus are really more similar than they might seem. It is an early forerunner of the hero meeting the villain at the end of the movie: 'We are not so different, you and I ...'

*Is this, then, where we can see some of that anti-Augustanism?*

It certainly is – on the one hand, Aeneas is bringer of order; on the other, he's a vicious murderer.

The poem's ending leaves us with Aeneas, enraged at the sight of his friend Pallas' belt round Turnus' waist, striking a fatal blow, and Turnus' soul fleeing to the Underworld.

Having started *in medias res*, we end in the middle of things too: we can only assume that Turnus' forces, having lost their leader, are routed; that Aeneas and his allies win comfortably; and that Lavinia and Aeneas marry and settle.

A very young medieval Italian called Maffeo Vegio did pen a poem in which these things happened; it's more a *jeu d'esprit*, however, and I think it misses the point. Virgil didn't want the poem to end with certainty. That final image confronts us with the specific violence and rage of a leader whom the Romans admired as their founder. This interplay between power and poetry is essential to any understanding of history and literature.

It was now getting dark, and I was feeling lazy. I could see a bus pootling its way towards us, and I staggered into a half-run to catch it.

*Well I do like the sound of the* Aeneid, said Una, as we jumped on the bus. *But there aren't as many dogs in it as Homer.*

No, I said. And that, in my view, is one of its great failings.

# Chapter 8

# CHANGING DOGS
## Ovid's *Metamorphoses*

Time was passing. September had vanished, as fast as Una when she's spotted a fox in the distance in the woods, and with it any remnant of the sun; it was now the middle of October.

I spent the weekend buried deep in various texts; Una, being rather left out of things, began to sulk, taking up her position by the window in the sitting room and keeping her eye out for passing enemies. If you have never seen a dog sulk, it's quite hard not to notice. But I had pressing things to do.

As I truffled through my books, I stumbled upon this:

'*saepe pater dixit: "studium quid inutile temptas?*
*Maeonides nullas ipse reliquit opes."*'

Una, I said.

She glanced my way. The term 'side-eye' was invented for dogs.

*What does it mean?*

It's from Ovid's *Tristia*, and its translation is as follows:

'Often my father said, "Why are you hacking away at that pointless fad?

Even Homer didn't leave behind any money."'

Maeonides is a name often used for Homer, as one tradition made him a native of Maeonia, or Lydia as it was otherwise known. The speaker is Ovid's father, ticking him off for wanting to be a poet. Ovid's brother, of course, is a successful lawyer. This kind of scenario is similar the world over.

Isn't it marvellous to hear the voice of the father roaring out across the centuries as his useless son messes about with ink and papyrus instead of swotting up on legal precedents?

*Sounds a bit like you,* said Una.

I ignored her, and put my work away. We got ready to go out. It was late afternoon, and Una's patience had been matched only by her ability to spot squirrels in the garden and bark furiously.

We had better go quickly, I said.

Our last conversation was about Virgil, and Augustan Rome, and the piety and duty of Aeneas, and also the complexities that result from a poet dealing with a regime that is on a knife-edge between tyrannical and restorative. If you only read Virgil, you might come away from it thinking that the Romans were awfully serious.

*That,* said Una, *is the impression I get from paintings. You know, white marble columns, dignified senators, chaste matrons…*

That is true. Those kinds of paintings, though, tend to reproduce the idea of the painter, rather than what Rome (or Ancient Greece) was actually like. It was a busy, messy, colourful place – all the buildings that popular imagination sees as white were actually gaudily bright, painted many colours. We get a sense of the bustling brouhaha from the poems of Catullus, which we'll talk about later, and also from the poems and satires of Martial and Juvenal. It's closer to the joyously cacophonous comedy of *A Funny Thing Happened on the Way to the Forum* (1966) than the severe portentousness of *Gladiator* (2000).

The idea that the Romans were all walking around brimming with virtue and honour is just as silly as the notion that the

Victorians were all sexually repressed and covered up the legs of their pianos because they might make men think of ladies.

Rome was as full of boors, bores, hypocrites and flatterers as any other city.

Ovid – or, to give him his full name, Publius Ovidius Naso – is best known for his wildly playful long poem, *Metamorphoses*. Which, thanks to David Bowie, we can translate as Ch-ch-ch-changes. Virgil and Homer both have a single theme, a single hero and (generally speaking) a single purpose. Here, all those conventions of epic are blithely smashed into smithereens.

To start with, there are about 250 stories, of differing length and import. It is essentially a handbook of myth – the closest thing we have to that notional Bible – and most of what you read as a child has its origin in Ovid.

Stories such as that of Echo and Narcissus, in which the beautiful boy falls in love with his own reflection and, unable to tear himself away, dies, leaving only a flower behind him; or Phaethon, who boasts to his friends that his father is the sun god, and comes to a terrible end when he's allowed to drive the chariot of the sun (having not had any driving lessons at all), have become deeply embedded into the cultural landscape.

In *Metamorphoses*, there isn't a straightforward narrative thrust. We've already mentioned the poignant section where Actaeon, having stumbled accidentally on the bathing Diana, is transformed into a stag and torn apart by his own hounds.

The transformations range from people turning into stones to birds to flowers, and many more, for a variety of reasons.

Ovid resists attempts to impose structures on him – the Middle Ages tried to moralise him, but could never quite make it stick. I'm reminded of Thetis or Proteus shifting into many forms to avoid capture. The poem itself transforms as it goes, switching tones and subject matter with ease.

We've been looking at all the first lines, since they tell us plenty about the poem's aims. That of *Metamorphoses* is:

'*In nova fert animus mutatas dicere formas*
*corpora…*'

Translated, fairly literally, as 'My mind' (*animus*) 'tends towards' (*fert*) 'telling' (*dicere*) 'of forms' (*formas*) 'changed' (*mutatas*) 'into new bodies' (*nova corpora*). See how the word order is all mixed up – *nova* and *corpora*, which grammatically agree with each other, are not even on the same line. Remember Lyra and her daemon, sensing each other over long distances? This is a good example of the Latin technique.

What Ovid is signalling to us is '*nova*' – new. Remember that previously we've been dealing with weapons, war and heroes, explicitly the subject matter of epic.

The Roman listener – as the poem was recited – would have been attuned to the grammatical functions of each word, and so would have been expecting something to agree with '*nova*'; and then would have been delighted and challenged by '*corpora*'. New bodies? What would those Romans, listening to this sophisticated, clever young poet, have thought? Would they have been unsettled, or titillated? Lacking contemporary accounts, we will never know, but note that the first word of Ovid's *Amores* is '*Arma*' – a direct challenge to Virgil. The Romans, unlike us, were not wildly excited about new things.

*What do you mean, unlike us? You hate new things.*

Well, that's true. I mean, they weren't so interested in novelties and everything being different all the time, as our general culture will have it. '*Novus*' also meant, approximately, 'strange'. Ovid doesn't pull any punches.

There were sources for Ovid – there is nothing in the ancient world (or ours) that was not related to something that had gone before. But none of them display Ovid's sheer, shimmering brilliance.

Ovid was a younger contemporary of Virgil's. He was born about a year after the assassination of Julius Caesar and, like Virgil, was from the provinces and of equestrian rank – that is, the wealthy land-owning class below the aristocratic senators, who had no political power.

Let's pause for a moment to think about the extraordinary flowering of literary culture under the reign of Augustus, largely facilitated by his friend Gaius Maecenas.

*That doesn't sound like a Roman name.*

It isn't, and he wasn't. He was thought to be Etruscan, and supported Augustus from very early on, growing very rich in the process; but more importantly (at least from the point of view of us grubby inkslingers), he was a great patron of the arts, including of Virgil, and the poets Horace and Propertius, who were lyric or elegiac poets. Ovid's own patron was Marcus Valerius Messalla Corvinus, a patrician. Corvinus means 'crow' – and given the subject matter of Ovid's great poem, it's a pleasing coincidence.

The lines I quoted earlier are from Ovid's biographical poem called the *Tristia* – I'll come to it, and the reasons he wrote it, in a minute, as they are important in understanding how powerful Augustus was, and how precarious life in the Roman Empire could be.

Firstly, *Metamorphoses*. Like Virgil, Ovid began with shorter works, and we are exceptionally lucky in having almost everything he wrote – he was always a popular author.

There were the *Amores*, a series of elegiac poems detailing his love for Corinna (possibly a real woman, or equally a poetic construct). The *Heroides*, or 'Heroines', seem remarkably modern, as they consist of a series of letters written from the heroines of myth to their lovers, variously accusing, demanding or plaintive. Ariadne, for instance, writes to Theseus when she's abandoned; although where, notes Stephen Hinds,[*] 'on her deserted shore... will Ariadne find a postman?' The *Medicamina Faciei Femineae* is a poem about make-up.

*Gosh. That sounds better than tutorials on YouTube.*

I completely agree with you. The *Ars Amatoria* tells its readers, men and women, how to court; which was swiftly followed by the *Remedia Amoris*, which told you how, once you'd become overly entangled, to get out of affairs. Now, Una, can you remember what kind of programme the Emperor Augustus wanted to impose in Rome?

Una thought. Her brow, had she got one, would have been furrowed. *Temples, morality...*

Got it in one. Remember the *Ars Amatoria*, as it will become important later.

Then we come to *Metamorphoses*. Perhaps because of the vast breadth of its subject matter, the poem takes up fifteen books – more than Virgil, but less than Homer. The books don't necessarily mark divisions in the cycles of stories – the Trojan War, for example, encompasses more than one.

Many scholars have attempted to divine unity in its theme, giving rise to the usual questions about what kind of poem it actually is. Is it an epic? Is it a romance? Or is it something new and entirely different?

---

[*] *The Oxford Classical Dictionary*, p. 1084.

Una was looking thoughtful. *Why did he call it* Metamorphoses? *That doesn't sound like Latin.*

You're right, it's not. The word *transformatio*, which would have done the job brilliantly, didn't make its debut in Latin until the time of St Augustine in the fourth century AD. By using the Greek word he was making a comment, too, about his sources – many of which were Greek – and about the relation of his poetry and Latin poetry in general to the Greeks.

*But couldn't the unity of the poem be transformations?*

Well, you'd think that, wouldn't you, but, as I'm sure you'll have realised by now, nothing is ever easy. Not all the stories result in a transformation, and very often the change happens more as the garnish to the tale rather than the meat of it. The olive in the martini.

The story of Cephalus and Procris has only the transformation of the dog into stone at the end of it – rather a flimsy pretext, perhaps, but one that allows Ovid to delve deeply into the love between the two of them.

Some, given Ovid's yen for wordplay, have spotted the word '*amor*', 'love', in the title, and have taken it to suggest that the poem is about different kinds of love, mostly excessive or perverse; but not all of them are. How do you fit the tale of Hecuba murdering Polymestor into this scheme? Or Perseus, in a nod to Ulysses, taking his revenge and wholesale slaughtering when he gets home?[†] Or Ajax and Ulysses bickering over Achilles' armour?

---

†   Chronologically, Perseus comes before Ulysses. But Ovid is referring to the scene in Homer when Odysseus/Ulysses takes his revenge on the suitors. So you have a case where a myth is looking forwards with hindsight.

# Changing Dogs

*You can't.*

The sheer range of variety in the poem is part of its charm. It flows, with wit, eroticism and tragedy, glancing from subject to subject, and yet never feeling shallow or jejune. It's ambivalent and playful, and that's partly why he was so popular, and why he remains widely read today, in translations and in many responses, such as Ted Hughes' *Tales from Ovid*.

A lot of art engages with Ovid: wander into the National Gallery, and you will see there Titian's *Diana and Actaeon*, which is based on the Ovidian tale; Bernini's sculpture *Apollo and Daphne* describes the moment the nymph starts to turn into a laurel.

Broadly speaking, *Metamorphoses* follows an ambitious chronological order. Where Homer was content to suggest the cosmos on Achilles' shield, and where Virgil was happy to talk about the past and the present through various other means, such as the visit to the site of the future Rome, or the shield of Aeneas, Ovid has thrown down the poetical gauntlet and said, well, chaps, I'm going to do the whole bloody lot. This makes it as allusive as Virgil, if not more so.

*Metamorphoses* is highly attuned to itself as a piece of poetry – it is as much about poetry as it is about its ostensible subject matter. Many have pointed to the moment when Narcissus, in love with his own reflection, realises that it is actually himself as the first modernist moment in poetry.

Art and artistry are central themes, as we see in the story of Arachne, who spins better than Athena, and is turned into a spider for her trouble; Orpheus, who sings so beautifully that the trees will come to him; Pygmalion, who shapes a lover out of stone; and Marsyas, who claims to be a better musician than Apollo, and is slain for his presumption. You can see a depiction of his punishment in Titian's *The Flaying of Marsyas*.

That Ovid plays with the notion of what it means to be an artist is also part of why he appeals to us in our twenty-first century, because he seems the most ironically aware of what he's doing. And what is art, but a form of transformation?

Una spluttered. And then she hacked a few times, sounding like an octogenarian on twenty Marlboro Reds a day.

*Sorry*, she said.

That's OK. Though there are overt political references in *Metamorphoses* – even a direct address to Augustus, and, of course, the fact that Julius Caesar is catasterised—

*He what?*

Er, sorry. I just like using that word. I mean, I hardly ever get a chance to use it.

*What does it mean?*

It means 'turned into a star'. It's a huge compliment to Augustus; an even greater one is that Ovid suggests the emperor will become a god himself, and take his place amongst the immortals.

In many ways, though, the poem undermines the *Aeneid* – a stable, serious world where Rome rules for ever, replaced with a fictional place where things are constantly shifting. Because of this, it has sometimes fallen out of favour with more high-minded critics, not just because of its perceived immorality and interest in human extremes, but also with those who see it as less substantial in theme than its predecessors. It has never fallen out of favour with more general readers.

Ovid begins with the world being formed out of chaos; he then follows the trials of early mankind, including the story of

Deucalion and Pyrrha, who are marked out by Jupiter for salvation from a flood.

*That sounds remarkably familiar.*

Yes, it is similar to the story of Noah's Ark. When they land, after the waters have receded, they are ordered to chuck the 'bones of their mother' over their shoulders; this being the world of prophecies, of course, this means not their mother's actual bones, but the rocks and stones of the Earth. Behind them springs up a race of hardy men.

To attempt to summarise *Metamorphoses* is like, in the words of the singing nuns, trying to catch a cloud and pin it down.[‡]

But in brief: the loves of the gods come next. You will remember that the gods in Homer were not questioned; silly though they sometimes could be, they were treated with awe and respect. Similarly, the divine mechanism in Virgil serves to throw Aeneas into a more serious light. Here, however, the behaviour of the gods is very much open to question.

They are often the prime movers of the metamorphoses. Ovid asks us, with, one imagines, a little glint of amusement in his eyes: are the gods just?

We meet Jupiter, running after anything that moves, quite literally.

---

[‡]  The wicked Ixion did once catch a cloud and pin it down – it was in the shape of Hera, whom he lusted after. It didn't go too well for him.

## JUPITER HAD NO IDEALS: HOW TO REMEMBER THE LOVES OF THE GOD

**Io:** J. takes the form of a cloud, and then changes her into a white heifer. Hera sends a fly (in most versions) to torture her; to avoid it, Io eventually crosses the Ionian Sea, which takes her name.

**Danaë:** J. takes the form of a shower of gold; Perseus is born.

**Europa:** J. comes as a bull; she gives birth to Minos.

**Alcmene:** J. disguises himself as her husband; she bears him Hercules.

**Leda:** J. as a swan; from the eggs are born Helen, Clytemnestra, Castor and Pollux.

**Semele:** J appears in all his splendour; Semele is consumed. Dionysus born.

Those are the most memorable, but we don't really know how many children were knocking about who might have claimed Jupiter as an absent father. It's certainly dozens, if not hundreds. Even Alexander the Great said his mother had been raped by the god, in the form of a serpent. Jupiter, not his mother.

Apollo is another reprobate, haring after the nymph Daphne. Now, if you're used to thinking of him as a god of order and dignity, it's shocking to see him as a lustful brute. Here the transformation is effected by Daphne's father, a river god; but she, as the laurel, is used as Apollo's symbol for ever more – the pursued vaunted by the pursuer.

Following the standard mythological pattern we saw earlier in our conversations, after the gods come the heroes, including the Trojan War. Ovid follows this pattern too, and we meet Aeneas (who turns into a god, natch), and, after a long section on Pythagoras—

*You mean, triangles and stuff? The square on the side of the hypotenuse is... er...*

The sum of the squares on the other two sides? Una, you obviously haven't been paying much attention in your maths classes either. Nope. Pythagoras – and it is the same one as the geometrist – talks about his theory that souls leap from body to body after death. And also, vegetarianism. I was rather tickled by the fact that Pythagoreans refused to eat kidney beans because they looked like human foetuses.

After all this, we get some Roman legends: the story of Vertumnus and Pomona, thought to be the first bona fide Latin myth, in which Vertumnus, a god of the seasons, seduces Pomona, an orchard goddess. We finish with the transformation of Julius Caesar into a star, and Ovid's proud statement that wherever Rome's power will extend, his song will be sung – a *carmen perpetuum*, or eternal song.

We're not dealing with a straightforward narrative layer here, as in the *Aeneid*, where we know that it's the 'poet' who's directing everything – and indeed, Virgil several times inserts his own opinions (we assume they are his) into the lines, such as the scene with Cleopatra, where we are told in no uncertain terms that she is '*nefas*', or, basically, unspeakable.

*Harsh.*

I know. But you'll remember that things are more complex: behind Cleopatra stands Dido. We can transfer the nobility and passion of Dido onto Cleopatra, as well as her negative qualities.

In Ovid, we begin with a narrative on one level, with the poet telling the story; but soon the levels multiply, so much so that if you're reading it, as many do, in sections, you can lose track of who's talking. Other narrators take over, such as the daughters of Minyas, and within stories there are other stories, inset, glittering like jewels in a necklace.

Una, ignoring my simile, was straining to ask something. She had put her bone down, having ceased gnawing a while ago, and had come to butt her nose against my leg. She does this when she wants something, not unlike a small child.

Una, I said. Are you waiting to ask if any of them turn into a dog?

She nodded.

I ruffled her neck. Only one person does turn into a dog. That's not to say that there are no dogs in the poem – as we know from Actaeon, there is the lovingly described list of hounds, and there are plenty of other hunting scenes. The monstrous Scylla, who also appeared in the *Odyssey*, has the top part of a woman, and her bottom part comprises six dogs.

*That's very specific.*

I know. There is a human-to-wolf transformation very early on, which we'll look at in detail, and then the metamorphosis of Hecuba, Priam's wife, into a dog comes later. We can see Ovid's techniques in both.

At first, says Ovid, men lived in a Golden Age. There was no need for laws, judges; ships had not yet sailed; there were no weapons, and the Earth itself gave forth plenty of nourishment without needing to be cultivated. This is the Golden Age, which Saturn ruled, that Augustus was so keen on evoking.

After this, came the Silver Age; the seasons, which previously had not existed, started their yearly round, bringing the freezing winter, and driving men to build houses and till the land. The Bronze Age followed, which Ovid treats briefly – humans were wilder, but not yet impious.

The arrival of the Iron Age, or specifically, as Ovid calls it, Hard Iron, brought evils, as mankind delved into the Earth and discovered gold, and therefore greed.

Jupiter, appalled at the savagery he sees, pops down to Earth disguised as a mortal, and comes to the land of the impious Lycaon, where he reveals himself as a god. But, though the people worship him, Lycaon mocks him and, planning to kill Jupiter whilst he sleeps, serves up a recently killed hostage on a plate.

*More cannibalism.*

That's enough for Jupiter, who immediately destroys the house with a thunderbolt, causing Lycaon to flee.

*Why didn't he just throw a thunderbolt at Lycaon?*

Well, the implication is that he might have tried to do so, but missed. Jupiter's starting to look a little bit less powerful, isn't he?

Let's look at what happens next to Lycaon:

> Who, seeing that, slipped out of doors amazed for fear
> and fled
> Into the wild and desert woods where, being all alone,
> As he endeavoured (but in vain) to speak and make his
> moan,
> He fell a-howling. Wherewithal for very rage and
> mood
> He ran me quite out of his wits and waxèd furious
> wood,
> Still practising his wonted lust of slaughter on the poor

And silly cattle, thirsting still for blood as heretofore.
His garments turned to shaggy hair, his arms to rugged
  paws;
So is he made a ravening wolf whose shape expressly
  draws
To that the which he was before. His skin is hoary grey,
His look still grim with glaring eyes; and every kind of
  way
His cruel heart in outward shape doth well itself
  bewray.

This is the Golding translation again – and it's Jupiter speaking. Lycaon is transformed into a wolf, thirsting for blood. Here, Ovid makes explicit that Lycaon's inner savagery is now displayed in his outward form. Very often, after the transformation, some aspect of the transformed person is retained in the new body. We begin, then, with something that appears to be a just punishment. Soon, things change.

Una gave me a glance. *Well, you would expect that, wouldn't you?*

I mean, this isn't always the case, though – not every transformation does a similar thing. That of Io into a cow, for example: Jupiter rapes her, concealing her from Juno by means of a cloud; Juno suspects, but Jupiter's got there already, and poor Io becomes rather more interested in grass than she used to be. Does Io deserve this?

Ovid displays all his comic genius in the way that Io as a cow tries to communicate with her father; eventually using her hoof to scrawl the letters IO into the dirt. Her father's reaction is that now he won't be able to marry her off to anyone except a bull, and will have calves as grandchildren.

The pregnant Io's guard, Argus, falls asleep, and is brutally murdered; Io, beset by a Fury – and you will remember that Furies are usually set on those who have sinned, and Io can hardly be said to have done so – is chased until, exhausted, she begs Jupiter for aid. He must negotiate with his wife, and it's only when he promises that he won't sin again (caveat: with this particular nymph) that Io is restored.

Far from being interested in morality, as in the *Odyssey*, or the agent of a divine fate, as in the *Aeneid*, Jupiter here is simply a duplicitous cad, a moustache-twiddling rake.

Hecuba's transformation comes in Book XIII. This book is absolutely aware of itself in relation to its predecessors, since it deals with the Trojan War; more specifically, with its aftermath. The book begins with the heroes Ajax and Ulysses arguing over who should get Achilles' armour – Ajax, poor chap, doesn't quite have Ulysses' debating skills. I was Achilles' cousin, he says, so I should have his armour. Imagine an American high school jock up against the captain of the debating team, and you'll have some idea.

Ulysses wins with ease. He even recounts an episode from the *Iliad*, in which he attacked the camp of Rhesus by night – a strange episode, known as the Doloneia – the joke here being that this slightly unheroic event is being used for Ulysses' advantage.

Ajax is devastated, and drives a blade into himself; from his blood springs a flower – the same one, notes Ovid, that came from Hyacinthus' blood, allowing a clever explanation for two origin stories for the hyacinth. Ovid really can both keep his cake and eat it.

The Greeks now once more wait for a favourable wind. Achilles' ghost rises up from the earth and – as large as he was in life – demands the sacrifice of Polyxena, Hecuba's one remaining daughter. In return, he will raise the winds to send them home. As Ovid tells it, she meets her fate with remarkable self-possession, saying she would prefer to die rather than live in slavery.[§] Her speech makes the assembled Greeks weep, though she restrains her own tears.

The effect on Hecuba is devastating. Once a proud queen with many children, she now has only one left: the prince Polydorus, who was despatched away to an ally for safe keeping.

Ovid's skill in pathos comes into play: just as Hecuba reaches the shoreline, asking for an urn so that she can take some water from the sea to wash the blood from her daughter, she sees a body on the shore.

It's Polydorus, mutilated by the spears of their allies.

Powered by rage, Hecuba tricks Polymestor, the murderer, into meeting her and, along with her women, tears his eyeballs out. So incensed is she that she even plucks out the eye sockets. It is one of the more gruesome moments in Ovid.

*Yikes*, said Una.

Set upon by the Thracians, she begins to growl, and bites at the stones thrown at her; she tries to speak, but instead barks – '*latravit*' – and becomes a dog, roaming the plains and howling, eventually lending her name, says Ovid, to the place – Cynomessa, or Monument of the Dog. This same transformation happens in Euripides' play *Hekabe*.

*So what happened to Ovid?* I could tell that Una was secretly thinking about having her own monument.

---

§   Remember what Achilles said about death, and how he'd prefer to live as the lowest of the low rather than be dead.

Nobody's really sure exactly what happened, but we know that Augustus exiled him from Rome.

*That seems a bit excessive. He's only a poet, isn't he?*

Poets, apparently, can be dangerous. Remember Plato? Ovid might have had an affair with Augustus' daughter Julia, who was accused of being exceptionally lax in the moral department, even conducting orgies in public.

Others think that Augustus also took exception to the loose morals as displayed in Ovid's earlier love poetry, the *Ars Amatoria*, which gives instructions on picking up girls at the games, amongst other things. He himself wrote that the cause was '*carmen et error*'– his poem and a mistake. We do not have the specifics; there may have been a conspiracy against Augustus, which Ovid might have known about. It's this kind of uncertainty that is so tantalising to the classicist.

Either way, the poor chap, sophisticated, urban, intelligent, was packed away to the coast of the Black Sea, where he had nothing to do but write sad poems. Hence the *Tristia*, and other works. It was lucky for us that he did do so, as they contain plenty of information about his life, although there are gaps: he says he wrote a poem in the language of the people of Tomis, which, alas, we do not have. He was still creating, still experimenting, and did so until his death.

Ovid's *Metamorphoses* bring an end to the Latin epic progression.

Afterwards, in the Silver Latin Age, there was Lucan's *Civil War*, which is an epic not only a few sandwiches short of a picnic, but also lacking a rug, a hamper and a cruet set. It contains a fantastically weird scene where a witch calls up a prophetic corpse; but it's unfinished, and has three heroes, and there are questions as to whether it's really an epic at all.⁋

The multifaceted, glimmering *Metamorphoses* is inimitable: no poet could ever hope to cover such a range of emotions and stories again. And no poet could hope to be so influential.

Imagine a bookshelf. Imagine that on it you have Geoffrey Chaucer, Edmund Spenser, William Shakespeare, Christopher Marlowe, John Donne, John Milton and Alexander Pope. That you also have Ali Smith, Ted Hughes, from more recent times, amongst others. Then imagine that Ovid did not exist: and watch those books vanish, one by one. That is partly why we need to continue to read and understand Ovid.

He is the most accessible to any modern reader of all the poets we've looked at so far – both in that he chimes with our ideas of selfhood and mutability, and that we can also find in him and his tapestries subjects that are challenging, ironical and, most of all, gorgeous.

A cyclist whizzed past us, ringing his bell in the dusk.

We'd better head back, I said to Una.

*The Silver Latin Age – what did you mean by that?*

The era after the death of Augustus, in AD 14. There is no more Virgil, no more Horace, no more Ovid. We have Seneca's gory tragedies; the aforementioned Lucan; and the witty, satirical novels of Petronius and Apuleius.

It's that sense of passing and change, once more – the greats sing no more.

---

⁋   *Momentary Monsters: Lucan and His Heroes* by W.R. Johnson really opened my eyes as to what literary criticism could do, reappraising Lucan and placing him back into the epic tradition.

We wended our way home, past all those multitudes of contemporary Narcissi glaring into their phones, seeking confirmation of themselves and, just like their literary forebears, listening to echoes.

*If only*, said Una, *they would look up.*

I know, I answered. I know.

# Chapter 9

# IT'S A DOG'S LIFE
## The Ancient Greek Tragedians

Throughout October and November, Una and I had abandoned our conversations. Term time was in full swing. I had seen her, though, instructing a fellow lurcher in the art of *latro, latras, latrat*.

Now, it was December. We had been to a funeral. Or rather, I, my wife and my son had been to a funeral; Una, dogs not generally being allowed at funerals, had not.

My grandmother had died at the age of ninety-nine. She was a great dog lover: her first was called Marcus Aurelius, after the Roman philosopher-emperor, and she used to ride on the beach with him galloping behind her. She was partly the mainspring of my interest in the classics: she had given my father a book on Greek myth, which he had passed down to me, and which I will, in time, read with my own son.

When we returned home, in the rainy dark of the afternoon, Una, who had been patiently waiting for us, was more eager to go for a walk than usual. Her sideways skip when we entered the house and switched on the lights raised my spirits a little – even if it meant trudging out again into the cold and the wet.

Come on then, I said. We can go round the block.

*You're sombre today*, said Una, when we'd reached the High Street. My breath was forming clouds in the air. The pavements were slick; a woman making a phone call was splashed by a car going slightly too fast through a puddle. We exchanged looks of resignation.

I suppose my thoughts are tending towards the big questions. Mortality, and, you know, that kind of thing. It reminds me of something in a Sophocles play: *Ajax*. I'd memorised it a long time ago, and it seemed particularly appropriate today.

> *horo gar hemas ouden ontas allo plen*
> *eidol' hosoiper zomen he kouphen skian.*

I was silent as a bus snaked by us, lit up from within, packed with passengers hanging on to the straps, windows steaming up with condensation. The streets were busy, many people flowing up and down. It was sometimes hard to avoid their shoves. I stepped aside to allow a woman with a pushchair to go by, a little bundled-up child peeking out from within.

*You'll have to translate*, said Una.

Sorry. We continued, heading into the throngs. It means something like: 'For I see we who are alive are nothing but ghosts, or empty shadows.'

*That's cheerful.*

Well it is tragedy.

*Ajax*, said Una. *Wasn't he the one who killed himself when Odysseus took Achilles' armour and he thought it should have gone to him?*

It was him. The quote comes from Odysseus. *Ajax* is a good example of what is perhaps Greek literature's most enduring, and accessible, monument.[*]

*What would that be?*

Tragedy. I say so because hardly a year goes by in London without at least one production. I have seen the *Oresteia*, the *Bacchae*, *Antigone* and a version of *Medea* in the last few years. There were even two *Oresteia*s being produced at the same time.

*Tell me about Greek tragedy,* said Una.

We ploughed on, past the Tube station, where Christmas trees were lining the pavements.

Aristotle thought that even the summary of a tragedy's plot should make us shudder. And that's certainly the case when you describe most of them.

Medea kills her own children. Oedipus blinds himself. Orestes murders his mother. The word 'tragedy' itself is thought to mean 'goat song'.

*Goat song?*

Yes, goat song.

*As far as I know,* said Una, *goats are not particularly good at singing. In fact they can hardly be said to sing at all.*

They don't, and you are right. But it doesn't mean singing goats, more's the pity. I had a sudden vision of a thousand Alpine goats bleating out verses by Aeschylus in a deranged version of *The Sound of Music*. It meant, we think, the song sung at the sacrifice of a goat.

*Ah.*

---

[*] The Emperor Augustus himself tried to write a tragedy about Ajax. It was not successful.

The origins of Greek tragedy as a genre are shrouded in mystery. The Romans didn't go in for it as much, and we only have later writers from the Silver Age, such as Seneca, who wrote ornate, literary tragedies, very much in the same vein as the Greeks, but much more self-conscious. When we talk of tragedy, we usually mean 'Greek tragedy'.

I've only seen one Latin play in performance – Seneca's blood-filled *Thyestes*. Seneca had more of an influence on Shakespeare than the Greeks, since he didn't have the Greek originals.

Oliver Taplin has a brilliantly trenchant view on the subject of Greek tragedy's origins: 'unknown and irrelevant'.[†] But something like the following was the case. Cult priests would sacrifice a goat – perhaps an apotropaic or propitiatory one—

*Apotrohuh?*

Apotropaic – it means to ward off evil. To start with, one priest would sing a song in praise of the god, or perhaps of the local hero, if it was a hero cult. As time went on, that song, known, Aristotle tells us, as a *dithyramb*, would take in some of the exploits of the hero.

These songs were probably performed in honour of Dionysus, and those participating would have worn masks, which later became part of the apparatus of the stage.

Soon the dramatic form was conceived – two characters on a stage, showing (and I use that word very specifically, since the ancients made a distinction between *mimesis*, or showing, which is what drama did, and telling, which is what epic did) – a story that was linked to the local history of the *polis*, or with a relevant ancestral theme.

---

† Oliver Taplin, *Greek Tragedy in Action*.

This must have gone on for centuries, and that's why Taplin thinks the origin doesn't matter, since the form of what we come to know as tragedy must surely have altered drastically over these years.

The playwright Aeschylus was the first to suggest using two actors.

*He must have been a bright guy*, said Una.

Now now, I said. I forgot to mention that before then, a single actor would have been interacting with the chorus – a group of singers, who took part in the action (and commented on it too). Sophocles added a third actor. Remember that masks meant different parts could be played by the same actor.

Tragedy is most explicitly linked with Athens, where it's thought to have begun; the tragedies we have are firmly Athenian in perspective.

We think of Athens' most enduring legacy as democracy; but over the years it had many different systems of rule, including tyrannies.

Cleisthenes, an elder statesman who had a hand in deposing the tyrant Hippias, was the chap who suggested that from now on power should lie with the people.

It was the first time that this had happened in the world, that we know of. The vote was denied to women and slaves; and there was also an empire that covered many islands. It was hardly a model democratic republic.

This is the era of the popular statesman and general Pericles, who encouraged democracy and the arts, and who helped to build the Parthenon, with its unforgettable statues by Phidias. If you were to walk through the streets, you might see a gaggle of young men listening eagerly to the philosopher Socrates as he challenged the way that they thought. You might bump into an actor on his way to rehearse a play by Aeschylus, or even see the tragedian himself, scratching his head as he worked through the problems of his plays. You might see a courtesan preparing herself to receive gentlemanly suitors. All around was intellectual and artistic fervour. It is not hard to get dewy-eyed about the magnificence and energy of the times.

## THE ACROPOLIS: LOSING ITS MARBLES?

'*Acropolis*' means the highest point in the city (*acro* = high, *polis* = city), and many Greek cities had one. The one in Athens was called Cecropia, after Cecrops, the half-man half-snake. The Parthenon is a temple, dedicated to Athena, decorated with friezes showing the battle of the gods with the giants, the Athenians fighting the Amazons (a legend), and the battle of Theseus against the centaurs. The north side, though it's much damaged, probably shows the Trojan War. Many of the statues and friezes, known as the Elgin Marbles, are in the British Museum; the Greek government has been campaigning for years for their return. It has become a hot political point, relating to all antiquities: where do they go, and what is a museum for?

This extraordinary profusion of tragedies, as if the teeth of a dragon had been sown in the soil beneath the Acropolis, and from them sprung thousands of poets at the same time, is a very Athenian thing.

Sparta was not known for its literary productions: anything that wasn't of the basic bash-your-spear-against-your-shield-and-love-your-country sort was actively discouraged. It was the Spartans who came up with the first version of TL;DR, on hearing a lengthy speech: 'Forgotten the beginning, don't understand the end.' The Spartans hailed from Laconia; so 'laconic' became synonymous with terseness.

*Not like you then*, said Una.

I ignored her. Towards the end of the sixth century BC, the Athenians performed tragedies at a festival known as the City Dionysia, which took place over three days in the spring.

The god Dionysus was an integral part of this, wild and unpredictable as he was, with his leopard skins and his unsuitable companions, the Maenads. His statue sat in the front row. Everybody in the city thronged to see the plays (though we are still not sure whether this also meant women and slaves. Scholars differ in their opinions).

*That*, said Una, *seems to be rather a theme.*

Dionysus is a god of paradoxes and transcendence: violent, strange, enchanted and enchanting, son of the king of the gods and of a mortal woman, whose rites included the tearing apart of living creatures; he himself is a mystical god who dies, is torn apart and is reborn.

This transmuting, transformative god is highly appropriate to the stage: much more so than Apollo, who, though god of music and the Muses, has more to do with order and clarity. Some see tragedy as a continuous struggle between Apollo and Dionysus, between order and chaos.

*Why did his followers tear animals apart?*

They thought that by doing so they could absorb Dionysus' gifts. Some think that through the stage, on which a form of

Dionysus is ritually dismembered, we can be restored to psychological wholeness. Think of that next time you're ripping a carcass apart.

*I shall*, said Una, clearly delighted that her carnivorous habits were immensely therapeutic as well as physically nourishing.

Tragedies were exceptionally popular. Scholars estimate that up to fourteen thousand or more would be gathered in the audience, enjoying a full day's worth of performances.

Though the subject matter was elevated, there is absolutely no suggestion that the theatre was considered an occupation of the elite. It was for everyone, and yet without the notion of 'dumbing down'.

It's very hard to think of something today that has similar resonance. Perhaps the opening ceremony of the 2012 London Olympic Games came within a whisker, as people across the country held parties to watch it on television; it was certainly an occasion that celebrated national, cultural and civic pride.

**THE OLYMPIC GAMES**

First contest – 200m sprint (the *stadion*).
Other contests – horse races, the pentathlon, wrestling, boxing.
Contest we should bring back – the race in full armour.
Most dangerous – the *pankration*, a mixture of wrestling and boxing. No holds barred, except you couldn't gouge out your opponent's eyes.

Prizes – a crown of wild olive.
Mascot – none, but they were in honour of Zeus.

If you couldn't afford a ticket to the Dionysia, there was a special fund to subsidise you (instituted from about the 420s BC). We're talking state-sponsored theatre here, on a huge scale. It really is political, dealing with matters that concern being a part of the *polis*, rather than in the sense that it's making particular points about contemporary politicians. That was the preserve of comedians such as Aristophanes, who freely lampooned living politicians watching in the audience.

The Dionysia was fully part of civic life. There would also be sacrifices, processions, comedies and a parade of war orphans – young men about to join the army, whose fathers had died in battle in service of Athens.

The stage was called the *skene* and was a wooden construction often representing a royal palace. This faced the *orchestra*, the dancing floor beneath the stage, where the chorus and their leader pranced. The audience occupied the slopes. We can imagine them pretty hugger-mugger, and no doubt chattering amongst themselves.

Whether they, like bottom-numbed visitors to Shakespeare's Globe, brought cushions or not we do not know, but I can envisage an elderly Athenian burgher making sure his slave provided at least two or three to keep him comfortable, with a plate of juicy figs nearby. As for relieving yourself– well, that can be left to the imagination.

The stage itself would have been large enough for props, such as the chariot in *Agamemnon*. There were two bits of machinery, the *ekkyklema*, a kind of trolley that rolled out from the central stage doors, usually bearing a body or a tableau of some kind, and the *mechane*, which was a crane used for flying characters, such as our friend Pegasus in a play by Euripides about Bellerophon, sadly lost to the ravages of time.

It may also have been used for the *deus ex machina*, when a god would appear at the end of a play and sort everything out. We've seen how Athena zips down to the rescue at the end of the *Odyssey*. In drama, impossible situations were often resolved by divine intervention.

Only three tragedians have survived the centuries, all hailing from the fifth century BC. In order of age, they are Aeschylus, Sophocles and Euripides. Think of them as the Premier League.

*Why only these three?*

Their contemporaries considered them the best. In Aristophanes' comedy *The Frogs*, Aeschylus and Euripides compete in the Underworld for the poet's throne. Sophocles declines to join in.

We know there were many others who battled to win the prizes offered at the Dionysia for the best play. These, including plays by Aeschylus' son, have long been food for weevils. The competition was known as an *agon*; the winner was crowned with ivy leaves, the plant of Dionysus.

Each playwright would have staged a trilogy, based around a theme, and followed by a 'satyr play', which, drawing on the same theme, was a burlesque. The satyrs, followers of Dionysus, had horse tails and large phalluses. The only one we have is Euripides' *Cyclops*, which features much boorishness and drunkenness.

## DEATHS IN GREEK TRAGEDY

*Medea* by Euripides – 4. Poisoned dress. Knife.

*Hippolytus* by Euripides – 2. Suicide by hanging. Chariot crash.

*Bacchae* by Euripides – 1. Torn apart by crazed Maenads.

*Oedipus Rex* by Sophocles – 1. Suicide by hanging.

*Antigone* by Sophocles – 3. Suicides by knives and hanging.

*Agamemnon* by Aeschylus – 2. Both murdered in baths.

Taplin makes the point that the tragedians were 'practical men of the theatre', fully involved in rehearsing, overseeing every aspect of the production from music (which there was plenty of) to the choreography, and were often even actors.[‡] In this sense they were very similar to William Shakespeare.

Much work has been done recently on what the music would have sounded like. An *aulos* is a reedy instrument that sounds, I am sorry to report, rather like a kazoo; the accompanying chanting is at once droning and exhilarating. It's a tantalising glimpse into the ancient world: shut your eyes and you could, just for a minute, be sitting in the front row at the Athenian performances. The music is freely available on YouTube.

We have only one extant trilogy, which is Aeschylus' *Oresteia* ('The plays concerning Orestes') comprising *Agamemnon*, *The*

---

‡    Oliver Taplin, *Greek Tragedy in Action*.

*Libation Bearers* and *The Kindly Ones*, and dealing with the fall-out of the murder of Agamemnon.

It's responding to Homer, both the *Iliad* – Agamemnon quite literally steps out of the poem, fresh from the fallen city, and onto the stage – and the *Odyssey*, where the deed of Orestes in killing Aegisthus is celebrated and offered as a paradigm to Telemachus.

We do also have – by wondrous chance – an *Electra* by Sophocles and one by Euripides, which cover the same ground as *The Libation Bearers*, and which allow us to compare the three playwrights and their varying takes. We'll look at that in more detail in a minute.

Nearly every single one of the tragedies we have is based on myth – and that, Una, is why a good working knowledge of them is so important.

Remember, though, that the playwrights were *working* with myth: they weren't simply dramatising a canonical version, but composing their own interpretations, which dealt with aspects of the stories that lent themselves to their own purposes.

It wouldn't have mattered that the audience would have known the story of Orestes from the *Odyssey*: Aeschylus sidelines Aegisthus and gives Clytemnestra the murderous starring role.

It's hardly surprising that the plays we do have usually concern heroes who had major cult presences in Athens itself. Crucially, barely any are actually set within the precincts of Athens, but take place in other cities such as Corinth or Thebes. This, many think, is a way of examining the city through a lens, in the same way that Shakespeare set many of his plays abroad, the better to glance safely at domestic issues.

Only *The Kindly Ones* finishes with Orestes in Athens, under the judgement of Athena. As for other perspectives, the only play that isn't myth-based is Aeschylus' *Persians*, which concerns the Persian War from the Persian perspective. A few hundred lines survive from the *Exagoge* by Ezechiel – a Hellenised Jew, writing later on – which tells the story of Exodus. Once more, we wonder at what we have lost, and what might still be uncovered.

In tragedy there are many things that modern audiences find difficult to process. Mother-killing! Madness! Incest! Cannibalism! Infanticide! Human sacrifice! Murder! Suicide! Self-mutilation! Dismemberment! Supernatural bulls rising from the sea and causing chariot crashes!

These headline events can obscure what tragedies are really about. They usually deal with a protagonist whose character is in some way excessive; this is called the tragic flaw or, in Greek, *hamartia*.

Oedipus is relentless in his pursuit of finding out the truth, only to discover that he is the cause of the troubles in Thebes. Antigone unflinchingly stands up against tyranny to bury her brother, only to be walled up by Creon, and to kill herself. Agamemnon commits hubris, and is punished for his past crimes. Pentheus refuses to worship Bacchus, and is killed.

Vast and sudden reversals of fortune, called *peripateia* by Aristotle, are common to all: Agamemnon, a king returning home triumphantly, instead of receiving the honours due to him (and the kind of life that Odysseus yearns for) is murdered in his bath; Oedipus begins as a king who has saved the city from a monster and is favoured by the gods, and ends as a patricide and a perpetrator of incest, self-blinded, the lowest of all. In *Antigone*, it's arguably Creon who suffers the *peripateia*, losing his wife and son at a stroke.

The plots, as considered by Aristotle, are compelled by *ananke*, or necessity: the things that must happen because of the particular arrangement of events. There's no escaping anything: Oedipus must fall; Antigone must kill herself; Pentheus must be torn apart.

*It's pretty bleak.*

It is. Tragedy deals with the transgressive or, in the eyes of the Athenians, polluting, as well as with larger, universal questions such as the way you should behave; or indeed, like *Hamlet*, with existence itself.

Like epic, and because of their heavy reliance on myth, the characters are kings, queens and heroes.

*What about the rest of us?* said Una.

Euripides, the later playwright, introduces some plebeian personas, such as an old farmer, and an exotic Phrygian eunuch in Helen's retinue.

In tone and action, the plays can seem very stylised to modern audiences: they proceed through choral odes, with speech in between those episodes. Euripides feels the most modern, with more characters and a greater variety of speeches. Events, as we understand them from a Shakespeare play – battles, murders, and so on – don't happen onstage (though the characters wouldn't have been standing still, but often came into contact with each other, and the chorus would have been dancing). This is why the messenger speech in which the crucial turning point of the play is described is so important.

Let's consider, now, the eldest of the ancient playwrights, Aeschylus. Despite the rumour that he croaked when an eagle dropped a tortoise on his head (no joke), he actually died when visiting the court of a tyrant in Sicily, we presume in an untortoise-related incident. His epitaph records his deeds at the

Battle of Marathon – he was a soldier, and was proud of being a loyal and brave citizen of Athens.

*The Battle of Marathon?*

This was a decisive moment in the Greeks' long-running war against Persia, in 490 BC. About 6,400 Persians were killed; the Greeks only lost 192.

*Pretty comprehensive.*

Indeed. He also fought at Salamis, the sea-battle, ten years later in 480 BC, and at Plataea; at those two battles, the Persians were defeated.

Had the Persians been victorious, the Greek world would have suffered under enslavement and tyranny. This feeds into Aeschylus' plays: freedom and justice are hewn from trauma.

Aeschylus wrote somewhere between sixty and ninety plays. Only seven survive. It's like having one tiny fragment of the limb of a famous statue.

We are very lucky to have the *Oresteia*, a haunting, brutal, beautiful trilogy, from the latter part of his career.

As a whole, it charts a movement from darkness to light: from the brutality of a world where a wife thinks it is right to kill her husband, and a son can murder his mother in turn, to a civic order where Justice reigns.

We travel, pursued by the wild, ancient forces of revenge, into civilisation: the red blood of Agamemnon is transmuted into the red cloaks of the celebrants at the end of the final play, as Orestes is absolved of guilt and the Erinyes, the Furies, become the Eumenides, the Kindly Ones, who lend their new name to the title of the final part.

Aeschylus' language, in the Greek, can be impenetrable. For students starting out, once you've mastered the grammar and the tragic vocabulary, which is quite specific and tends towards a lot of 'oh wretched me!'s, Euripides and Sophocles are much easier to grasp.

## THE TRAGEDIES OF THE HOUSE OF ATREUS

(*Thyestes*, Seneca – Roman play)

| Aeschylus | Sophocles | Euripides |
|---|---|---|
| *Agamemnon* | | *Iphigenia in Aulis* |
| *Libation Bearers* | *Electra* | *Electra* |
| | | *Orestes* |
| *The Furies* | | *Iphigenia in Tauris* |
| | | *Andromache* |

When, many years ago, I was considering setting up a Greek reading club and wanted to start with *Agamemnon*, my old tutor, Dr Christina Kraus, noted that it's 'barely in Greek' and that it might be wiser to begin with something more straightforward. The poet A.E. Housman brilliantly parodies this (and translators) in his 'A Fragment of a Greek Tragedy':

CHORUS: O suitably-attired-in-leather-boots
Head of a traveller, wherefore seeking whom
Whence by what way how purposed art thou come
To this well-nightingaled vicinity?
My object in inquiring is to know.
But if you happen to be deaf and dumb
And do not understand a word I say,
Then wave your hand, to signify as much.

If we look at the opening section of *Agamemnon*, you'll see why. We start with a watchman, on the roof of Agamemnon's house, waiting for a beacon fire that will tell him and the rest of Argos that Troy has fallen.[§]

In the third line he compares himself to a hound: the loyalty and watchfulness of the palace dog.

*And quite right too*, said Una, who was beginning to wonder when one of her kind might appear.

He describes his weary task; and then the blaze of the signal fire appears. It is a message, leaping across the seas and the hills. Hail! he calls out. This welcome light will bring many choral dances!

*Huh?*

Well, the people of Argos will be so chuffed that Troy has finally fallen and King Agamemnon will be back that they'll have an enormous beano. If only! It sets up an irony that sustains the play: what should be a cause for delight is in fact a harbinger of disaster.

After spending some considerable time informing us how happy he is, the watchman says that when Agamemnon comes home, he'll clasp his hand; but, he continues, I won't say anything else, because 'a big ox has gone on my tongue.'

*Right.* I could see Una trying to imagine that, and failing.

This is a good example of when ancient idiom doesn't map onto anything we have today. We assume it means that he's being forced to keep silent about the shady stuff that's been going on inside the palace – that Clytemnestra has been

---

§    Note the similarity to the beginning of *Hamlet*, with its watchers on the ramparts, and its themes of internecine conflict.

plotting with Aegisthus, brooding on her revenge, and that Agamemnon's homecoming will be problematic.

Think of Clytemnestra as an anti-Penelope: instead of weaving a tapestry, she catches her husband in a web of her own (and a literal net, which she throws over him when he's having a bath). She's also called a 'watchdog' of the gates of the palace, making her very much in control of what's going on. In the background looms all the bloody history of the House of Atreus, which, hopefully, you'll remember from the early chapters.

Una nodded. *Yes, I remember. The throne of blood, you might say.*

Aeschylus' language is all but impossible to render into English. It's richly archaic, and spattered with strange metaphors. Despite this extraordinary energy, many use words like 'monumental' to describe his verse, even comparing his surviving plays to the Parthenon itself.

Some translators adopt a high register, full of thees, thous and hithertofores – hence (you see, it's infectious) the Housman parody.

Others aim for poetical intensity over literal meaning. Here's a couple of samples. I fumbled for my phone, from which I can access the Loeb Library online whenever I wish. This, I continued to Una, is a prose version translated by Herbert Weir Smyth, first published in 1926:

> Ah well, may the master of the house come home and may I clasp his welcome hand in mine! For the rest I'm dumb; a great ox stands upon my tongue – yet the house itself, could it but speak, might tell a tale full of pain; since, for my part, of mine own choice I have words for such as know, and to those who know not I've lost my memory.

*That seems a bit… overwrought*, said Una.

'Exactly. And this'… I switched to the Kindle app, and did a bit of scrolling… 'is from Robert Fagles's verse translation, forty years later.'

> Just bring him home. My king,
> I'll take your loving hand in mine and then…
> the rest is silence. The ox is on my tongue.
> Aye, but the house and these old stones,
> give them a voice and what a tale they'd tell.
> And so would I, gladly…
> I speak to those who know; to those who don't
> my mind's a blank. I never say a word.

*That's easier to follow*, said Una.

It is, and there's a reference to *Hamlet*'s last words (sparking a literary circuit: Aeschylus influences Shakespeare influences Fagles influences Aeschylus), but it's no closer to the Greek. Both of these translations bear the marks of their translators much more than they do that of Aeschylus. Even a glimpse into the Greek offers something wilder, stranger.

So what's going on in the play? It's a revenge tragedy. Revenge, by its very nature, is endless, since one death simply activates the need for another. The Elizabethan playwrights were well aware of this; and Aeschylus was too.

The crux of *Agamemnon* is when the titular hero is invited by Clytemnestra to tread on the purple (or reddish – the word is *porphura* and, as you know, it covers a range of hues) cloths on the ground: to do so would be an act of hubris.

He does, and his fate is sealed; Clytemnestra murders him, and then seizes control of the palace, along with Aegisthus, who is also a member of the House of Atreus, being a surviving son of Thyestes, and who has been acting with vengeful motives of his own.

The next part of the trilogy is *The Libation Bearers*, (*Choephoroi* in Greek) where Orestes returns home from exile. Note the similarity between the returning Agamemnon and his son (and compare to the returning Odysseus and Telemachus); yet whilst Agamemnon returns in triumph, Orestes is forced to arrive in disguise.

The title refers to Electra, Orestes' sister, and the chorus, who bring libations to pour on Agamemnon's tomb. In *The Libation Bearers*, Clytemnestra is no longer an avenging spouse; she is now a mother, facing death at the hands of her own son.

All three versions of the Electra story have a 'recognition scene' between Orestes and Electra, which means we can see how the different dramatists handled the same material, especially as they all use the same device of a lock of hair.

*Sounds strange.*

I'll tell you about it in a minute. The final play in Aeschylus' trilogy, *The Kindly Ones* (*Eumenides* in Greek), sees Orestes hounded by the doglike Furies, who form the chorus; eventually Orestes pitches up in Athens, where he is put on trial and absolved. 'Athens rules!' shouts the crowd.

The second playwright of the three surviving greats is Sophocles. Only seven of Sophocles' plays are extant, out of about ninety. He is best known today for *Oedipus Rex* and *Antigone*, which both deal with the House of Cadmus. Like Aeschylus, he was a soldier, and was a general in the Samian War alongside Pericles.

He is known for his deployment of irony, particularly in *Oedipus Rex*, where the blind seer Teiresias knows the truth.

Oedipus, the detective, pursues the truth, only to find out that the perpetrator is himself: a supreme example of the technique.

Euripides was younger than Sophocles, though they were contemporaries. Facts about his life are scantier than a nymph's negligée, but unlike his two colleagues he was never a soldier and never held any office.

Where Sophocles and Aeschylus tend to hold Athens up in admiration, and to deal in heroics, Euripides is an underminer.

So many of his plays – nineteen of them, some of which are fairly slight – survived, possibly because a librarian rescued a whole shelf when the Library of Alexandria burned down. Nine of his plays withstood the ravages of time, in alphabetical order, from *Helen* to *Cyclops*.

*That's not alphabetical.*

It is in the Greek alphabet, going from Eta to Kappa.⁋ There was no H; the sound was indicated by something called a 'rough breathing'.

*Oh yes, sorry.*

Let's look at the recognition scene in Aeschylus' *Libation Bearers* first.

At the start of the play, Orestes, returning from long exile, snips off a lock of his hair and leaves it by his father's grave. Electra and the chorus arrive; Orestes recognises her immediately.

Electra, bringing her own libations to the grave, stumbles on the lock, and notes its similarity to her own. Whoever left it must be related to her! she assumes – not unreasonably.

Taplin suggests that the cutting of hair was connected to 'important social rituals: entry to adulthood, mourning… and,

⁋  The Greek alphabet: see Appendix C.

perhaps, on claiming paternal heritage. What seems odd to us would not have seemed so strange to the audience.

Electra also notices footprints by the tomb: one set matches hers perfectly! Modern readers often laugh at this; but, as has been suggested, the scene should not be taken literally, and should be read in a more ritualistic and metaphorical light.[**]

Electra follows the footsteps, the very image of a nineteenth-century amateur sleuth, and comes face-to-face with Orestes. The recognition is over before you can say knife. Orestes confirms his identity with a piece of cloth (decorated with a beast) that Electra wove for him.

It has the gravity of ritual; there isn't any sense of the problems of revenge, only that it is righteous to avenge Agamemnon.

Electra and the chorus need Orestes; he is on Apollo's mission; he also invokes Zeus, the father of the gods himself. Orestes and Electra are the children of the eagle, about to annihilate the viper who destroyed him. The stage is set for their revenge, which is accomplished quickly.

Sophocles introduces a different device. He's more interested in layers of narrative than Aeschylus: something he does exceptionally deftly in *Philoctetes*, where Odysseus has to retrieve the bow, and, in directing Neoptolemus in what to say and do, effectively becomes a dramatist himself. In *Electra*, Orestes arrives with his old tutor and tells him to give out notice that he, Orestes, has died in a chariot accident (obviously a fairly common form of death).

This adds another layer of tension, as well as showing an awareness of dramatic form. Orestes will still pour libations on Agamemnon's tomb, and leave a lock of his hair.

---

[**] Jane Draycott and Emma-Jayne Graham, *Bodies of Evidence*.

Electra is a much more intense figure in Sophocles' version, consumed with hatred for Clytemnestra and Aegisthus.

The focus is very much on her character – which is lacking in Aeschylus – and on what she has suffered whilst Orestes has been in exile. Electra's sister Chrysothemis is introduced; she informs Electra that Clytemnestra is planning to send libations herself to Agamemnon's tomb. We see the killer Clytemnestra in a different light: she's having qualms.

One of the masterstrokes in Sophocles' version is the speech, delivered by the old tutor, in which he relates the death of Orestes. Only, of course, it's a lie. The characters onstage are spellbound by the tension of the story; we watch them, spellbound at a further remove. Sophocles understood something profound about the nature of drama and its layers of deception.

This also allows Sophocles to show Electra at the depth of despair: her only hope, she believes, has been quashed. Dramatic irony: we, the audience, know that Orestes is waiting, just offstage.

Sophocles has Chrysothemis find the lock of hair. She assumes it belongs to Orestes – not because it looks like hers, but because only a member of the House of Atreus would make such an offering.

The moment of recognition between Electra and Orestes is delayed further. When he does arrive, Orestes carries with him an urn, in which he claims lie the ashes of Orestes.

The tension crackles, until, unable to keep his secret from Electra any longer, he shows her a signet ring that belonged to Agamemnon: a surer sign than Aeschylus' piece of cloth. Orestes remains a heroic figure, though Electra's motivation for revenge (especially set against the temperance of Chrysothemis) seems excessive, transforming her into something very like a Fury.

When we come to Euripides' *Electra*, all bets are off. It's as if Aeschylus is the sensible, dutiful older brother; Sophocles tries to follow him in the same fashion, but wants to make his own mark; and then Euripides is the teen tearaway. You can almost see the Athenians asking him, 'But what are you rebelling against?' And Euripides, chewing a leaf, snarling 'Whaddya got?'

The play begins with a farmer, who is now Electra's husband – such is her lowly state, a royal princess forced to marry a peasant. When we meet Orestes, he talks of laying his offerings; but he also says that he's ready to escape, should he be recognised. This is far from the purposeful hero of the other two plays.

On seeing Electra, he grabs her by the hand; Electra fears for her life. It's hardly propitious.

An old man takes the role that Sophocles gave to Chrysothemis. He arrives bearing a lock of hair found at Agamemnon's tomb.

Now we see Euripides laying into his predecessors. Hold up the hair against yours, he says, and see if it matches! Ridiculous, replies Electra, mine is combed; Orestes grew up in the wrestling schools, it would be very different.

Well, answers the Old Man, put your foot into his footprint and see if they match.

But his would be larger, wouldn't they? answers Electra.

Mightn't there be some bit of weaving that you could recognise him by? continues the Old Man.

Don't be silly, replies Electra. I was a child at the time: how could I have been weaving?

It's at moments like this I wish I was able to slip back in time and watch the audience as they saw this. Would they have laughed, in acknowledgement of Euripides' wit? And how would this have affected what they felt about the nature of the tragedy? We know from Aristophanes that Euripides' plays scandalised the Athenians. But in exactly what way would be fascinating to find out.

This is why Euripides appeals so much to us; he asks the questions that we as modern readers and spectators ask of Aeschylus. In the end, Euripides relies on the same device as Homer in the *Odyssey*: there is a scar above Orestes' eyebrow that the Old Man recognises. He sustained it from falling over as a child, when chasing a fawn.

*Hardly heroic*, sniffed Una, who has been known to chase after fully grown deer.

There lie the essential differences between the three great tragedians.

Aeschylus is grand, ritualistic and mystic; a master of the dramatic form, but interested more in abstracts than character. He spoke to the Athenian audience of their movement from darkness and wildness towards justice.

Sophocles developed ironies, examining subjects in a clear, stark manner, allowing his audience to grapple with thorny ethical problems to do with tyranny and the state.

Euripides undercuts everything and plays with the very notion of what drama is, interested in psychology and realism (as much as that can be allowed for on the stage).

We were now trotting down Camden Road.

We've discussed some of the plays in detail, so it might be useful to have an idea of what tragedy is. The central question of all being: why do we watch it? Why do we *enjoy* – if that is even the right word – watching the sufferings of others?

The Aristotelian view was that the plays provided a 'catharsis'. This word is now widely misunderstood, and used in all sorts of pop-psychological situations.

*I heard someone saying that their holiday in Tibet was, like, so cathartic…* said Una.

Well, I hope it wasn't. Some think it means a medical purging of emotions like pity and fear. If you went to the theatre and saw people experiencing terrible things, your body would be cleared of these things. It's a bit like medieval physicians bleeding people when they were ill. Others think it means something more like purification. Many readers (including me) find this interpretation reductive: that you watch a tragedy solely to be 'purged' of the emotions of pity and fear, and that you come out of them cured.

*What did Aristotle think provoked fear and pity?*

He thought the sufferings should involve close kin; that the wicked deed should be done with conscious and full knowledge (such as Medea killing her children); or that they must discover what they've done later (Oedipus killing his father).

We were now approaching home, coming round the corner into our street. The drizzle had levelled off a little, and the windows of the houses were bright with Christmas lights and trees.

The late A.D. Nuttall was one of my tutors in my first term at Oxford. I remember so vividly sitting in his comfortable rooms in New College, with the fire burning, in the autumn afternoons.

He was a kindly presence, and very patient with undergraduates and our follies. One of his short books, *Why Does Tragedy Give Pleasure?*, attempts an answer to this eternal question. He suggests that instead of the passive 'catharsis', you should substitute 'exercise'. Dreams are said to prepare you for future horrors;

a similar sort of thing may be happening in tragedy. That seems very persuasive to me: that they enact horrors, exercising our minds in the same way as dreams and nightmares.

If you're looking for relevance, then I can point you in the direction of a 2014 production of Euripides' *Trojan Women*, which was performed entirely by a cast of amateur Syrian women refugees. Its themes of revenge and war spoke to them as loudly today as they did to the first audiences, all those thousands of years ago.

We were home. The cold air had done us both good. And soon we had settled into the sitting room, warm now, Una curled into her favourite armchair, whilst I opened a copy of *Oedipus Rex* and began to read.

## Chapter 10

# HOUNDED BY LOVE
## Catullus and Sappho

Sometimes Una and I take our exercise right into the centre of London. I don't think she particularly enjoys the rammed streets and the surging tourists; but I am always amenable to visiting the charming offices of the *Literary Review* with her when business of a bookish sort leads me there.

I have suggested to the editor that Una should have her own column, perhaps on matters of interest to dogs; however, this has not yet been taken up with as much enthusiasm as I, or Una, might have liked.

We were on our way there one morning when I stopped to dawdle on the steps of the British Museum. An exhibition about Troy was on. I was wondering why the museum doesn't allow dogs inside, and thinking about writing a letter to the trustees, when I spotted a familiar figure hurrying down the great marble stairs towards the street.

It was Daisy Dunn, a young classicist and writer of much-admired biographies of the poet Catullus and the two Plinys (the Elder and the Younger), and she had just come from seeing the exhibition. She beamed, and brushed away a lock of blond hair from her face. Daisy is rather a fixture on the classical scene, and certainly living proof that we are not all fusty old fuddy-duddies, hem hem.

'*Salve! Salvete!*' said Daisy, remembering to include Una.

Una leapt up to greet her, and we fell into step, heading towards the Tube station.

I told Daisy about my conversations with Una.

Una would very much like to know about Catullus, I said. We've got over the slightly feline appellation. I've mentioned him before to Una, and in fact we were just reading about him this morning. 'You ought really to like Catullus anyway,' I said to Una, 'because his name is only one letter away from *catulus*, which means puppy.'

*Sure*, said Una.

'We've been dealing,' I said to Daisy as we walked, 'with the epics and the tragedies.'

'The big stuff,' said Daisy.

'I was reading Catullus 64 to Una this morning, the poem about Theseus and the Minotaur, which has got all – or at least most – of Greek mythology in it, and I was thinking it's so complicated – what would you say to someone who wanted to approach Catullus, where would they start?'

'I would say,' said Daisy, in her measured, gentle voice, as we reached some traffic lights and paused for a moment, 'that Catullus 64 is my absolute number one favourite poem in the world. But,' she looked down at Una, 'if I was going to teach Una Catullus, that's probably the last one I would turn to, because it's so complex.'

Duly reprimanded, we crossed. Daisy continued, 'Catullus as a poet, out of all the Latin poets, is the first one you can really engage with as a modern reader, because he speaks like us. He writes about his feelings and his emotions. And that kind of thing wasn't really being done in Rome when he started doing it.'

*So which poem would you recommend?* asked Una.

Daisy smiled. 'I would probably start, great romantic that I am, with some of the love poems. Catullus fell in love with a married woman, whom he called Lesbia in his poems, and he wrote her a number of very, very romantic poems. There's Poem 5, which begins "Let us live, my Lesbia, and let us love."

In Latin it's really, really languid, I think you've got to read it in Latin. It's '*vivamus, mea Lesbia, atque amemus,*' and those last three words are elided, they run into each other, and that's very typical of Catullus as a poet.

He came from Verona, which was part of Gaul at this time in the Late Republic, and there they spoke slightly differently from at Rome. I think when Catullus writes a line like that, you hear the longer vowel sounds, you hear something of his dialect.'

*So he was an outsider?* said Una.

'Yes, and he embraces the fact that he is an outsider, he's not someone who's been brought up in Rome. He's come from the north. And that feels very modern to me. It's very much the thing now to embrace your roots and your dialect. You can hear in "*Lesbia atque amemus*" a real lover's drawl.'

*Tell us,* said Una, *was Lesbia a real person? I remember Ovid's Corinna might not have been.*

'I think so,' answered Daisy. 'And this is one of those questions that has divided people for centuries. Is Lesbia real? Is anything about Catullus' life real? The simple answer is it's impossible to know. We only have about six facts about Catullus' life. The poems are all we've got to go on, so I think we've got to read them closely. They tell their own story, and within that story – whether it's fictional or not – he falls in love, deeply in love, obsessed with this woman called Lesbia. A lot of people think that she is modelled on a real woman, who was Clodia Metelli.'

*Who was she?* asked Una.

'She was an aristocratic woman from one of the oldest senatorial families in Rome, and her ancestors were very prominent. Catullus was from a very different background, so you've got this whole idea of there being a class mismatch between them, and you can see these poems as a medium to bridge that gap.'

'He was from the equestrian class, wasn't he? The one below the senators?'

'Yes, that's right,' answered Daisy. 'You get the impression, whether Lesbia is real or not, that he's addressing these poems to a very, very intelligent and very witty woman, who's able to understand the allusions to other poets in his work. She's quite a clued-up character. Clodia was, apparently, married to a senator in Rome, and then he died in slightly uncertain circumstances. A rumour arose that she'd actually murdered him. Cicero took her down in court, and presented her as a prostitute as well, so you see that if you're a woman at the time and fall foul of a man, then you've got very little comeback really.'

*Oh,* said Una. *One of the things I noticed, as Philip and I were reading Catullus, was that sometimes he addresses boys as objects of love.*

'He does. There's a series of poems to a boy called Juventius. It's too basic for us to say he's bisexual, Romans don't really think in those terms. It's completely normal in that culture that you might find a boy attractive, and therefore praise him. That was sometimes sexual, but it wasn't necessarily. It wasn't frowned upon. You can have the two simultaneously – he doesn't really distinguish, and I think what comes out is he describes Juventius as being young, whereas Lesbia is an older woman. The relationship with Lesbia eventually comes to an end, and he's absolutely devastated.'

*Tell us about the end of the affair.*

'The end of the affair is just the end of Catullus' world, really. He turns against her, quite viciously. He'd written all these love poems, about kisses – my favourite ones – *da mi basia mille, deinde… deinde* – give me a thousand kisses, then more! – you get that, and then you get this whole other stream of poems where he's talking about her standing on street corners and there are queues of men – he presents her pretty much as a prostitute.'

*That doesn't sound very nice*, said Una.

'It's really cutting and it's quite horrible to read, particularly if you do try to equate her with Clodia Metelli. I think this comes from a place of absolute deep devastation. So if I was to teach Una, I'd start with *vivamus, mea Lesbia, atque amemus*. I would then use Poem 85, which is *odi et amo*, I hate and I love. "*Odi et amo. Quare id faciam fortasse requiris. Nescio, sed fieri sentio et excrucior,*"' Daisy recited.

'He actually uses the literal word crucified, *excrucior*, and the clever thing is this poem is a couplet and he's presenting himself actually on a cross. If you think of this couplet as two lines, he's presenting the poem like this.' She crossed one arm in front of the other. 'And he's on the point where the cross intersects, where love and hate intersect. It's quite an easy poem to read, I think, if you're starting Latin, but then there's so much there beneath the surface, it's quite deep. It seems so simple but no one else has really said it better.' We were near the Tube station. Daisy glanced at her watch.

Una had one more question. *We've been looking at epic so far – we've looked at the* Iliad, *the* Odyssey *and so on; if we're looking at Catullus, and he's got this poem, 64, does that count as epic?*

Daisy smiled. 'I think it's epic, it's a sort of anti-epic. Scholars would call it a miniature epic, an epyllion, because it has got a heroic theme. It deals with the age of heroes, just like Homer did. But Catullus is turning that on its head, so the heroes aren't being embraced as heroes, as Hector would be, and Achilles; he's actually looking at the flaws in these people. Particularly of Theseus, who isn't being praised for going and killing the Minotaur.'

Someone stopped to comment on how beautiful Una was. She's used to this. Slightly embarrassed, she turned to Daisy.

*What is he being praised for?*

'He's not – he's being presented as a heartless character who's abandoning a woman who's helped him to achieve his feat. He couldn't have done it without Ariadne: she gave him a ball of thread and helped him escape the labyrinth after he killed her half-brother, the Minotaur, and without her he's nothing, in Catullus' poem. Most of the poem's dwelling on his shortcomings. So I think also looking at the shape of the poem, it's four hundred and something lines, significantly shorter than the *Odyssey*, but plays with the idea of epic.'

*Thank you Daisy*, said Una. I concurred.

Daisy had to run to get her train. '*Valete!*' she said, and we waved her off.

That poem, 64, I said, is a masterpiece of ingenuity. It begins with the Argonauts, then it moves to the wedding of Peleus and Thetis…

*I remember them*, said Una. *The parents of Achilles.*

Exactly. And then the poet, as if he were behind a camera, moves through the house of Peleus and pauses in front of a couch, on which is a coverlet. And on this coverlet is a representation of Ariadne. Suddenly, we're in that story. That's the *ekphrasis* I was talking about earlier. It's an extraordinary piece of work.

*I'd like to read it*, said Una. *Once I've done the easier ones.*

Come on. Let's go. Catullus, I said to Una, as Daisy disappeared down the Tube station steps and we continued on towards Soho, was very much influenced by Greek poets. He and his contemporaries were known, we think, as the Neoterics, since they adopted Greek styles. One of his poems is a direct imitation of one by the poet Sappho.

*Who was that?*

She is pretty much our only surviving woman poet from antiquity, apart from the later Roman Sulpicia, and she hailed from the island of Lesbos, near what is Turkey today, in the latter part of the seventh century BC – so a good few hundred years before Catullus.

We know practically nothing about the world she lived in. And indeed, few people know of her. A friend of mine, a classicist, was officiating at a humanist lesbian wedding. He chose Poem 31, which we'll look at in a minute, to read out afterwards instead of a religious blessing. He introduced her as the earliest great lyric poet of Western civilisation, who was writing on the Greek island of Lesbos in around 600 BC.

There was tittering in the congregation. In fact amongst certain members, more than just tittering. My friend assumed that they had just enjoyed its appropriateness. He found out afterwards that a number of people thought he had made the whole thing up. They were astounded to discover that there really is an island called Lesbos, and that its very earliest great citizen had been a female poet called Sappho who expressed love for women.

There is much debate, as you would expect, about her poetry, which is usually addressed to women and is overflowing with deeply felt passion. Were these emotions sincere? Or was she writing in a particular kind of style, taking on a persona, as if she were a male poet?

Was she a chaste schoolmistress (as the Victorians liked to paint her) or a sensual court poet? Her sexuality is much discussed: many later sources endow her with male lovers, and she was meant to have killed herself for unrequited love; her name has become synonymous with love between women.

Her poetry is intimate and idiomatic, and we just don't know whether it was meant to reach a small group or was part of public ritual. Just the same sorts of arguments, by the way, happen with Catullus: the pendulum swings between reading his poems as faithful records of his own life and loves, and more literary constructions that bear no relation to life. Personally, I think that we know – really know – Catullus through his poems, just as we garner a sense of Ovid through his *Tristia*, and Horace through his lyric poems, and Pliny through his letters, which are essentially an autobiography; but we don't really know much about the actual character of Virgil from what he wrote, though I suspect, Una, that he was hardly a laugh a minute. Although we can, of course, intuit his mighty soul, though we do but tremble before it.

Catullus, on the other hand, would have been very amenable to all of the things that I enjoy doing, such as loafing about. Sometimes he's claiming to have nothing in his wallet but cobwebs, other times he's delighting in the friendship and excitement of the literary productions of his circle, staying up all night and chattering over his latest compositions. He's merciless in teasing both friends and enemies, and has a marvellously wide range of insults. It is he who pokes fun at a provincial who struggles to say his Hs.

*Did he have a dog?*

Unfortunately there's no poem to a dog, but there is one to Lesbia's pet sparrow.

*Well then*, said Una.

We had reached Tottenham Court Road, where builders held the waiting pedestrians back with extendable barriers, whilst enormous bulldozers, like leviathans, eased slowly out of construction sites. Una and I picked our way through the mob and passed by Foyles, where there is a good selection of Loebs.

I wanted to see if there were any new classical books anyway. 'Let's pop in and have a look at some Catullus and Sappho,' I said to Una. She agreed, wagging her tail gently.

'And just like Sappho,' I continued, as we passed through the gleaming hall, almost a temple to the gods of literature, up to the classical level, 'Catullus' fate hung in the balance: we might have only had a few lines if it hadn't been for a complete manuscript that surfaced in his home town, Verona.

There's a lovely tradition that it was found stopping up a hole in a barrel of wine, which is undoubtedly not true, but enjoyable nevertheless, and we thank the thirsty monk who, looking about for something to save his wine, lighted on Catullus.

We rose in the lift, and entered the classical section – now, sadly, much reduced, but still fairly extensive.

We'll look, I said to Una, at one of Sappho's poems, and then compare it to Catullus' version, and this will give you a good idea of how the poets worked. We've already seen how Virgil and the Greek playwrights vied with Homer; Catullus is both translating and competing with Sappho. Here is Catullus:

*Ille mi par esse deo videtur,*
*ille, si fas est, superare divos,*
*qui sedens adversus identidem te*
*spectat et audit*
*dulce ridentem, misero quod omnes*
*eripit sensus mihi: nam simul te,*
*Lesbia, aspexi, nihil est super mi*
*<vocis in ore;>*
*lingua sed torpet, tenuis sub artus*
*flamma demanat, sonitu suopte*
*tintinant aures, gemina teguntur*
*lumina nocte.*
*otium, Catulle, tibi molestum est:*
*otio exsultas nimiumque gestis:*
*otium et reges prius et beatas*
*perdidit urbes.*

I translated it for Una, in a slightly halting prose version: 'That man seems to me to be equal to a god; that man, if it can be said, to sur-pass the gods, who, sitting opposite you, again and again, watches and hears you, laughing sweetly, which snatches all my senses away from wretched me. For as soon as I see you, Lesbia, then nothing is left of speech in my mouth; my tongue seizes up, a slender flame rushes through my limbs, my ears sound with their own ringing, and my eyes are covered with twin nights. Leisure, Catullus, is a pain for you. At leisure, you're restless, and you do too much. Leisure, in the past, destroyed both kings and blessed cities.'

And here, Sappho. I showed Una the page.

φαίνεταί μοι κῆνος ἴσος θέοισιν
ἔμμεν᾽ ὤνηρ, ὄττις ἐνάντιός τοι

ἰσδάνει καὶ πλάσιον ἆδυ φωνεί-
σας ὐπακούει
καὶ γελαίσας ἰμέροεν, τό μ᾽ ἦ μὰν
καρδίαν ἐν στήθεσιν ἐπτόαισεν·
ὡς γὰρ ἔς σ᾽ ἴδω βρόχε᾽, ὤς με φώναι-
σ᾽ οὐδ᾽ ἒν ἔτ᾽ εἴκει,
ἀλλ᾽ ἄκαν μὲν γλῶσσα †ἔαγε†, λέπτον
δ᾽ αὔτικα χρῶι πῦρ ὐπαδεδρόμηκεν,
ὀππάτεσσι δ᾽ οὐδ᾽ ἒν ὄρημμ᾽, ἐπιρρόμ-
βεισι δ᾽ ἄκουαι,
†έκαδε μ᾽ ἴδρως ψῦχρος κακχέεται†, τρόμος δὲ
παῖσαν ἄγρει, χλωροτέρα δὲ ποίας
ἔμμι, τεθνάκην δ᾽ ὀλίγω ᾽πιδεύης
φαίνομ᾽ ἔμ᾽ αὔται·
ἀλλὰ πὰν τόλματον ἐπεὶ †καὶ πένητα†

*Well*, said Una, *that's, er, all Greek to me. Read it out.*

And so I found myself reading out Sappho's poem about jealous passion to my dog, at 11:30a.m. on a weekday morning, in the main branch of Foyles on the Charing Cross Road. Still, I expect they've seen stranger things. And to be fair, the bookseller barely gave us a glance. I then translated it for her, again, slightly haltingly, as my Greek's a little rusty:

'That man seems to me to be equal to the gods, who, sitting opposite you, hears you speaking sweetly, and delightfully laughing. My heart flutters in my chest; even when I look at you for a short while, it's not possible any more for me to speak; but it's as if my tongue is [broken], and a light flame runs over my skin. My eyes can't see, and my ears resound; a cold sweat covers me, trembling seizes me everywhere, I'm paler than grass, and I almost seem to be dead. But everything must be endured, since even a poor man...' and there it breaks off.

*What do the funny crosses mean?* asked Una, when I'd finished.

They mean that there's a gap in the text – shown by a 'crux' – and that a scholar (or many scholars) has suggested words that will complete the sense whilst being true to the theme and style of the poet. It's a brilliantly complex (and taxing) business, doing this.

If we read the two poems next to each other, you'll see that Catullus is almost directly translating the Sappho.

In both poems a man is sitting opposite the beloved, who, because of his proximity, seems endowed with divinity. The poets both express, in richly physical language, their inability to speak because of the effects of their passion. Both appear intimate, and express jealous love. The question remains why Catullus chooses to translate or emphasise certain things differently from Sappho. We assume that the Lesbia he is addressing is Clodia. The name, of course, has extra resonance in a translation of Sappho, as she was the woman from Lesbos.

Catullus' setting is, perhaps, even at the house of Clodia and her husband; that man sitting opposite her may even be him. Thus the sense of delicious envy is heightened.

You'll see in his second line that Catullus uses the word '*ille*' again – 'That man'. Sappho only has '*kenos*', which means the same thing, and does not repeat it. Immediately for Catullus the sense of competition is heightened: that man – him!

Sappho says that he's equal to the gods; Catullus goes further, and asks, if it be '*fas*', that man might seem to surpass the gods. We've met the concept of '*nefas*' before – something that is transgressive – and '*fas*' means something that is sanctioned by the gods. Catullus doesn't want to cause divine conniptions by his excessive statements. Why, then, does he say it? It's a little ironic touch of the sort that makes Catullus so attractive.

Sappho's may have been composed for a wedding; it may also be entirely sincere. The specificity of Catullus gives extra frisson. He also talks about *otium* – a subject that was dear to Romans' hearts and which meant, essentially, leisure time. Some people think that this stanza was stuck on by accident; others see in it an extension of his themes. He berates himself ironically, claiming that all this leisure is bad for him. Of course, we know it's not.

The poems interact with each other: they show that jealous love is both universal and specific; that time is no barrier to emotion.

I placed the Loebs back on the shelf. It was time to head to the *Literary Review* offices.

We'd come through Soho, which is always in a process of transformation, and now is beginning to lose many of its flesh-pots and to resemble something very much like an extension of Regent Street. But the *Literary Review* offices, above the print shop Andrew Edmunds, still exist in a different time zone altogether.

The door buzzer; the rickety stairs; the warm fug; the piles of books teetering on every available surface. It was time to leave off our conversation, and for Una to take up her position under-neath one of the desks, whilst I scoured the shelves for books to review. Our conversations would have to be put on hold for a moment, as my *otium* was rapidly about to become *negotium*. But soon, I promised Una, we would return.

## Chapter II

# A PAINTED DOG
## The Beginning of History

Christmas had been and gone, in the mysterious way that it does, seeming to be at once the longest period of time you've ever spent eating mince pies and mainlining port, as well as a blur of wrapping paper and tiny bits of Sellotape. I had attempted to amuse my relatives with an Ancient Greek version of 'Jingle Bells', translated by, no less, the Emeritus Regius Professor of Greek at Oxford:

> *Klangedon, klangedon*
> *klange panta-che;*
> *elaunomen kai chairomen*
> *monozugo harmati;*
> *klangedon, klangedon*
> *klange panta-che;*
> *elaunomen kai chairomen*
> *monozugo harmati.*

Whether they were as tickled by this as I was is unclear, given that most of them had left the room by the time I had finished. Only Una remained, *canis fidelis* that she is.

It was the start of a new year, with all its attendant sense of possibility. Janus, the Roman two-headed god whose function was, amongst other things, to guard thresholds, was invoked, and I'd poured him a small libation of my own. Not on the actual doorstep, of course, but down my throat.

The crackers had been pulled, the debris cleared away, the presents received and admired, the empty wine bottles chucked in the recycling, and we were back in London, having spent much of the holiday period in the country, where Una had reverted to her Iliadic purpose, and I to a sybaritic one.

*Sybaritic?*

Yes, after the inhabitants of Sybaris, a Greek colony in southern Italy, who were meant to be more luxurious than anyone else, at least in the eyes of the Romans.

And so we were facing the new year feeling rather like some Roman who'd overdone it on the dormice at the dinner table, ready for a diet of lettuce leaves. Of course what this also meant was lots more walks for Una, as I strove to make my now adipose frame resemble more nearly the classical ideal.

*Chance would be a fine thing*, said Una, who somehow manages to stay lithe and sleek.

*So how do we know what we know?* she went on, as we sprang out of the front door, brimming with good cheer and ready to take on any squirrel that dared show its face.

How do we know what we know? That's not really the kind of thing that we're talking about here, I said. That's more like epistemology.

Una left a silence that was simply begging to be filled.

Which is the philosophy of knowledge. For that kind of thing, you need to talk to Monty.

Monty is a dog who belongs to a writer called Anthony McGowan. He's small, rather scruffy.

*McGowan?*

No, Monty. He's a terrier. We sometimes bump into both of them on the Heath, and McGowan's always muttering away to Monty about philosophy. At least, I think that's what he's doing.

I last saw him shouting 'Kierkegaard!' in rather a wild-eyed frenzy somewhere near the loos by Parliament Hill. He could also tell you about Diogenes the Cynic, which means, by the way, Diogenes the Doggy. I'll just tell you one thing about him: when Plato defined man as a 'featherless biped', Diogenes went and plucked a chicken and said, 'Look, a man!'

*OK, I'll ask Monty, then*, said Una. *What I mean*, she continued, through her teeth, *is how do we know about what happened in the classical era. It's so long ago.*

And yes, for you, Una, it really is exceptionally long ago, as the generations of dogs are many more than the generations of humans.

Much of what we can glean from antiquity springs from the historians, and it's certainly worth knowing who were the major contributors, and what they told us.

Herodotus of Halicarnassus – a coastal Greek city in Asia Minor (modern-day Turkey) – was the very first, who seems to have invented the genre. I think it's important not to underestimate this, as can often happen with students, who accuse him of being insufficiently rigorous: he called his work '*historia*', or in English, 'history', which means 'inquiry'.

His main theme was the ongoing war between the Greeks and the Persians, which we've glanced at briefly when discussing Aeschylus. This is when the Greek forces, doughty, small and mostly united, succeed supremely against the vast array of the Persian forces. Perhaps the most famous episode is the battle of Thermopylae, or the Hot Gates, for which Herodotus is our major source, although the Greeks didn't win this one.

*What happened there?*

It's one of those moments that's almost passed into legend, and it has provided the meat for the recent film *300* – which does bear some resemblance to the facts. And here a force of about six thousand Greeks tried to hold back the Persians, some time in 480 BC. Imagine a cork trying to stop a hole in a dam that's about to burst. It wasn't just curtains for the Greeks, but an interior designer's whole remaindered stock.

The Persians believed the Hot Gates were the only way through the mountains. There was another route, which the Greeks were keeping shtum about – until somebody betrayed its existence. Armed with this new knowledge of the terrain, the Persians were bound to sweep devastatingly through, and they crept behind the Greek army.

It was a crucial moment. Most of the Greeks fled; the Spartans, led by King Leonidas, remained to take their stand. There were three hundred Spartans, against what were probably one hundred thousand Persians.

*Did they win?*

Spartan mothers used to say to their sons, come back with your shield, or on it. The Spartan code demanded honour and ferocity in battle. If they fled, they would be shamed. They fought with spears, until they broke; they fought with swords; when they were pressed to the last, they fought with their hands and teeth.

It was impossible. They had no chance. They were defeated, and killed, and the Persians took Thermopylae.

Herodotus probably composed his work sometime in the fifth century BC; he was a friend of Sophocles.

He conceived happenings as part of a divine pattern: commit hubris, and you will receive your comeuppance. You'll remember this from myth, of course. He was trying to work out what it meant to be 'Greek' (though that wasn't the word he used, as you know) in relation to the other cultures that rubbed up against them.

He was entirely innovative in his approach, and assiduous in using oral sources. He went around interviewing the grandchildren of people involved in the events of the late sixth century BC. Herodotus also travelled widely, including into Egypt (pharaohs! a river that floods in summer!), asking locals for their memories of events; this has, however, led many over the centuries to call him a liar. Aristotle even calls him 'the storyteller', noting that Herodotus claims that the spermatozoa of Ethiopians are black.

They aren't, says Aristotle.

Una, who at this point had been paying attention to a suspicious movement in the long grass, turned round. *How did he know that it wasn't?* she asked.

Well, that we would all like to know, I replied. Aristotle was an empiricist, after all. Perhaps he experimented with lots of different kinds of people as controls. Anyway, it's in Herodotus that we find the famous story of King Croesus, who went to the oracle at Delphi and asked it whether he should fight the Persians. The oracle replied (in rather clearer fashion than it usually does, it must be said) that if he did, he would destroy a mighty empire. Croesus duly went to war and, well, the bell was tolling for Croesus: he was defeated and captured.

I can well imagine his letter of complaint to the Delphic Pythia. But you *said*! Aha, came the reply. If only you'd listened properly. The mighty empire, *naturellement*, was yours.

Herodotus was full of wonder and admiration for mankind's achievements. His worldview is very much a symmetrical one, and he looks back into the far past of myth and legend for reasons why the Greeks and the Persians are at odds. It is entirely possible, says Herodotus, for people to be punished for what their ancestors did.

He tried to view different peoples even-handedly (bar the nomads, whom he admits he couldn't stand. Perhaps it was the smell). A good example of this is when Herodotus tells us that King Darius of the Persians asked some Greeks how much they would have to be paid in order to eat the bodies of their fathers; the Greeks reacted with horror. Darius then asked some Indians, called the Callatians, who were used to eating the dead, how much it would cost for them to burn their fathers; they reacted with similar dread.

Herodotus says that each culture will naturally prefer its own customs (or '*nomos*'): he doesn't try to suggest that the Greeks are any better (or worse) than the Indians (or any other culture).

Una snuffled. She is well aware that some of her habits might appear a little odd to those who are not dogs. Whilst she is quite happy, for instance, to lick her own posterior, she turns her nose up when offered a bath.

*Who came after Herodotus?* she enquired.

Thucydides, a little later in the fifth century BC. Like Aeschylus, he was a soldier, even a *strategos*, or general, and by most accounts a mightily successful one. He is often considered the first proper historian, because his methods were more analytical, and he rejected the idea of an overarching divine plan; but this is rather unfair on poor old Herodotus, who did, ultimately, invent the whole historical caboodle.

Thucydides' subject was the Peloponnesian War between Athens and Sparta, which rolled onwards between 431 and 404 BC; he himself was born probably somewhere around 460 BC; and so he was writing about contemporary events.

*Does that make them more reliable?*

Yes and no – he's still got his own axes to grind. He's too much of a fan of Pericles, and so isn't very critical of him.

In contrast to the oral nature of Herodotus, Thucydides has a more scientific approach; unlike Herodotus, he likes to compare different accounts in order to attempt to achieve the truth. Thucydides never finished his work, for reasons we don't know. Another loss for our libraries. Both set a high standard for the historians who were to follow them.

*What about the Romans?*

Well, of course there is Livy. I will freely admit that I never much liked Livy at school: too many long, wet afternoons spent staring at his exceptionally complicated sentences about what seemed to me to be exceptionally boring subjects. In recent years, I've grown to like the old fellow. His style, which was called '*lactea ubertas*' – milky richness – by a Roman critic, was what I found off-putting as a teenager; yet now, I find pleasure in delving through those same sentences.

Now, Una, we must leap forwards a few hundred years in time, from the glories of the fifth century BC in Athens; remember that about this time, the Romans were chucking out their kings, and then gradually expanding in Italy, without much notice being taken of them. They were also hard at work promoting their own particular brand of austere virtue.

It's easy to contrast the Greeks and the Romans: the first as frivolous and liking their luxuries; the second as hatchet-faced bureaucrats, interested only in expanding their rule. It isn't quite so easy as that though– the Spartans, for example, don't fit into this scheme. The Romans certainly liked to present themselves, through their stories and their histories, as exemplars of a particular kind of virtue. You will remember Aeneas and his pious refusal of Dido's entreaties; you can only imagine what would have happened had it been a Greek.

*He would have slept with her, built a city, had some children, and then buggered off again, I should think,* said Una.

When Livy was born, during the Republic, probably in 59 BC, the rule of an emperor like Augustus was an impossible future; he died in AD 17, a few years after Augustus, having seen the Civil Wars, and the fall of Julius Caesar and the rise of Octavian. An equivalent might be someone who was born in 1600 in London, and just caught the end of the reign of Elizabeth I; if she died in 1688, she'd have seen a king beheaded, a Republic, a restoration, and the start of the Glorious Revolution.

Livy's work is called *Ab Urbe Condita* – '*From the founding of the city*' – and covers events from then all the way up to 9 BC, within his own lifetime.

It's got all the classics. Here you'll find the rape of Lucretia, which as you'll remember catalysed the fall of the Tarquins; here you'll find the horrific tale of Verginia—

*Why horrific?*

It's certainly horrific to our ears. Verginia's father killed her rather than let her be raped by a magistrate.

*Why would he do that?*

To save her honour. The Romans had many such stories. Another involves a girl called Tarpeia. She was the daughter of the commander of the Roman forces. The Sabines promised her, if she betrayed Rome, what they bore on their left arms. Thinking it meant their gold bracelets, she readily betrayed the city; only to be squashed by the Sabines' shields as they entered. I once taught this story to a twelve-year-old boy, and asked him what he thought the Romans meant to show by it. The boy said, instantly, 'The terms of your contract should be more certain.'

*He has a point.*

Coriolanus the traitor is here too, whose tale is told in the Shakespeare play that bears his name; and, much later on, the masterly passages describing the Second Punic* War, and the defeat of Hannibal the Carthaginian, with his war-elephants.

There are many, many, many books of Livy, mostly intended to show the reader how the moral backbone of the Romans ensured their success.

*Where should I start?*

With the self-contained stories from Rome's early history, and then Hannibal. We can all get excited about Hannibal, because he was such a legend: still in his twenties, he crossed the Alps – with elephants! – and marched through the plains of Italy, winning a huge victory at Cannae against the Romans in 216 BC. Robin Lane Fox calls him a 'consummate trickster, more of an Odysseus' – and once again we see myth and history reflecting each other. Hannibal didn't win, though; he was beaten in the end by the brilliant young general Scipio, who invaded Africa to conquer him.

---

* Punic comes from the word for Phoenician; the Carthaginians were settlers from Phoenicia.

And now we must hurtle forwards again. I have zero qualms in saying that we will be meeting my favourite of the historians, Tacitus, who was born in about AD 56. Augustus is long gone, and the reign of the emperors has been in full spate a while now; the entire Julio-Claudian dynasty, which has managed to grip on to power since Augustus won the battle of Actium in 31 BC, is about to come to an end with the suicide of Nero in AD 68. Almost a hundred years of Roman history; and that's not even counting Julius Caesar. There is one dynastic irony: quite a lot of the later Julio-Claudians were descended from Mark Antony. And so, in a sense, his legacy did live on.

## THE JULIO-CLAUDIAN FAMILY

Julius Caesar – end of the Roman Republic
Augustus – first emperor, d. AD 14
Tiberius AD 14–37
Caligula AD 37–41
Claudius AD 41–54
Nero AD 54–68

The Julio-Claudian family is much more complicated than a spider's web, or even the genealogical tree of the Kardashians. This was nowhere near as easy as a straightforward father-to-eldest-child monarchy. The Romans were still getting to grips with what an emperor was, and what that kind of power entailed.

*Can you explain the family?*
The Kardashians?
*No, the Julio-Claudians.*

I'll have a go… Adoption was very common, and you might adopt your nephew or great-nephew or even grandson as an heir, and refer to them as your son. Augustus, the great instigator of moral crusades and temple-building, and the very first 'emperor', crucially, had no sons, and so he adopted his grandchildren Lucius and Gaius; however, they both kicked the bucket rather young.

*In suspicious circumstances?*

Well, it depends on whom you read. Certainly, intrigue, murder and political infighting took place on a massive scale. And that's why we were all told *not* to read Robert Graves' *I, Claudius* before we'd done our finals, because Graves supplies the motives for all the deaths (and points the finger at Livia). Augustus' wife Livia had two boys from a previous marriage, who were then tipped as his heirs: Drusus and Tiberius; Drusus, however, fell off a horse and died.

*Ouch.*

Eventually, Augustus, though rather reluctantly, was compelled to recognise Tiberius as his heir.

Tiberius, who preferred to take an indirect approach to ruling, did have his own natural son, Drusus; but Augustus had forced him to adopt his nephew Germanicus. Germanicus was immensely popular with the Roman people, as well as being a brilliant military leader; however, he too soon shuffled off this mortal coil. Some said he accused Tiberius on his deathbed. *Accuso!*

Drusus also died; he had been at odds with Tiberius' henchman Sejanus. Did he die of natural causes, or was he poisoned?

We can never know. Meanwhile, the two elder sons of Germanicus had also been killed, on charges of treason. If you have seen the film *Kind Hearts and Coronets*, in which a minor heir to a dukedom murders his way through his relatives in order to gain the ermine robes, then it's hard not to see a similar pattern here.

In any case, Caligula, Germanicus' youngest son, was then made Tiberius' heir. The historian Suetonius (whom, however, we must take with a pinch of the salt stuff) tells us that Tiberius was almost immediately smothered with a pillow so that Caligula could be accelerated up the imperial rankings.

Caligula is a nickname, meaning 'little boots'. His rule was short and violent; he was murdered, sordidly, in a back corridor of his palace; his wife and little daughter were killed on the same day; and the Praetorian Guards proposed Claudius, Drusus' son and the uncle of Caligula, as emperor.

*The Praetorian Guards?*

Yes, it's extraordinary how much power they had. Throughout the history of the later Roman Empire, if you had the Praetorian Guards on your side you were a dead cert. Think of them as Molossian hounds. Claudius, thought to be rather incompetent, in fact ruled well and for a fairly long time, even conquering Britain; he adopted Nero, his great-nephew. Nero is the figure who we associate with extravagance, building his golden palace on the ruins of the burned city of Rome. Did he fiddle whilst Rome burned? Nope; but it's certain that he died because he believed the Senate had declared him an enemy of Rome. Unable to do it himself, he begged one of his companions to help. And so the last member of the Julio-Claudian dynasty died in ignominy, amongst confusion, whilst chaos waited around the corner. Now, can you remember all their names?

*I think I've got it. Augustus, Tiberius, Caligula, Claudius, Nero. ATCCN.*

Good. All The Claudians: Chant Now!

After the death of Nero, Rome was once more ravaged by fighting, in what is known as the Year of Four Emperors: Galba, Otho, Vitellius and, finally, Vespasian.

Vespasian, and his two sons Titus and Domitian, comprise the Flavian dynasty, which lasted until Domitian, authoritarian and excessively concerned with his baldness, was assassinated in AD 96.

The reason I have such a fondness for Tacitus is that his style remains unsurpassed for elegance, vividness, wit and compression. When Galba is murdered, Tacitus says of him: '*omnium consensu capax imperii, nisi imperasset*' – by the consent of all he was capable of ruling; if he had not ruled. Sublimely pithy in the Latin.

It's partly from Tacitus that we get the extraordinary stories about Nero: depraved and un-Roman, he made a mock-marriage to a eunuch called, some say, Pythagoras, and took the female role. The scene in Tacitus where Nero tries to murder his mother Agrippina with a collapsible boat—

Una interrupted. *What?*

Yes, I know. They were nothing if not inventive. And why not try a collapsible boat? Who on earth would ever guess that you had tried to kill your mother with a collapsible boat? It's like something out of *Midsomer Murders*.

*But why did he want to kill his mother?*

She disapproved of his goings-on with a woman called Poppaea Sabina.[†]

---

[†]  Though her father was Titus Ollius, Poppaea took the name of her famous grandfather, C. Poppaeus Sabinus – something that did sometimes happen amongst aristocratic women.

*Still, that doesn't seem like quite enough…*

Tacitus supplies the motive; we don't really know why. The scene is fantastically gripping and atmospheric, and made even more brilliant by the fact that Agrippina survives and swims to shore; one of her handmaidens pretends to be her, thinking that she will be saved, and is clubbed to death. Agrippina makes it home. By this time you're really egging her on. Nero's agents corner her. '*Fere ventrem!*' she says to them – strike my womb – defiant to the last.

*Isn't that your Latin surname?* Venter?

It is. But don't take it as an invitation to hit me.

*I won't.*

Tacitus conjures up deathly internecine violence of the type you might find in Aeschylus, yet it teeters on the edge of sinister comedy.

Then you've got the Year of Four Emperors: GOVV. Get Out! Vamoose, Vamoose!

Una, startled, looked up.

No, not you. It's a mnemonic, for Galba, Otho, Vitellius, Vespasian. That brings you neatly down to the other two Flavians: Titus and Domitian; so all you need to do is add Touch Down! and you've got the first twelve Caesars.

*Why are they called Flavians?*

Because Vespasian's full name was Titus Flavius Vespasianus.

And after the Flavians there came at last a breather. The Nerva-Antonine dynasty presided over what many call the best age of the Roman Empire, ruled by Trajan, Hadrian and Marcus Aurelius (amongst others); this dynasty saw an expansion and consolidation of Roman power. This is what Edward Gibbon says about it:

In the second century of the Christian era, the empire of Rome comprehended the fairest part of the earth, and the most civilised portion of mankind. The frontiers of that extensive monarchy were guarded by ancient renown and disciplined valour. The gentle but powerful influence of laws and manners had gradually cemented the union of the provinces. Their peaceful inhabitants enjoyed and abused the advantages of wealth and luxury. The image of a free constitution was preserved with decent reverence: the Roman senate appeared to possess the sovereign authority, and devolved on the emperors all the executive powers of government. During a happy period [AD 98–180] of more than fourscore years, the public administration was conducted by the virtue and abilities of Nerva, Trajan, Hadrian, and the two Antonines. It is the design of this, and of the two succeeding chapters, to describe the prosperous condition of their empire; and afterwards, from the death of Marcus Antoninus, to deduce the most important circumstances of its decline and fall; a revolution which will ever be remembered, and is still felt by the nations of the earth.

It was the beginning of the end. On the literature side, no new Virgil took up the stylus; and certainly no new Homer. It's easy to feel melancholy about this, and to think in terms of a general decline. Another explanation may simply be that the form of the epic no longer suited the times.

This is the age of Pliny the Younger, the letter-writer, who served under Hadrian (and whose description of the eruption of Vesuvius, in which his uncle, Pliny the Elder, died, is on a par with Samuel Pepys' exceptionally vivid account of the Great Fire of London); and the poet and epigrammatist Martial, as well as the satirist Juvenal.

If you remember your Catullus, you will be familiar with Martial's world of chancers, dinner parties and love affairs, though his seems saltier. You can see how quickly the language shifts, too: '*Cotile, bellus homo es*' begins one poem, which doesn't take a Latin language degree to translate if you know a bit of Italian.

*I don't*, said Una.

Sorry – it means Cotilus, you're a handsome chap. We might as well take a look at one of his shorter epigrams, since it's the kind of thing that you can read pretty well even when you've only got a basic grasp of Latin:

> *Bella es, novimus, et puella, verum est,*
> *et dives, quis enim potest negare?*
> *sed cum te nimium, Fabulla, laudas,*
> *nec dives neque bella nec puella es.*

> You're pretty, we know, and young, it's true,
> and rich. Who can say you're not?
> But when you praise yourself too much, Fabulla,
> you're neither rich, pretty, nor young.

It lacks the bite, if you'll excuse me, of a classic Catullan epigram. The critic William Fitzgerald thinks that Martial is very much a poet for our age: he lends himself very well to soundbites and pithiness.

There is one poem we should look at more closely.

I loaded up the SPQR app on my phone, which lets me pull up classical texts as swiftly as Mercury:

*Issa est passere nequior Catulli,*
*Issa est purior osculo columbae,*
*Issa est blandior omnibus puellis,*
*Issa est carior Indicis lapillis,*
*Issa est deliciae catella Publi.*
*hanc tu, si queritur, loqui putabis;*
*sentit tristitiamque gaudiumque.*
*collo nixa cubat capitque somnos,*
*ut suspiria nulla sentiantur;*
*et desiderio coacta ventris*
*gutta pallia non fefellit ulla,*
*sed blando pede suscitat toroque*
*deponi monet et rogat levari.*
*castae tantus inest pudor catellae,*
*ignorat Venerem; nec invenimus*
*dignum tam tenera virum puella.*
*hanc ne lux rapiat suprema totam,*
*picta Publius exprimit tabella,*
*in qua tam similem videbis Issam,*
*ut sit tam similis sibi nec ipsa.*
*Issam denique pone cum tabella:*
*aut utramque putabis esse veram,*
*aut utramque putabis esse pictam.*

It's a poem about a little dog, called Issa, who is more badly behaved than Catullus' sparrow (a nice intertextual reference there). She's purer than the kiss of a dove; more pleasing than any girl or Indian pearls. If she whines, you'd think she was talking; she feels the '*tristitiamque gaudiumque*' – the sadness and joy – of her master, Publius.

*Well that is partly what we dogs are for*, said Una, rather primly.

264

She rests on his neck – she must have been a toy dog – and sleeps. In a lovely touch, Martial tells us that she never pees on the bed, but asks to be let out. Publius loves her so much that he's actually getting a picture painted of her.

*Well quite right too*, said Una.

We were reaching the entrance to our street. Home was within sight. The end of Roman history was in sight, too. The age of the Antonines, as it's often known, comes rocketing to an end with Commodus, an emperor whom you may have seen in *Gladiator*. He is the one who chopped ostriches' heads off in the middle of the Colosseum, and then displayed them to the senators, as if to say: you're next.

### WHAT'S ON AT THE COLOSSEUM

This was the medieval name for the Amphitheatrum Flavium, or Flavian Amphitheatre, so called as it was built by the Flavian emperors. It was a massive public spectacle. Roll up, roll up, for extreme violence, extraordinary pain and supreme misery!

Morning: Wake up, have breakfast. Talk to clients. Go to Colosseum.

AM: Animal fights and hunts – camels, leopards, lions, tigers, pigs, boar, crocodiles… even a rhinoceros. You could see a bull duking it out with an elephant.

Lunchtime: Criminals executed. By crucifixion or by being thrown to wild beasts.

PM: Gladiators and re-enactments of myths and battles. The Emperor Titus even re-enacted a sea-battle, filling the whole theatre with water.

Evening: Home. Time to put your feet up.

After that, it's really rather a mess. People were proclaimed emperor left, right and centre. Were you simply passing by on the wrong day you might get a tap on the shoulder and find yourself suddenly shrouded in the imperial purple. Amongst this motley lot is the extraordinary Elagabalus, who was a mere teenager when proclaimed emperor, and who, according at least to some sources, had a particularly intimate relationship with his blond charioteer, and liked to pretend to be a female prostitute, standing behind a fringed curtain in his palace and waiting for clients to pass by.

Home was in sight. I let Una off the lead. And here is where, usually, most classicists' studies end. And that, Una, is really a very long answer to your original question about classics.

*Well, thank you*, said Una. I climbed up the stairs, looking forward to a nice cup of Earl Grey. She pattered up beside me, and I tickled her under the ruff.

*Briefly …* she said, as I put my key in the door.

What?

*Briefly – what happened afterwards? You said the Roman Empire lasted until 1453?*

You have a good memory, Una. Which is true, as she can remember where she buried a bone at least a year after she's done so.

The Empire was split in half, I said, entering the house, by the Emperor Diocletian, in AD 286.

Too large to control, it was divided into eastern and western halves. Alaric the Visigoth laid waste the city of Rome in AD 410. It was the beginning of the end.

It's one of the strange coincidences of history, I said, hanging my coat up, that the last Roman emperor was called Romulus Augustulus – the latter being a diminutive of Augustus. He ruled for a year, between AD 475 and AD 476.

Bizarrely, his father was called Orestes. It feels as if things were coming full circle; that the legendary figures who began the classical cycle had returned to see the end. Of course that is nothing more than fancy. But where would we be without fancy?

And then Odoacer, a Germanic princeling, deposed him, followed by waves of Goths and Vandals. The Eastern Roman Empire continued for another thousand years as what we call the Byzantine Empire, after the city of Byzantium (modern Istanbul), until it was defeated by the Turks. And the complexities of the Byzantines, Una, are well beyond my short span of knowledge.

It's still extraordinary to me that a political entity begun in the dust and heat of Rome before Augustus was even heard of could have lasted until so near our own times. I danced with a man who danced with a girl who danced with the Prince of Wales...

I needed that cup of tea and a biscuit – preferably a bit of shortbread. It was actually nearly lunchtime. Was a glass of wine out of the question? Surely not, and rather appropriate after all this talk about Greeks and Romans.

*There's just one more thing*, she said.

Oh really? I said. What?

*How did they live?*

# Chapter 12

# DOGGY STYLE?
## Sex and Sewers

How did they live? How did the Romans live? How did the ancient Greeks live? Questions that have consumed historians and classicists for decades, even centuries; questions that are hard to answer without either assuming that they were indeed very much *not* like us... or that they were essentially twenty-first-century people in togas and tunics.

Una just had to save that most difficult of questions till last.

I had to put her off for a while. She kept reminding me of it. When I filled her bowl with little titbits of partridge, she would look at me, questioningly. I knew what she was thinking.

*Did the Romans eat partridge?*

Well, that I could answer, as there is a recipe in a cookbook by Apicius. You use plenty of herbs, honey and wine, and make sure you baste it. Then I went up to bed.

She would haunt me in the corridors. When I put on my boots, about to go and get the papers, she would stare at me, obviously wondering how the Romans got their news.

Well, I began to answer, there was indeed imperial post, a system set up by Augustus himself, used for official messages; you could, if you were a diplomat, misuse it.

Then I tied my laces and went out.

Eventually, I came to a day that was relatively free from any other disturbance, and so I decided to take Una out for a long walk. Or rather, she decided, as she prodded me out of my study one morning.

*It still gets dark early, you know,* she said.

I know, I answered. But I was pleased to get out into the biting cold air.

There was no escaping her. Your question from the other day, I said. How they lived. It's really rather a broad one, as we're dealing with such a huge range of experience. How the Mycenaeans of the pre-Athenian age lived in palace complexes would have been very different from that of Romans of the Silver Latin period, and of course across the classes, and for men and women.

But let's start with time. One of my favourite things about time is that there were several different systems going on at once in different cities across Greece. Even the words for time didn't have specific meanings – '*hora*' in Latin could mean anything from 'hour' to 'season'; the word for 'winter' in Latin, '*hiems*', is also the word for storm.

*So if a farmer said to his friend, I'll meet you in an hour, you wouldn't know if he meant that day or the year after?*

No, of course you could guess from the context. But their concept of time was much more closely linked to weather than to a rigidly observed system of counting days. Whilst astronomers and observers noted the movements of the stars, the Athenian calendar never corresponded to the phases of the moon, and the Roman months – before they were reformed – were often out by about a quarter of a year.

*So what did they do?*

They just stuck in another month, until it lined up again with the seasons.

*So they probably never kept appointments*, said Una.

Indeed. If you were a Roman in the Augustan age and later, I said, passing the bookshop (the Owl Bookshop, which I hope is in homage to Athena), a surprisingly large range of occupations was available to you; many of which would involve servicing the needs of the rich. Why, you might even turn your hand to fattening peacocks for the table.

Both Martial and Juvenal complain in their poems about the endless noise of the Roman streets: much of which came from craftsmen and so on going about their daily business. Were you to amble down a street in ancient Rome, you would find it was split into various quarters: carpenters had their workshops in one place, perfumers in another, and so on. Fast-food joints sold you sausages, bread or chickpeas. Monkeys might entice you to a fig stall. Diamonds, crystal, clay figures, songbirds, snails... It would have been a ramshackle, gloriously busy vision. There was plenty of fashion to buy: a cloak embroidered with feathers, or gold, or a fur coat.

*Fancy.* Una preened, no doubt imagining herself in a gold collar.

Slaves provided a huge amount of free labour. Domestic slaves were called *famuli*. The popular image is of a rich, well-fed man enthroned, whilst a slave fans him with palm leaves. When I was doing work experience at a weekly magazine, a cartoon with this very image was pinned up on the wall. The caption read: 'Slave is such a nasty word. Let's call you an intern.'

And of course slaves would have helped with hairdressing, nursing, and all kinds of other tasks of this nature.

# Doggy Style?

*Like the people who dry Mark Zuckerberg's armpits when he's sweaty?*

Just like them. A hairdresser would also pluck your armpit hairs.

*Ouch.*

Whilst it's passed into popular culture that the Roman paterfamilias – the head of the family – had the power of life or death over slaves, in reality it was barely ever exercised; although the notoriously austere Cato (he who appears on the shield of Aeneas), who was around in the second century BC, used to send away his slaves if they got too ill or old to work.

*Gosh.*

Yes – again something that makes them seem absolutely alien to us. The family, by the way (*familia*) meant the household, rather than people related by blood to the paterfamilias. You get that meaning in nineteenth-century novels. Slavery was a condition of the ancient world, found in almost every culture.

*How did you become one?*

You could be captured by pirates; this meant that you could start off as an aristocrat and end up a slave. This could happen whether you were a man, woman or child.

Una shuddered.

I know. It's awful. Remember the swineherd in the *Odyssey*, Eumaeus? He was meant to have been of princely birth. If you conquered a city, you'd probably enslave its inhabitants, too. If your mother was a slave, then you were also considered to be born one. And you could also be enslaved if you committed a crime – condemned to work in the mines, become a gladiator, or to join in one of the hunts in the Colosseum.

## WHO WANTS TO BE A GLADIATOR?

**Do you enjoy:**
…fighting beasts? Then become a *bestiarius*.
…chariots? Then *essedarius* is the job for you.
…wearing lots of armour? You'll want to be a *murmillo*, the most heavily protected of the lot, with a distinctive helmet shaped like a fish; failing that, you could be a *secutor*, who wore a helmet with protection for his face.
…using a net? That would be a *retiarius*. You wouldn't just have a net, you'd have a trident too.

Obviously, if you were working in an industrial capacity you'd have had a terrible time of it, and there's no question that conditions would have been appalling. For domestic slaves in a Roman household, on the other hand, things were much better. They were often highly trained – they could be wet nurses, hairdressers, teachers or financial agents, amongst many other roles – and very often ended up by buying their freedom. Many ex-slaves went on to become wealthy and prominent, and their children too.

*How did you get freed?*

In Rome, by a process known as manumission – literally being freed from the hand of your master. We know that manumission (or rather a form of it) also happened across the Greek world. Many took place every year in Rome – so many, in fact, that Augustus passed a law limiting the number of slaves you could free in your will to 100. You could also buy your own freedom. Your master would let you accumulate money and even land, and when you could, you paid up, and then became a full Roman citizen, and you could use the rest of your savings to start up a business.

Of course, this meant that you had obligations to your former master: you still had to do a bit of work for him, and you were duty-bound to support them. As a freedman, you became your patron's client. Imagine the scene: as an aristocratic man you are never alone, but are followed about everywhere by a crowd of attendants, who all want something from you or whom you can use to do something. Never a moment's peace! I'm not sure, Una, that I would have enjoyed being either a patron or a client.

A good example of a slave relationship is found in Cicero's Tiro – who was effectively his secretary; Cicero writes to him with tender affection and concern about his health. Nobody questioned the institution of slavery: it was part of the texture of the world. Even when the famous Spartacus, the Thracian slave, escaped and rebelled in 72/73 BC, he didn't want to end the practice of slavery; he and his companions wanted their freedom.

What we would find more troubling is that babies were quite often abandoned on rubbish dumps – good places to find a new supply of slaves. Exposure was common across Ancient Greece and Rome – that's partly why it crops up in so many myths, such as that of Oedipus. It was still being done as late as the Emperor Justinian (the Eastern Roman emperor in the sixth century AD), who passed a law declaring all exposed children were free.

*That's… awful.*

It is, to us. And it's one of the ways in which we are furthest from them. Now don't get it into your head that they didn't love their children – that's something else that has seeped into the popular imagination. There is plenty of evidence of deep affection for babies or young children who died.

We passed a rubbish lorry, moving, leviathan-like, along the road. You will be pleased to hear, Una, that you weren't allowed to throw excrement or dead bodies into the street in Roman law.

*That's good. But there was that hand that the dog brought in?*

Well you can see that laws were not always kept. The historian Polybius also notes that when the Romans attacked and took a city, you would find in the streets the bodies not just of people, but also of dogs cut in half.

*Horrible!*

Indeed. And I do remember a story of a senator being pelted with poo so that he wouldn't vote…

*Sounds like things haven't changed much. What if you wanted to… you know, go?*

Well there were public loos, and the famous sewer system, presided over by Cloacina, the goddess of the sewers.

*She drew the short straw too?*

You can imagine that when the more favourable particular duties were being handed out, Cloacina might have been otherwise engaged.

There was a short pause. Una raised an eyebrow.

Pliny tells us that many of the Romans who built the Cloaca Maxima under the reign of the Tarquins were so exhausted by it that they killed themselves. So important was the Cloaca Maxima – the Very Big Sewer – that in 33 BC, when Octavian was still Octavian and was doing plenty of public works, he cleared out the sewers and his trusty lieutenant, Agrippa, made a journey down them. There were particular slaves called the *stercorarii*, whose job it was to collect human excrement.

*What did they do with it?*

They sold it to farmers, who used it as fertiliser. Cloacina, incidentally, was also a protector of marital sex, and some say an aspect of Venus – because the name is actually to do with cleanliness. Talking dirty, indeed.

And now, talking of sex, let's get one thing out of the way. An enduring idea about the ancient Greeks – though not the Romans – is that they were pretty much only interested in sex between older, bearded men and younger, beardless boys. This tends to be based on images from a painted vase here, or a drinking bowl there.

The classicist Sir Kenneth Dover (who once masturbated over a mountain) wrote a famous book called *Greek Homosexuality*, in which he propounded a theory that sex was all about power: the lover, or *erastes*, would be an older man who, penetrating his younger beloved, or *eromenos*, in a process known as 'intercrural sex' (that is, between the thighs), would be showing his superiority. The penetrator would not gain shame in this way; whereas the penetratee would be in a definite subordinate position.

Davidson, in his book *The Greeks and Greek Love*, argues that the reality was much more complex. The first thing to clear up is that the definition of the word '*pais*', or 'boy', doesn't mean what we assume it means.

We had reached the Heath, and we passed a group of youths playing football. One of them had a slightly unfortunate scrubby moustache, the sort that looks like toothbrush bristles. Their voices were on the edge of breaking.

The Athenians, in particular, are often accused of this particular vice. But puberty happened about four years later than it does now, meaning that youths 'in their first beards' would in fact have been not like those gawky adolescents, but about eighteen years old. (The Greeks were vague about specific ages, and grouped people in general age divisions.) In Athens there were many restrictions on interaction with boys under this particular age group, who were protected by slaves.

Davidson makes a distinction between Greek Homosexuality – that is, political and ritualised sex between men – and homosexuality in Greece. The first took place in special contexts outside of a married man's life. In the second, of course, there were always men who fell in love with other men. It seems that the very fact that Greek Homosexuality was so prevalent actually highlighted the type of man who only prefers men, that is, what we would now call a homosexual man.

The forms of sex between men that we see on cups and vases, argues Davidson, are often ritualised forms of Greek Homosexuality. And these were localised, so that different city states would have had different approaches.

A vase from Elis shows two youths of the same age, about to engage in intercourse. One of them is sitting on a chair, the other is about to position himself on top, in what I am told is a cowboy position. They are facing each other. A smiling woman watches, whilst a man listens outside.

Is this a piece of smut? Does it show what the Greeks liked to do all the time? Elis was a mysterious place, where holy secret rites were celebrated. This scene, Davidson argues, shows a religious ceremony, which needed silence to take place properly.

# Doggy Style?

Other vases show scenes of sexual excess: what might seem like a description of a common act, with a man lusting after a youth, is actually a warning against it.

The Spartans had a different system altogether. They effectively institutionalised homosexuality. Adolescent boys, kept closely governed in schools, were encouraged to have relationships with older boys: this is why their wives shaved their heads and wore men's cloaks when they came home for sex.

*Blimey.*

An Athenian man was freer. He might court a beautiful *pais* – about eighteen years old – with a cockerel or a new cloak. There was the *hetaira*, or courtesan, a sophisticated woman who would often be serenaded late at night. At a *symposium* – a dinner party, effectively, of which we have a wonderful fictionalised account by Plato, with Alcibiades turning up late and drunk – you might even get fondled by your neighbour or a flute-player or dancing girl. Wives are rather less celebrated, and tended to be kept off the scene in most of the literature that we have (the most famous example being Xanthippe, Socrates' wife, who, as he lay dying, was sent away because she was crying too much).

*What about the Romans?*

They lacked the same ritualised forms of male–male love as the Greeks; but that doesn't mean they didn't go in for it, especially after contact with the Greeks.

Catullus the poet was just as capable of loving the young Juventius – and of being annoyed that he wouldn't return his kisses – as he was of loving the beautiful, civilised and mature lady Lesbia. The Emperor Hadrian, who very much modelled himself on the Greeks, had a boy lover, Antinous; he even named a city after him when the boy drowned.

There were plenty of female prostitutes in Rome, too, and a Roman man might, as would a Greek, find sexual partners amongst his domestic household.

Women in Rome were meant to be chaste, and only sleep with their husbands – but there is a squib by Martial in which he accuses a chaste maiden of sleeping with her maidenly friends. And of course we know of Julia, Augustus' daughter, who may well have been a keen attender of orgies and committed adultery (and was exiled for it, poor thing). We also know that a law was passed, in AD 54, that aimed to prevent free women having affairs with slaves (owing to the complications arising from the legal status of the children).

We were now back at the top of Parliament Hill, where we'd started, towards the end of the summer. I needed to catch my breath.

The grass was muddy and churned. A Labrador, glistening with water, lolloped past in search of a chewed tennis ball. The trees were still bare, reaching twigs into the air as if they had only just escaped from a god and transformed from nymphs; but the sky was clear and blue.

Persephone, for the moment, still remained with Hades. Soon she would be returning to the Earth, and to her mother's embrace. Seeds, long hidden in the earth, would be sprouting.

I inhaled, deeply. We'd covered myths, language, epic poetry, tragedy, love poetry and history. We'd glanced at some philosophy. We'd talked of emperors and slaves, lavatories and peacocks.

There was still more to discuss: with Classics, the conversation is endless.

We had come to a natural end, though. Our chariot race was run. The good horse and the wild had been pulling us in different directions for long enough, and it was time for this soul to have a rest.

In any case, Una had moved her attentions towards a handsome lurcher, swaggering past with all the elan of a Roman orator in the forum who's just won an important case.

You know, Una, I said. She turned to look at me. The handsome male lurcher hung around for a bit, and then sped off after his owner.

There's one person I haven't mentioned much, who is still one of the most important figures in myth. He was an Argonaut – the mystic Orpheus: the man endowed with such great skill in music that he could calm the beasts, and make the trees and rocks move to hear him.

His wife, Eurydice, was bitten by a snake, and died from the poison. Devastated, Orpheus begged Hades to let her come back to life. The god of the Underworld, moved by his gorgeous, plangent singing, agreed. There was a condition: Orpheus was not allowed to look back at her until they reached the upper air.

Eurydice followed him all the way to the entrance to our world. Orpheus couldn't help himself: he turned back just at the edge of the tunnel. His music couldn't save her in the end, and Eurydice was snatched away from him, and returned to the dead for ever.

Orpheus lived on. He refused the love of women in his grief, and turned to men. One day, some Maenads, maddened followers of Bacchus, found him and tried to seduce him. He refused their advances, and so they chased after him, and tore him limb from limb.

His head, as it floated down the river, still carried on singing. It's Ovid's *carmen perpetuum*.

At one and the same time Orpheus is a mortal whose music failed to stop his killers; and an immortal whose singing will last for ever.

That, really, is what Classics is about, Una. That friction, that paradox, that ambiguity. The classicist searches for meaning, delving through the evidence, detective, critic, dreamer all at once. Wherever there is a gap in our knowledge, the classicist aims to fill it. Wherever there's another way of looking at something, the classicist will try to see it.

Whatever turbulence happens in the world, whatever texts are lost, Classics will continue. All we have to do is listen.

Una, pattering gently by my side, bent her head, and pricked up her ears.

And then shot away, chasing after the flash of a squirrel's tail.

# Appendix A

# Some Useful Latin Phrases

Canis latrat – the dog is barking
Canis exire vult – she wants to go out
Heri eam exercui – I walked her yesterday
Veni! – Come!
Sede! – Sit!
Neca! – Kill!
Adiuve! Est lupa in villa! – Help! There is a wolf in the house!

**Some slightly more useful Latin phrases:**

AD – Anno Domini – In the Year of our Lord
ad hoc – for this purpose
ad infinitum – for ever
   *Great fleas have little fleas upon their backs to bite 'em,*
   *And little fleas have lesser fleas, and so ad infinitum.*
am – ante meridiem – before noon. I never get up ante meridiem.
a priori – from the cause to the effect
bona fide – in good faith
c. – circa, around. Una has chased c. 100 squirrels.
caveat emptor – let the buyer beware
CV – curriculum vitae – course of life. Una's CV left a little to be
   desired.
deus ex machina – a god from the machine

e.g. – exempli gratia – for example

etc. – et cetera – and the rest

flagrante delicto – in the act of committing a crime. I caught Una eating the chicken, in flagrante delicto.

ibid. – in the same place

i.e. – id est – that is

infra dig. – beneath your dignity. Una considers terriers rather infra dig.

ipso facto – by the fact itself

modus operandi – plan of working. In stalking the shrew, Una's modus operandi was stealth.

nb – nota bene – note well

nem. con. – nemine contradicente – with no one opposing. The motion was passed nem. con.

non sequitur – doesn't follow logically

pm – post meridiem – after noon. I like to nap in the pm.

prima facie – at first sight

pro bono publico – for the public good

pro rata – in proportion

p.s. – post scriptum – written afterwards

q.e.d. – quod erat demonstrandum – which was proved. Useful in arguments.

quid pro quo – one thing for another

sic – thus, literally

sine qua non – indispensable

status quo – the same state as now

v. – versus – against

vice versa – the position reversed

viz. – videlicet, namely

volte face – reversing your opinion. Una made a volte face about cats.

vox populi – the voice of the people

# Appendix B

# Latin Grammar

**Present tense of Latro, latrare, latravi**

Latro – I bark
Latras – You (s.) bark
Latrat – He, she or it barks
Latramus – We bark
Latratis – You (pl) bark
Latrant – They bark
Present infinitive: Latrare, to bark
Present participle: Latrans, -antis – barking
Una latrat – Una barks
Latrans canis currit – The barking dog runs
Una latrare vult – Una wishes to bark

## NOUNS

**First declension**
Lupa, f. – A she-wolf

*Singular*
Nominative: Lupa – A she-wolf (subject)
Vocative: Lupa – O she-wolf!
Accusative: Lupam – A she-wolf (object)
Genitive: Lupae – Of a she-wolf
Dative: Lupae – To or for a she-wolf
Ablative: Lupa – By, with or from a she-wolf

*Plural*

Nom: Lupae – She-wolves (subject)
Voc: Lupae – She-wolves! (addressing)
Acc: Lupas – She-wolves (object)
Gen: Luparum – Of she-wolves
Dat: Lupis – To or for she-wolves
Abl: Lupis – By, with, or from she-wolves

*But how*, said Una, *do you tell the difference between the genitive and dative singulars, and the nominative and vocative plurals?*

Well, I answered, it's all to do with context. '*Lupae veniunt!*' really can only mean 'The she-wolves are coming!' Whereas '*clamor lupae*' can only mean 'howl of the she-wolf'. The same goes for the other declensions.

If you think that's a lot of stuff to learn, note that Ancient Greek only has five cases. But it catches you in other ways. And be glad that, unlike some Australasian languages, there is no aversive case: 'for fear of…'; or, like a Himalayan language, an altitudinal one. Which must be helpful in the mountains.

## Second declension

Catulus, m. – A puppy

*Singular*

Nom: Catulus – A puppy
Voc: Catule – O puppy!
Acc: Catulum – A puppy (obj.)
Gen: Catuli – Of the puppy
Dat: Catulo – To or for the puppy
Abl: Catulo – By, with or from the puppy

*Plural*

Nom: Catuli – Puppies
Voc: Catuli – Puppies!

Acc: Catulos – Puppies (obj.)
Gen: Catulorum – Of the puppies
Dat: Catulis – To or for the puppies
Abl: Catulis – By, with or from the puppies

The masculine plural, *catuli*, is the source of all the misapprehensions in English about whether a noun ending in -us should be pluralised with an -i or not. The problem is that not all -us nouns are second declension. I saw someone on Facebook referring to his 'stati' – but 'status' is actually a fourth declension noun, whose plural happens to be 'status'. So best to anglicise it if you can; although sometimes convention means that an -i is acceptable. For example, you would talk of narcissi. However, octopi is egregious and must be stamped out.

And now you know this, you can enjoy my favourite joke. A Roman goes into a bar and asks for a *martinus*. 'Don't you mean a martini?' answers the bartender. 'If I wanted two, I'd have said,' answers the Roman.

### Third declension

Canis, canis, m/f. – A dog

#### *Singular*

Nom: Canis – A dog
Voc: Canis – O dog!
Acc: Canem – A dog (obj.)
Gen: Canis – Of a dog
Dat: Cani – To or for a dog
Abl: Cane – by, with or from a dog

#### *Plural*

Nom: Canes – Dogs
Voc: Canes – O Dogs!
Acc: Canes – Dogs (obj.)

Gen: Canum – Of dogs
Dat: Canibus – To or for dogs
Abl: Canibus – By, with or from dogs

# Appendix C

# The Greek Alphabet

| | |
|---|---|
| A, α | Alpha |
| B, β | Beta |
| Γ, γ | Gamma |
| Δ, δ | Delta |
| E, ε | Epsilon |
| Z, ζ | Zeta |
| H, η | Eta |
| Θ, θ | Theta |
| I, ι | Iota |
| K, κ | Kappa |
| Λ, λ | Lambda |
| M, μ | Mu |
| N, ν | Nu |
| Ξ, ξ | Xi |
| O, ο | Omicron |
| Π, π | Pi |
| P, ρ | Rho |
| Σ, σ, ς | Sigma |
| T, τ | Tau |
| Υ, υ | Upsilon |
| Φ, φ | Phi |
| X, χ | Chi |

Ψ, ψ        Psi
Ω, ω        Omega

All words that begin with a vowel have a smooth breathing (like a small backwards c) above them; if a word begins with an 'h' sound, then that becomes a 'rough' breathing (which you also find on words starting with a rho).

# Appendix D

# Author, Author

Many of these authors have been mentioned in our conversations: you might want to have a look at them in more detail. I haven't listed everyone (we'd be here all day), but these are places where you can start with confidence.

### Aeschylus
Greek playwright. Didn't die by virtue of having a tortoise dropped on his head. Seven plays survive, all tragedies.

Must-read: *Agamemnon*.

### Aristophanes
Greek playwright. Bawdy, and full of local idioms and references, which makes it hard to translate into English. However, they are still hilarious.

Must-read: *The Frogs*.

### Aristotle
Greek philosopher. Pupil of Socrates. Taught Alexander the Great. Usually thought of as the moment when the Classical Greek era ends.

Must-read: *Poetics*.

### Catullus
Roman poet of the late Republic. Would have been fun at a dinner party. Sexy and usually broke, so not marriage

material, plus he'd always be mooning over that Clodia Metelli.

Must-read: the Lesbia poems.

## Cicero

Roman lawyer, letter-writer, philosopher: the man could do everything. A range of defence and prosecution speeches survive, including the fabulous *Pro Caelio*, in which he defends the play-boy Marcus Caelius Rufus. His letters are also brilliant. If you start reading a Cicero sentence, be very much aware that it will probably take a week or so before you get to the verb at the end.

Must-read: *In Catilinam*.

## Euripides

Greek playwright. The intense younger sibling of the great trio of tragedians who wants to do everything differently.

Must-read: *The Bacchae*.

## Herodotus

Greek historian. In fact, inventor of history, NO LESS, so you'd better watch it when you're dissing his methods.

Must-read: his only text, *Histories*.

## Homer

Greek poet (arguably). Might have been more than one person. Might have been blind. Probably did compose both the *Iliad* and the *Odyssey*; probably didn't compose the *Homeric Hymns* or the mini mock-epic, *The Battle of Frogs and Mice*.

Must-read: the *Iliad*.

## Livy

Roman historian. Much inflicted on schoolchildren. Grows on you.

Must-read: the account of Hannibal crossing the Alps.

**Lucretius**

Roman philosopher. My personal favourite. An Epicurean who wrote about atomic theory in hexameters.

Must-read: *De Rerum Natura*, his account of the entire universe.

**Ovid**

Roman poet. Publius Ovidius Naso. A personal fave for many. Much of his work survives, and the Latin is more straightforward (in my view) than, say, Virgil, so it's a good place to cut your teeth.

Must-read: *Metamorphoses*.

**Plato**

Greek philosopher. Of huge importance to any understanding of the ancient world, and of the development of philosophy. I would start with the *Symposium*.

Must-read: *The Republic*.

**Plautus**

Roman playwright. See Terence. Full of mistaken identities, lovers, and the kind of tortuous plot that was so influential on Shakespeare's comedies. The 'clever slave' is a trope that found its apotheosis in Bertie Wooster's valet, Jeeves.

Must-read: *Menaechmi*.

**Pliny the Younger**

Roman belle-lettrist. An extraordinary insight into the mind and life of someone from the reign of Hadrian.

Must-read: his account of the eruption of Vesuvius.

**Propertius**

Roman poet (Augustan). A particular favourite of mine: vivid and strange, full of bizarre imagery and urbane scandal.

Must-read: Book I of his poems.

**Sallust**
Roman historian. Best avoided, if you ask me. But if you must, read his account of Catiline.

**Sappho**
Greek poet. More Sappho has been discovered recently, offering gorgeous insight into this ancient and influential woman's supreme artistry.

Must-read: *The Complete Poems*.

**Sophocles**
Greek playwright. His most popular surviving plays deal with the House of Cadmus: Oedipus and his daughter Antigone.

Must-read: *Oedipus Rex*, but give *Philoctetes* a go too.

**Tacitus**
Roman historian. Supreme stylist. Full of scandal, intrigue and vivid, gripping scenes. If you want to know who got killed by a feather down his throat, this is where to go.

Must-read: *Annals*.

**Terence**
Roman playwright. The Latin language in Terence, being in dialogue, can be easy to pick up, and it's an interesting insight into what Romans found funny.

Must-read: *Adelphoe*.

**Virgil**
Roman poet. Endlessly fascinating: you'll find, once you get into the *Aeneid*, yourself returning to it again and again, and the language, though it's fairly stylised and rich with imagery, becoming easier and easier to grasp.

Must-read: the *Aeneid*.

**Xenophon**

Greek military historian. Probably the first proper prose text you'll read in Ancient Greek, if you decide to take it up. Straightforward sentence constructions and military vocab mean it's relatively easy to pick up.

Must-read: *Anabasis*, an account of how Xenophon and his army left Asia Minor.

# Appendix E

# The Amyclae Throne

The myths, heroes and divinities shown on the Amyclae Throne at Sparta, which also had a huge bronze statue of Apollo, are as follows:

The Graces
The Seasons
Echidna and Typhos
The Tritons
Poseidon and Zeus carrying Taygete
The Pleiades
Alcyone
Atlas
Heracles and Cycnus
Heracles and the Centaurs
The Minotaur and Theseus
The Dance of the Phaeacians
Demodocus singing about Ares and Aphrodite
Perseus and Medusa
Heracles and the giant Thurius
Tyndareus and Eurytus
The Rape of the Leucippides by Castor and Pollux
Hermes carrying Dionysus to heaven

## The Amyclae Throne

Athena taking Heracles to heaven
Peleus giving Achilles to Chiron the centaur
Cephalus abducted by Eos
The wedding of Harmonia
The duel between Achilles and Memnon
Heracles' revenge on Dionysius the Thracian and Nessus the
    centaur
The Judgement of Paris
Adrastus and Tydeus
Hera and Io
Athena and Hephaestus
The Hydra
Heracles and Cerberus
Anaxias and Mnasinous
Megapenthes and Nicostratus, sons of Menelaus
Bellerophon killing the chimera
Heracles driving away the Cattle of Geryon
Castor and Pollux on horseback
Sphinxes
A band of Magnesians
The Calydonian Boar Hunt
Heracles killing the children of Actor
Calais and Zetes, the twin sons of the north wind, driving away
    the Harpies
Pirithous and Theseus abducting Helen
Heracles strangling the Nemean lion
Apollo and Artemis shooting Tityus
Heracles fighting Orius the centaur
Theseus fighting the Minotaur
Heracles wrestling the River Achelous
Hephaestus binding Hera

The Funeral Games of Pelias, Medea's brother
Menelaus and Proteus
Admetus yoking a boar and lion
The Trojans bringing libations to Hector.

# Bibliography

**Primary Texts**

I have, mostly, used the excellent Loeb Classical Library for reading the primary texts.

These are always a good place to start, and can help you to anchor yourself in the general meaning of something before you delve further into it. These are available online, but there's nothing quite like the feel of an actual print Loeb.

Another excellent resource is the Perseus website, at perseus.tufts.edu, which has every text uploaded alongside translations, as well as a brilliant lexicological tool so you can look up every word: it's not always right, though, so it's worth checking things yourself in a dictionary if things seem a little odd.

The following editions have proved very useful in terms of commentary. When you read a Latin or Greek text you'll find that, to start with, you'll need two or three books: one is the text itself, which you can usually find in an Oxford edition. The second is a commentary, which provides information about the text, line by line, that helps you to make sense of specific parts of the text, glossing obscure terms or grammatical phrases or idioms. I am always astounded by the scholarship, love and energy that go into commentaries.

And the third is a translation, which, as you progress, you will find you need to use less and less: these can often be beautiful in their own right (such as the Fagles version of Aeschylus) as well as providing interpretations of their own.

*Iliad I–XII* by Homer, edited and with introduction and commentary by M.M. Willcock (Bristol: Bristol Classical Press, 1998).

*Iliad XIII–XXIV* by Homer, edited and with introduction and commentary by M.M. Willcock (Bristol: Bristol Classical Press, 1999).

*Ovid's Metamorphoses: Books 1–5*, edited and with introduction and commentary by William S. Anderson (Norman, OK: Oklahoma Press, 1997).

*Catullus: The Poems*, edited and with introduction, revised text and commentary by Kenneth Quinn (London: St Martin's Press, 1977).

Many excellent translations are available, with good critical introductions, published by both Penguin Classics and Oxford World's Classics. I have used the following:

Aeschylus, *The Oresteia*, trans. Robert Fagles (London: Penguin Classics, 1966).

Homer, *The Iliad*, trans. E.V. Rieu (London: Penguin Classics, 2014).

Homer, *The Odyssey*, trans. Martin Hammond (London: Penguin Classics, 1987).

Virgil, *The Aeneid*, trans. David West (London: Penguin Classics, 1990).

# Bibliography

## Secondary Literature

A fine place to start is *The Oxford Classical Dictionary* eds. Simon Hornblower and Antony Spawforth (third edition, Oxford: Oxford University Press, 1999). My parents gave me this edition as a present for getting into Oxford. It sits on my desk, still providing help and guidance.

The following books are all scholarly yet accessible, and I have drawn freely from them:

Catherine Bates (ed.), *The Cambridge Companion to the Epic* (Cambridge: CUP, 2010).

Mary Beard, *SPQR: A History of Ancient Rome* (London: Profile, 2015).

—*Confronting the Classics: Traditions, Adventures and Innovations* (London: Profile, 2013).

Alastair Blanshard, *Hercules: A Heroic Life* (London: Granta, 2005).

Alan Cameron, *Greek Mythography in the Roman World* (Oxford: OUP, 2004).

James Davidson, *The Greeks and Greek Love: A Radical Reappraisal of Homosexuality in Ancient Greece* (London: Phoenix, 2008).

Guy Deutscher, *The Unfolding of Language: The Evolution of Mankind's Greatest Invention* (London: Arrow, 2006).

Jane Draycott and Emma-Jayne Graham (eds.), *Bodies of Evidence: Ancient Anatomical Votives Past, Present and Future* (Abingdon: Routledge, 2017).

Paul Erdkamp (ed.), *The Cambridge Companion to Ancient Rome* (Cambridge: CUP, 2013).

Iain Ferris, *Cave Canem: Animals and Roman Society* (Stroud: Amberley, 2018).

M.I. Finlay, *The World of Odysseus* (London: Chatto & Windus, 1977).

William Fitzgerald, *Martial: The World of the Epigram* (Chicago, IL: University of Chicago Press, 2007).

Simon Goldhill, *How to Stage Greek Tragedy* (Chicago, IL: University of Chicago Press, 2007).

Robert Graves, *The Greek Myths: The Complete and Definitive Edition* (London: Penguin, 2011).

Barbara Graziosi, *The Gods of Olympus: A History* (London: Profile, 2013).

Jasper Griffin, *Homer on Life and Death* (Oxford: OUP, 1980).

—*Homer* (Oxford: OUP, 1980).

—*Homer: The Odyssey* (Cambridge: CUP, 1987).

Judith P. Hallett and Marilyn B. Skinner (eds.), *Roman Sexualities* (Princeton, NJ: Princeton University Press, 1997).

James C. Hogan, *A Commentary on the Complete Greek Tragedies: Aeschylus* (Chicago, IL: University of Chicago Press, 1984).

W.R. Johnson, *Momentary Monsters: Lucan and His Heroes*, vol. 47 (Ithaca, NY: Cornell University Press, 1987).

Robin Lane Fox, *The Classical World: An Epic History from Homer to Hadrian* (London: Allen Lane, 2005).

William Stuart Maguinness (ed.), *The Thirteenth Book of the Aeneid by Mapheus Vegius*, (London: Virgil Society, 1957).

Charles Martindale (ed.), *Ovid Renewed: Ovidian influences on literature and art from the Middle Ages to the twentieth century* (Cambridge: CUP, 1988).

Nicholas Ostler, *Ad Infinitum: A Biography of Latin* (London: HarperPress, 2007).

E.T. Owen, *The Story of the Iliad* (Bristol: Bristol Classical Press, 1994).

# Bibliography

Adam Parry (ed.), *The Making of Homeric Verse: The Collected Papers of Milman Parry* (Oxford: Clarendon Press, 1971).

Charles Segal, *Singers, Heroes, and Gods in the Odyssey* (Ithaca, NY: Cornell University Press, 1994).

Oliver Taplin, *Greek Tragedy in Action* (London: Methuen, 1978).

Tim Whitmarsh, *Ancient Greek Literature* (Cambridge: Polity, 2004).

Bernhard Zimmermann, *Greek Tragedy: An Introduction*, trans. Thomas Marier (Baltimore, MD: Johns Hopkins University Press, 1991).

C.B.R. Pelling (ed.), *Plutarch: Life of Antony* (Cambridge: CUP, 1988).

Winston Spencer-Churchill, *My Early Life* (London: T. Butterworth, 1930).

## Fiction and Poetry

Charles Dickens, *Captain Boldheart and the Latin-Grammar Master*, https://www.gutenberg.org/files/23765/23765-h/23765-h.htm.

Ronald Firbank, *Vainglory* (London: Grant Richards, 1915, reissued Penguin Classics, 2012).

Robert Graves, *I, Claudius* (London: Arthur Baker, 1934, reissued Penguin Classics, 2006).

Ted Hughes, *The Oresteia* (London: Faber & Faber 1999).

Ted Hughes, *Tales from Ovid* (London: Faber & Faber, 1997).

Seamus Heaney, *Opened Ground: Poems 1966–1996* (London: Faber & Faber, 2002).

Andrew Lang, *The Violet Fairy Book* (London: Longmans & Co, 1901).

Alexander Pope, *The Iliad of Homer* (reissued London: Penguin Classics, 1996).

Dodie Smith, *The Starlight Barking* (London: William Heinemann, 1967, reissued Egmont, 2011).

Diana Wynne Jones, *Dogsbody* (London: Macmillan, 1975, reissued 2010).

**General Articles**

'Keeping Up the Classics', *The Times* (online), 19 January 1887, p. 10. Retrieved from *The Times* Digital Archive, http://tinyurl.gale.com/tinyurl/BcdbF0.

**Scholarly Articles**

These are for the specialist.

Anderson, William S., 'Multiple Change in the *Metamorphoses*', *Transactions and Proceedings of the American Philological Association*, vol. 94, 1963, pp. 1–27.

Beck, William, 'Dogs, Dwellings, and Masters: Ensemble and Symbol in the Odyssey', *Hermes*, vol. 119, no. 2, 1991, pp. 158–167.

Burnett, Anne Pippin, 'Hekabe the Dog', *Arethusa*, vol. 27, no. 2, 1994, pp. 151–164.

De Ste. Croix, G.E.M., 'Herodotus', *Greece & Rome*, vol. 24, no. 2, 1977, pp. 130–148.

Felton, D., 'On Reading *latrare* at Ovid *Met.* 7.791', *The Classical World*, vol. 95, no. 1, 2001, pp. 65–69.

Gosling, W.F., 'Pets in Classical Times', *Greece & Rome*, vol. 4, no. 11, 1935, pp. 109–113.

Graver, Margaret., 'Dog-Helen and Homeric Insult', *Classical Antiquity*, vol. 14, no. 1, 1995, pp. 41–61.

Lockwood, Laura E., '*Paradise Lost*, VII, 15–20', *Modern Language Notes*, vol. 28, no. 4, 1913, pp. 126–127.

Moulton, Carroll, 'Similes in the *Iliad*', *Hermes*, vol. 102, no. 3, 1974, pp. 381–397.

Schlam, Carl C., 'Diana and Actaeon: Metamorphoses of a Myth', *Classical Antiquity*, vol. 3, no. 1, 1984, pp. 82–110.

Scodel, Ruth, 'Odysseus' Dog and the Productive Household', *Hermes*, vol. 133, no. 4, 2005, pp. 401–408.

Scott, John A., 'Dogs in Homer', *The Classical Weekly*, vol. 41, no. 15, 1948, pp. 226–228.

Steadman, John M., 'Perseus upon Pegasus' and *Ovid Moralized*', *The Review of English Studies*, vol. 9, no. 36, 1958, pp. 407–410.

Stephens, Viola G., 'Like a Wolf on the Fold: Animal Imagery in Vergil', *Illinois Classical Studies*, vol. 15, no. 1, 1990, pp. 107–130.

Taplin, Oliver, 'The Shield of Achilles within the *Iliad*', *Greece & Rome*, vol. 27, no. 1, 1980, pp. 1–21.

Toynbee, J.M.C., 'Beasts and Their Names in the Roman Empire', *Papers of the British School at Rome*, vol. 16, 1948, pp. 24–37. JSTOR, www.jstor.org/stable/40310468. Accessed 6 March 2020.

Van Nortwick, Thomas, 'Aeneas, Turnus, and Achilles', *Transactions of the American Philological Association* (1974–2014), vol. 110, 1980, pp. 303–314.

# Acknowledgements

I would very much like to thank all of my masters and tutors, especially Andrew James, Michelle Martindale, Adrian Arnold, Bruce Mitchell, Jim Sheppe, Fr. John Hunwicke, Raymond Mew and Chris Kraus, for inspirational, kindly, challenging and understanding teaching, mentoring and guidance. And many apologies, too.

I'd also like to thank my editor, Sam Carter, and Juliana Pars, Rida Vaquas, Jacqui Lewis and all at Oneworld, and the following, who have variously offered encouragement, time, titbits and knowledge: Anthony McGowan, Melissa Katsoulis, Tatiana von Preussen, Beatrice von Preussen, Jeffrey Henderson (general editor of the Loeb Classical Library), Julia Gray, Mouse Allen, George MacPherson and Pindr, Daisy Dunn, Christopher Pelling (Regius Professor of Greek Emeritus), Nicholas Bowling, Robert Christie.

Thank you, especially, to those who have helped to give me the time and space to write: Richard and Marie Womack, Andrew von Preussen, and Antonia and Charles Wellington.

# Index

# Index

# Index

# Index

# Index

# Index

# Index

# Index

Mills and Boon 140
Milton, John 206
Minerva 60; see ATHENA
Minos 32–3, 44, 198
  owner of magic dog 31
Minotaur 32, 43–4, 68, 73, 74,
    86, 236, 240
Minyas, the daughters of 200
Molesworth, Nigel 98
Molossian hounds 154, 259
  mentioned by Aristotle 27
  by Virgil 27
  fitted with spiked collars 27
Monmouth, Geoffrey of 161
Muses, the 85, 214
Museum, British 213, 235
Mycenaean 124, 173

naming system, Roman 165
Narcissus 190–95
Nausicca 138, 141, 146
Neoptolemus 133, 229
Neptune 52; see POSEIDON
Nerva-Antonine dynasty 261
Nesbit, E. 63
  child characters steeped in
      Latin 105
Nestor 144, 146
Nero 44, 257, 259–61
Nike 46
  confused with Iris 46
  manufacturer of sportswear 46
Niobe 40, 44
Noah 197
*nostos / nostoi* 121, 154

nuns, singing 197
Nuttall, A.D. 233
nymphs 39, 63, 77, 118, 138,
    145, 180, 278

Octavia 171
Octavian 177, 184, 255, 274; see
    AUGUSTUS
Odoacer 267
Odysseus 3, 30–1, 54, 73, 80,
    83, 111–2, 117–8, 121, 126,
    134, 136, 138, 140–60, 172,
    179, 194, 209, 210, 220, 227,
    229, 256
*Odyssey*, the 30, 39, 53, 80, 82,
    103, 126, 135–46, 157–60
Oedipus 3, 33, 73, 78–9, 82, 121,
    126, 210, 218, 220, 221,
    227–8, 233–4, 273
  not a cat 82
  not a dog 82
Olympian Games 79
Olympus 11, 21–2, 51–3, 59, 61,
    67, 84, 146,
Onions 114
  heroic use of as garnish for
      drink 106
Orestes 73, 80, 124, 145, 210,
    218–23, 227–32, 267
Orpheus 73–4, 81, 139, 148, 153,
    195, 279–80
Orthrus 54
  neglected brother of Cerberus
      54
Oscan 94

316

# Index

# Index

# Index

# Index